T0330421

Capital Liberalization in Transition Countries

Capital Liberalization in Transition Countries

Lessons from the Past and for the Future

Edited by

Age F.P. Bakker

Deputy Executive Director, De Nederlandsche Bank and Professor of Money and Banking, Vrije Universiteit, Amsterdam

Bryan Chapple

Senior Economist, Monetary and Economic Policy Department, De Nederlandsche Bank, Amsterdam

Edward Elgar
Cheltenham, UK • Northampton, MA, USA

Published by
Edward Elgar Publishing Limited
Glensanda House
Montpellier Parade
Cheltenham
Glos GL50 1UA
UK

Edward Elgar Publishing, Inc.
136 West Street
Suite 202
Northampton
Massachusetts 01060
USA

A catalogue record for this book
is available from the British Library

Library of Congress Cataloguing in Publication Data
Capital liberalization in transition countries ; lessons from the past and for the future / edited by Age F.P. Bakker, Bryan Chapple.
  p. cm
  Includes bibliographical references and index.
  1. Capital movements—Congresses. 2. Capital movements—Europe, Eastern—Congresses. 3. Capital movements—Former Soviet republics—Congresses. I. Bakker, Age. II. Chapple, Bryan.

HG3891.C3695 2003
332'.041—dc21

2002044676

ISBN 1 84376 345 1

Printed and bound in Great Britain by MPG Books Ltd, Bodmin, Cornwall

Contents

Figures

Tables

Boxes

Contributors

Veronica Bacalu
Senior Economist, European II Department,
International Monetary Fund

Age Bakker
Deputy Executive Director
De Nederlandsche Bank
Professor of Money and Banking
Vrije Universiteit, Amsterdam

Willem Buiter
Chief Economist
European Bank for Reconstruction and Development

Bryan Chapple
Senior Economist, Monetary and Economic Policy Department
De Nederlandsche Bank

Vache Gabrielyan
Board Member
Central Bank of Armenia

Stefan Ingves
Director, Monetary and Exchange Affairs Department
International Monetary Fund

Armine Khachatryan
Advisor to Executive Director for Armenia, Bosnai and Herzegovina,
Bulgaria, Croatia, Cyprus, Georgia, Israel, Former Yugoslav Republic of
Macedonia, Moldova, Netherlands, Romania and Ukraine
World Bank

Roger Nord
Advisor, Management Communications,
International Monetary Fund

Yung Chul Park
Professor, Department of Economics
Korea University

Ewa Sadowska-Cieslak
Advisor, Research Department
National Bank of Poland

Anatolii Shapovalov
First Deputy Governor
National Bank of Ukraine

Chi-Young Song
Professor, School of Economics
Kookmin University

Anita Taci
Economist, Office of the Chief Economist
European Bank for Reconstruction and Development

Eva Thiel
Senior Economist, Directorate for Financial, Fiscal and Enterprise Affairs
Organization for Economic Cooperation and Development

Boris Vujčić
Deputy Governor
Croatian National Bank

Preface

This book has its genesis in a conference on capital account liberalization in transition economies in Kiev, Ukraine that took place in October 2001. The conference, jointly sponsored by the International Monetary Fund, the National Bank of Ukraine and De Nederlandsche Bank, brought together a wide range of policy makers and experts in the field of capital account liberalization. The intention was to allow participants to discuss earlier liberalization experiences and to exchange information regarding liberalization in a range of transition economies. Participants included senior representatives from the central banks of Armenia, Belarus, Bulgaria, Croatia, Moldova, the Netherlands, Poland and Ukraine. In addition, representatives of key international organizations such as the European Bank for Reconstruction and Development (EBRD), the International Monetary Fund (IMF), the Organisation for Economic Co-operation and Development (OECD) and the World Bank took part, as did an academic specializing in capital account liberalization in East Asia.

The various presentations at the conference were of such interest that we felt it would be appropriate to make the material available to a wider audience. The contributors have therefore expanded their presentations into chapters suitable for publication.

We are grateful to the contributors for their willingness to contribute to the book and to the National Bank of Ukraine for their role in hosting the conference that began the process. Here at the Nederlandsche Bank, Martin Admiraal, Ingrid van de Mortel and Pieter Rook expertly provided the assistance necessary to bring the project to a successful conclusion.

1. Capital account liberalization in the transition phase: an overview

Age Bakker and Bryan Chapple

1.1 INTRODUCTION

The challenges facing policy makers in transition countries have captured the interest of many in recent years. Capital liberalization is one of the key issues for these countries, given that a crucial part of the process of moving to a market-oriented economy is opening up to the outside world – not only for trade in goods and services, but also for capital flows. Access to direct investment, and to international financial markets more generally, is important in facilitating the modernization of transition country economies by providing access to technology, markets and financial resources. At the same time, capital account liberalization carries with it risks, particularly in terms of exchange rate volatility and financial system stability. The challenge of maximizing the benefits of liberalization, while minimizing the associated risks, is therefore a key issue in many transition countries and will continue to be so in coming years.

Progress in capital account liberalization to date varies considerably between transition countries. Many of those countries likely to enter the European Union (EU) in the near future have already substantially liberalized controls on capital flows. Other countries, and in particular those countries formerly part of the Soviet Union, tend to have more restrictive regimes. For both groups, the various issues associated with capital liberalization continue to be important. The ability to attract inward investment (and particularly direct investment) is an important objective of economic policy in transition countries, although success in doing so has varied widely. Institutional features other than the formal capital control regulations are also important influences on capital flows. Of course, attracting the inflows is only part of the story. For countries to make the most use of the flows, they need to be effectively intermediated by the financial system and directed to profitable uses. This point is made by several contributors, again emphasizing the importance of a sound institutional framework.

To date, much of the attention on the region has been focussed on developments in Russia. While Russia is, of course, an important influence on the wider region, the experiences of other countries are just as interesting, but have so far received less attention. Moreover, the country studies in this book illustrate that there is considerable variation across transition countries. We have, therefore, chosen not to focus on Russia directly in this book.

A feature of this book is that a wide variety of transition country liberalization experiences are described by central bank experts from those countries.[1] This allows us to understand the factors that influenced the choices made by policy makers as they experienced them. This 'first-hand' description is complemented by contributions by authors from international organizations or from outside the region, who in general seek to bring to bear the lessons from earlier experiences on the current challenges facing transition countries. One of the key questions facing countries yet to complete capital account liberalization is the extent to which they can reliably draw lessons from earlier experiences. The various chapters in the book illustrate both that each country's experience is in some ways unique, but also that there are some common lessons from liberalization experiences over recent decades. Drawing out these various lessons is one of the key objectives of the book.

This chapter discusses some of the key themes that emerge from the various contributions to the book. The following section considers the development of the broad consensus across advanced countries regarding the benefits of capital account liberalization. The liberalization experiences of these countries heavily influenced the positive attitudes of international organizations, such as the International Monetary Fund (IMF) and the Organisation for Economic Co-operation and Development (OECD), towards liberalization. More recently, financial markets crises, partially associated with capital account liberalization, have led to an increasing emphasis on the risks associated with liberalization, as discussed in Section 1.3. Section 1.4 considers the extent to which the circumstances in which transition countries must liberalize are in fact different from those of earlier liberalization episodes. The East Asian experiences are used to provide some insights into the extent to which the lessons from advanced countries remain relevant. Section 1.5 discusses the link between liberalization and financial market reform while Section 1.6 reviews the experiences of transition economies to date. Section 1.7 offers some concluding remarks.

1.2 THE DEVELOPMENT OF A LIBERALIZATION CONSENSUS

Age Bakker (Chapter 2) illustrates how industrialized countries came to gradually appreciate the benefits of capital account liberalization. Until the 1980s, capital controls were viewed by many as a normal part of the economic toolkit, to be used by countries when required. Although used to a different extent in different countries, controls were widely applied, including at times in countries that traditionally favored free capital flows (e.g., the United States and Germany in the 1960s). The defense of the exchange rate was a common goal of capital controls, along with a desire to maintain monetary policy autonomy. Industrial policy concerns and taxation were also relevant in some countries.

Within Europe, the goal of currency stability was important for facilitating the internal market within the European Union (EU). Diverging approaches to economic policy between countries resulted in substantial capital flows at times, leading to exchange rate tensions. Eventually European countries accepted the need for policy discipline to support stable exchange rates, allowing capital liberalization to occur, consistent with exchange rate stability. The goal of a common currency was an important motivating factor for liberalization in some countries. A similar situation exists for some transition countries, as will be discussed later in this chapter, with the prospect of EU accession and eventual European Monetary Union (EMU) membership acting as a spur for liberalization. For other countries, disillusionment with the (lack of) effectiveness of controls and increasing acceptance of the benefits of pursuing stability-oriented macroeconomic policies tilted the balance in favor of liberalization.

A key point to emerge from Bakker is that many different approaches to liberalization are possible. Some countries took a very gradual approach (e.g., France and Japan) while others removed capital controls within a few months once the decision to liberalize had been taken (e.g., the United Kingdom and New Zealand). As is also evident from a number of other contributions to this book, the overall policy environment is more important for the success of liberalization than the speed. In particular the link to macroeconomic policy settings (and the exchange rate regime) is critical, as are the state of financial market development and institutional settings. In general, there is now a widespread consensus in favor of maintaining free capital flows, at least in advanced countries. While initial movements towards liberalization were swiftly reversed in some advanced countries when the currency came under pressure, the extent of this tendency to reintroduce controls steadily declined as countries integrated further into international financial markets. Over the past decade there has been no move by advanced countries to reintroduce controls. Nevertheless, debate remains, particularly regarding the timing and sequencing of liberalization. In part this ongoing questioning stems from the impact of recent financial crises.

1.3 THE ROLE OF INTERNATIONAL ORGANIZATIONS

The experiences of advanced countries doubtless influenced the attitudes of international organizations. The IMF and the OECD have traditionally been strong supporters of open capital accounts, even though capital account liberalization does not form part of the IMF's Articles of Agreement. This has played a role in their advice to transition countries over the past decade. Quirk and Evans (1995) note that, particularly in Central and Eastern European countries, the Fund has encouraged developing countries to liberalize restrictions on capital account transactions. Foreign direct investment (FDI) was viewed in an especially favorable light, presumably given its role in facilitating the modernization of industries by providing not only finance, but also technological expertise and often access to export markets. In many transition countries, considerable industrial restructuring was required to allow these countries' exports to compete on international markets. FDI was essential in facilitating a rapid modernization.

Eva Thiel (Chapter 5) illustrates the fact that the OECD also takes a positive view of capital account liberalization and encourages countries to progressively liberalize capital flows. In particular, a certain minimum level of capital liberalization is required prior to OECD accession, along with a timetable for further liberalization. Peer review also ensures that member countries continue to have to justify remaining capital controls on a regular basis. To date, four transition countries have joined the OECD – the Czech Republic (1995), Hungary and Poland (1996) and Slovakia (2000). These countries had already begun working towards eventual EU accession, which requires complete capital liberalization. As Thiel notes, it is therefore difficult to assess the extent to which OECD membership acts as an independent spur to liberalization. However, it is likely that, at the very least, the OECD provides these countries with a forum in which progress towards the goal of free capital flows is regularly monitored and assessed.

In advocating liberalization, international institutions have pointed to the benefits that arise from liberalization in terms of increased integration in international financial markets, including the ability to attract funds from these markets. To some extent, liberalization is inevitable for countries wishing to participate in the global economy (Eichengreen and Mussa, 1998), given the fact that capital controls can lead to distortions in trade flows and handicap the competitive position of a country. A further reason for the skeptical approach taken towards capital controls by international institutions is that controls are perceived as not being particularly effective (aside from for short periods and in particular circumstances). Capital flows can also provide a useful discipline on national policy makers by encouraging sound economic policy management (Bakker and Chapple, 2002).[2]

Consistent with their doubts about the effectiveness of controls, the reimposition of capital controls has generally been discouraged. Instead, international organizations typically recommend adjustments in monetary, fiscal and exchange rate policies. For example, in reviewing the experiences of four countries which had reintroduced controls, Quirk and Evans conclude that, at best, reimposed controls had only a very short-term impact on capital flows. Thiel documents that the OECD approach to capital liberalization also discourages the reimposition of controls once a particular capital flow has been completely liberalized. As a general rule, the so-called standstill obligation of the OECD codes covering capital flows only permits a country to reintroduce controls in temporary economic or financial difficulties.

Although liberalization has clearly been encouraged by organizations, attention was also paid to the sequencing of reforms – both in terms of the order in which the various capital controls should be removed and in terms of how capital account liberalization should be sequenced with other reform measures.[3] The standard message that capital controls should be removed to the extent possible at the earliest opportunity was, therefore, tempered by the attention paid to potential risks associated with liberalization. The existence of these risks is clearly evident from the experiences of advanced economies, particularly during some of the liberalization experiences in the 1980s, as Bakker notes. International organizations therefore frequently noted the importance of macroeconomic stability and a sound financial system (including rigorous prudential management and banking supervision).[4]

However, there is less evidence that these factors were stressed as a necessary precondition for liberalization. Moreover, there may also have been insufficient acknowledgement of the importance of the exchange rate regime (and the consistency of that regime with other macroeconomic policies) and capital account liberalization.[5] That lesson was also slow to be learned by a number of industrialized countries during their liberalization processes, as financial and exchange rate crises in a number of Nordic countries illustrate. The extent of the Asian and Russian financial crises (beginning in 1997 and 1998, respectively) highlighted the importance of taking a broader perspective. Increasing attention was given to the fact that transition and emerging market economies begin liberalization from a different position than had advanced countries in previous decades. Moreover, increased financial integration and innovation has led to changes in financial markets that have important consequences for capital flows. These differences are discussed further in Section 1.4.

The increased attention on the necessary preconditions for a successful liberalization is evident in the chapter by Stefan Ingves (Chapter 3). He clearly sets out the need for reform in various areas of the economy – particularly in the financial system – to precede complete liberalization of short-term capital flows. The Ingves chapter also emphasizes Bakker's conclusion that a wide range of approaches to liberalization can be successful (or unsuccessful). Moreover, the context for liberalization varies considerably between countries – in terms of institutional and policy settings, the likely size of capital flows, current controls, and so forth. This makes it impossible to map out a simple prescription that all countries can follow to avoid the risk of crises. Ingves therefore sets out ten general principles to be taken into account in sequencing capital liberalization – focussing in particular on the relationship between liberalization and other policy areas. In order to allow for country-specific factors, Ingves suggests that each country should then develop an individual plan for their liberalization process, within the framework provided by the general principles.

The chapter by Ingves illustrates that the IMF is responding to the challenges of recent financial crises by suggesting a more cautious approach to liberalization.[6] Although capital liberalization continues to be viewed as an important goal for countries to pursue, there is a greater awareness of the risks associated with a liberalization process that is not well coordinated with policy moves in other areas. In addition, the importance of the exchange rate regime is highlighted. Ingves implies that a flexible exchange rate regime may often be preferable for countries with capital mobility. As he notes, day-to-day exchange rate volatility may impose some costs on the economy, but these could be less than an unsuccessful attempt to maintain an unsustainable exchange rate, as experiences in some advanced countries confirm (Bakker and Chapple, 2002). Thiel also emphasizes the importance of discussions on institutional reform as a part of the liberalization process in the OECD context.

1.4 LIBERALIZATION THEN AND NOW – WHAT ARE THE DIFFERENCES?

As noted above, the context for capital account liberalization in transition and emerging market economies is in many ways different from that faced by the advanced countries. First, the institutional situation is considerably different. Transition countries generally actively seek to attract inward capital flows (particularly direct investment) as domestic savings are insufficient. In addition, domestic financial systems may be less developed and more regulated than was the case in advanced countries, reducing the ability of countries to intermediate portfolio inflows to productive uses. The second key area of difference concerns the fact that global financial markets are now considerably larger and more integrated than was the case 20 years ago. Relatedly, innovation has resulted in the development of many new financial instruments.

The Institutional Situation

Although the benefits of opening up the capital account are generally well accepted, the less desirable side-effects in terms of increased vulnerability to financial shocks have made the authorities in most transition countries cautious about capital liberalization. From the country studies in this book it emerges that the balance of benefits and risks seems to be determined by the credibility of the exchange rate regime and complementary institutional and macroeconomic reforms. In the initial stages of transition, priority has been given to opening up the trade account, as advanced economies did after the Second World War, and to stabilizing the economy in the face of high inflation. Given this, the restoration of current account convertibility was the main priority, as this allowed the generation of scarce foreign exchange through external trade. Previous trade relations had typically focussed on trade in the non-convertible ruble area. The Baltic states were among the first to attain Article VIII status at the IMF (in 1994) and Romania and Bulgaria among the last (see Table 1.1).[7]

A second overriding motive was to attract FDI as domestic savings and the scarcity of foreign exchange were hindering domestic expansion. FDI was not only instrumental in acquiring capital, but also urgently needed in order to import technological innovation and know-how. All transition economies liberalized FDI flows first, including the repatriation of profits, although some countries maintain administrative restrictions in certain key sectors for industrial policy reasons. Trade credit has also been liberalized and residents have generally been allowed to open foreign exchange deposits. The latter is an interesting difference from the experience of advanced economies which typically lifted restrictions on foreign currency deposits for residents only at the end of their liberalization process, as they were eager to prevent residents from quickly converting domestic currency into foreign currency in the event of diminished confidence. In contrast, transition countries were already characterized by a high degree of dollarization and/or euroization as foreign banknotes were regarded as a safe haven for savings (Table 1.2). Allowing residents to hold foreign currency deposits at domestic banks helped overcome foreign exchange scarcity. The extent of foreign currency holdings

Table 1.1　Acceptance of IMF Article VIII status

Country	Date	Country	Date
Lithuania	May 1994	Hungary	January 1996
Latvia	June 1994	Mongolia	February 1996
Estonia	August 1994	Russia	June 1996
Kyrgyzstan	March 1995	Kazakhstan	July 1996
Croatia	May 1995	Ukraine	September 1996
Poland	June 1995	Georgia	December 1996
Moldova	June 1995	Armenia	May 1997
Slovenia	September 1995	Romania	March 1998
Czech Republic	October 1995	Macedonia	June 1998
Slovak Republic	October 1995	Bulgaria	September 1998

Source : International Monetary Fund.

varies considerably between transition countries. Croatia has a relatively high level, consistent with its quasi-currency board approach to monetary policy. For some countries there is a trend towards a reduction in the relative importance of foreign currency deposits as confidence in the domestic currency increases.[8]

Table 1.2　Foreign currency deposits (% of broad money[a])

	1994	2000
Croatia	50.7	64.2
Czech Republic	7.0	10.6
Hungary	18.4	16.9
Moldova[b]	10.2	28.0
Poland	28.5	14.6
Slovak Republic		15.5
Slovenia	38.1	31.9

Notes :

a: M3, or M4 for Croatia. End of period data.

b: Data for 2000 are for the January–September period.

Sources: Oesterreichische Nationalbank 'Focus on Transition 1/2000', Vujčić (Chapter 9) and International Monetary Fund.

Aside from the motives for liberalization and the different sequencing, the broader policy context also differed between transition and advanced countries. The process of changing from socialist economies to market-oriented economies requires reform across virtually all areas of the economy. In contrast, advanced countries did not have to make such significant changes. In most cases advanced countries had a well-developed financial sector and moved to indirect instruments for monetary policy implementation prior to liberalization. An additional complicating factor for transition countries is the fact that their banking sectors have frequently inherited loans to state-owned enterprises where the prospects for recovery can be small. Both corporate and banking sector restructuring have therefore been required in order to allow the development of a healthy financial sector. An indication of the magnitude of the challenges that transition economies have faced is provided in Table 1.3 which sets out the estimated level of real GDP in 2001 as a ratio of the 1989 level for a number of transition countries. For transition countries overall, real GDP is well below its 1989 level, despite steady growth over the past few years.

Table 1.3 Real GDP in 2001 as a ratio of 1989 level*

Armenia	0.69
Croatia	0.84
Czech Republic	1.1
Hungary	1.08
Moldova	0.35
Poland	1.28
Russia	0.62
Ukraine	0.44
All Central-Eastern Europe and Baltic states	1.1
All South-Eastern Europe	0.76
All Commonwealth of Independent States	0.62
All transition countries	0.74

Note :* Only selected countries shown. Regional averages include additional countries.
Data for 2001 are estimates.

Source : European Bank for Reconstruction and Development.

Financial Market Developments

Two important changes in financial markets over the last two decades are the extraordinary growth in global financial markets and the innovation that has occurred in those markets, in terms of the availability of new financial instruments. Financial flows are therefore considerably greater than when advanced countries liberalized (Figure 1.1), while new financial instruments can make it more difficult to maintain effective capital controls. As is evident from the country studies, many countries seek to limit short-term portfolio flows. However, longer-term portfolio flows or direct investment can also be rapidly withdrawn if financial markets in the country concerned are sufficiently liquid. Moreover, there is an increasing variety of financial instruments and markets in which investors can effectively speculate against the currency. One consequence is that the ability to defend a fixed exchange rate by seeking to limit so-called speculative flows is likely to be considerably more difficult now than 20 years ago. These changes also pose challenges for risk management by financial institutions and for prudential supervisors.

Figure 1.1 Growth in global capital flows (index 1982 = 100)

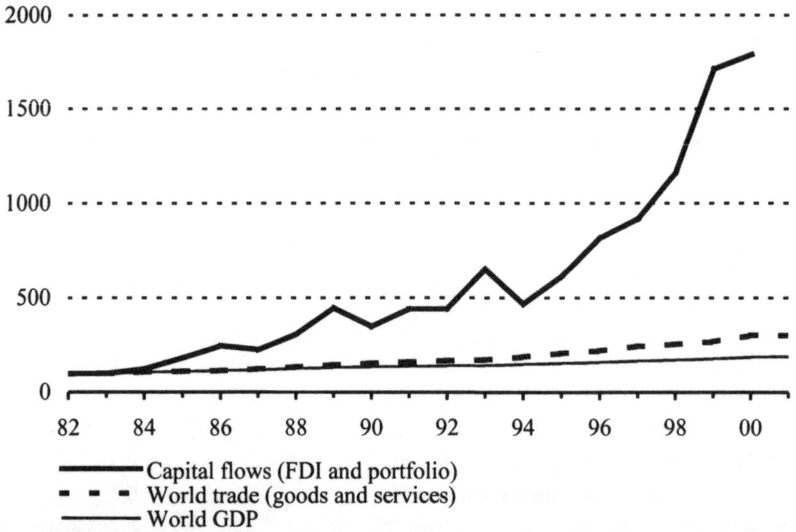

Source: International Monetary Fund. All series in volume terms.

The challenges of capital liberalization in this environment are evident in the contribution of Yung Chul Park and Chi-Young Song (Chapter 4). Park and Song discuss liberalization in four South-East Asian countries (Indonesia, Korea, Malaysia and Thailand). In discussing the case of Korea, the authors note the difficulties in considering the removal of capital controls while the infrastructure (including prudential supervision) was not sufficiently established to curb speculative behavior. Having relaxed controls to some extent by the beginning of the 1990s, Malaysia, Indonesia and Thailand each took measures to offset the adverse impact of large and (at times) volatile capital inflows prior to the crisis that began in 1997 – either via controls of one form or another, or (in the case of Thailand) by liberalizing outflows.

The focus of the Park and Song chapter is on responses to the crisis across the region and the possible impact of the differing responses on growth. The different reactions chosen by Korea (IMF assistance and further liberalization) and Malaysia (no IMF assistance and the reintroduction of capital controls) provide the opportunity for a comparison of the relative merits of the two approaches. After a careful examination of the data, Park and Song conclude that there is no real evidence to suggest that one approach was clearly better than the other. Both countries have recovered rapidly and strongly from the crisis. However, it is not obvious that the reintroduction of controls (in the case of Malaysia) or further liberalization (in the case of Korea) aided or hindered the speed and strength of the recovery. This ambiguity about the impact of capital controls in the current environment is seen by the authors as one factor behind the reluctance of South-East Asian countries to undertake extensive further liberalization in the near future, despite the encouragement of international and regional organization. Despite this questioning, the authors note that the real questions remains when, not if, these countries will further liberalize.

1.5 CAPITAL ACCOUNT LIBERALIZATION AND FINANCIAL REFORM

As noted above, this study confirms the view that sound financial institutions and markets are a precondition to benefit from financial integration and mitigate the risks associated with any reversals of investor sentiment. In most transition countries significant progress has been made in developing an efficient financial sector, but the progress has been uneven and the transition, even in the most advanced economies, is not yet complete. The pace and sequencing of banking reform have differed greatly. With the benefit of hindsight, voucher privatization schemes have been less successful, whereas countries allowing foreign ownership of banks have been among the most advanced. In the Czech Republic the privatization of banks through voucher auctions ended in a severe banking crisis and in the end all large banks were sold to foreign interests.

Country experiences show how difficult it has been in practice to establish domestic financial markets with sufficient depth and liquidity. Fixed-income capital markets have tended to be dominated by government issues. Although in all transition countries a Treasury bill market is functioning, issues of longer maturities and non-government debt have been few. Generally, stock markets remain underdeveloped. In Willem Buiter and Anita Taci's contribution (Chapter 6) the focus is on the need to build strong, stable and efficient domestic financial markets and institutions in order to reap the benefits and withstand the risks from cross-border capital flows. Even in the most advanced transition economies the development of the banking sector is still lagging compared to other emerging economies. Moreover, the establishment of the rules of the game is not sufficient – the rules need to be seen to be enforced in a transparent and credible manner.

Transition countries had no choice than to develop a relationship-based financial system in the absence of well-developed financial markets. Different privatization strategies were followed and Buiter and Taci are not enthusiastic about the voucher privatization schemes followed *inter alia* in the Czech Republic and a number of CIS (Commonwealth of Independent States) countries. These privatizations have contributed to connected lending and sectoral overconcentration. Countries which have allowed foreign ownership earliest, Hungary and the Baltic countries, have been most successful as foreign banks have spurred innovation and competition and brought about improved corporate governance practices. Although banks therefore dominate the financial sector, intermediation and efficiency levels are still low in comparison to advanced economies. Shortcomings in legal enforcement have also deterred bank intermediation. In recent years increased competition, privatization and foreign entry have increased the efficiency of the banking sector, but further consolidation seems unavoidable. If anything, Buiter and Taci are of the opinion that there are too many (small) banks in most transition economies.

Buiter and Taci strongly argue that capital liberalization should follow domestic financial sector reform and macroeconomic stabilization, echoing the conclusions of other authors. The risks associated with financial integration can be mitigated by institutional development, particularly of the legal and supervisory system. Strengthening supervision and increasing the autonomy of the supervisory authorities becomes particularly relevant when cross-border flows become relatively more important. Risks with respect to short-term inflows can be mitigated by prudential regulation, which is particularly important given the fact that these countries are bank dominated. Regarding the legal environment, the biggest obstacle is enforcement, not so much the formal legal framework itself. With the institutional environment strengthened in this way, a strong and sound banking sector can cope with capital mobility and allow the country to take full advantage of international capital flows. To this end, they argue that much more needs to be done to enhance consolidated reporting, improve the transparency and disclosure of financial operations and improve risk management by banks in transition countries.

1.6 LIBERALIZATION EXPERIENCES SO FAR

Apart from the common approach followed towards liberalization of current and FDI cross-border flows there have been marked differences in approach and speed towards the liberalization of other items of the capital account. Liberalization has often been made dependent on progress in other areas, such as financial sector deregulation, banking sector reform, monetary reform and establishing a credible exchange rate regime. As in the case of industrial countries, peer pressure by other countries and international organizations has been another factor which has determined the speed of capital account liberalization. An important motive has been the political imperative of speedy accession to international organizations, such as the OECD, and the European Community, which have created their own momentum for economic reform and liberalization.

Capital liberalization in many countries went hand in hand with the move towards a more flexible exchange rate regime (Armenia, Hungary, Poland), whereas in countries which stuck to capital controls, managed exchange rate regimes were maintained (Croatia, Ukraine). For the more advanced transition economies volatile short-term capital flows have been a matter of concern – lacking marketable domestic financial instruments the backward transition economies, such as Moldova, have not faced such problems. Countries such as the Czech Republic, Slovakia and Poland have faced large inflows of speculative short-term money and sharp reversals of investor climate which at times triggered currency crises. This has made countries such as Poland and Hungary, which have been slower in opening up the capital account, more cautious.

Categorizing the speed of liberalization can only be approximate and is complicated by the fact that some countries reintroduced exchange or capital controls following the Russian crisis. Similarly, progress to date in liberalizing flows varies considerably. Despite these limitations, it is clear that some countries have taken a gradual approach to liberalization, including Croatia, Hungary, Moldova, Poland, Russia, Slovenia and Ukraine. Of these countries, Moldova and Ukraine have been particularly slow. In contrast, liberalization has been more rapid in Armenia, the Czech Republic, Slovakia and the Baltic states. Regarding progress to date, Armenia, the Czech Republic, Hungary and the Baltic states have now largely liberalized capital flows, but in most other transition countries the liberalization of portfolio flows is still incomplete. It is difficult to establish whether the controls are effective and although most authors in this book refrain from a firm judgment in this respect, several do note that there is little indication that controls are binding. There seems to be agreement that controls are inefficient in the longer run, as loopholes (legally or illegally) are increasingly exploited. The sometimes enormous amounts of flight capital held by residents abroad suggests that controls are ineffective, especially in countries where law enforcement is weak and violators are not prosecuted. Nevertheless, controls are maintained (in some cases primarily to prevent tax evasion). As in advanced countries, a distinction can be made between the intensity of the formal controls and their actual implementation. Hungary and Poland, for example, made progress towards liberalization at times by streamlining and easing approval procedures, rather than by adjusting legislation.

Foreign direct investment inflows have varied considerably between transition countries in recent years (Figure 1.2). Although inflows declined somewhat in many countries over 2001, the total inflows to the region as a whole were little changed, despite the global economic downturn. To have maintained inflows in this environment is an indication of a degree of investor confidence in the outlook for the region. In cumulative terms over the 1989–2001 period, per capita inflows have been significantly higher in the average Central-Eastern European and Baltic country (US$1,365) than in either South-Eastern Europe (US$296) or the Commonwealth of Independent

Figure 1.2 Foreign direct investment inflows
(% of GDP, selected transition countries)

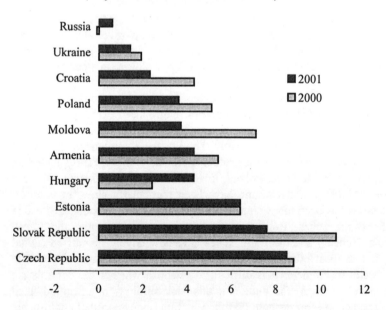

Source : European Bank for Reconstruction and Development.

States (US$196). This reflects not only relative progress made in liberalization and institutional reform, but also prospects for European Union accession.

Capital Liberalization in Selected Countries

Anatolii Shapovalov (Chapter 7) sketches a mixed picture for *Ukraine*. As domestic savings fell far short of investment needs, capital account liberalization was seen as instrumental in order to attract foreign capital. Ukraine suffered a major setback in the wake of the Asian and Russian crises as short-term portfolio investments were quickly withdrawn. Some of the previously liberalized capital restrictions were reintroduced and domestic financial sector development suffered a major setback. This experience has brought home the importance of a well-functioning domestic financial sector and a robust institutional setting, including appropriate legislation. The restructuring of external debt in 1999 has allowed a renewed gradual easing of capital restrictions. Nevertheless the authorities have been reluctant to liberalize cross-border portfolio flows because of their volatile nature and the still underdeveloped character of the domestic financial system.

The disappointing FDI flows into Ukraine to date (less than one-third of the levels attained by some Central European countries, relative to GDP) can be largely ascribed to lagging economic reforms, a less favorable investment climate due to fiscal disincentives and regulatory obstacles, and a faltering legal and institutional environment. In the Ukrainian context the lack of coordination between the state authorities, and more generally the unstable political environment, have also hindered FDI flows. Recently, better growth performance has improved the economic and financial climate. This may augur well for a repatriation of flight capital, which is estimated at US$10–20 billion.

The case of *Armenia*, described by Vache Gabrielyan and Armine Khachatryan in Chapter 8, provides an interesting and, among the CIS countries, rather isolated example of relatively rapid and eventually, in 1997, full capital account liberalization. After a dismal start, during which Armenia suffered hyperinflation, initially severe capital controls were established to underpin the stabilization efforts and support the introduction of a national currency. When inflation was under better control and the new currency consequently strengthened, these controls were gradually relaxed and eventually eliminated at the time the exchange rate was floated. However, the absence of a well-developed financial system at the time of capital liberalization has hindered the attraction of long-term foreign capital, as has the unstable political climate.

At the same time Armenia has weathered the shake-out of the subsequent international financial crises relatively well, despite its liberalized environment. Gabrielyan and Khachatryan argue that the floating exchange regime has functioned as a good shock absorber. Moreover, the authorities have strengthened the supervisory and regulatory framework following capital liberalization and have actively promoted prudential risk management by banks. At the same time, the build-up of foreign exchange reserves and the reluctance to use them for interventions in the foreign exchange market has helped underpin monetary and financial stability. All in all, Armenia has not been harmed by early capital liberalization, but the benefits of financial integration thus far have not yet been fully reaped.

At the other spectrum of the corner solutions for exchange rate regimes is *Croatia*, which has sought stabilization through the operation of a quasi-currency board. At a very high level of currency substitution (almost 75 per cent of broad money is foreign currency denominated), Croatia probably is the most euroized country among the Central and Eastern European countries. In Boris Vujčić's contribution (Chapter 9) it becomes clear that Croatia has regarded the development of a sound financial sector as a priority, having experienced a mini banking crisis in the early transition years, and puts much less emphasis on opening up the capital account than some of the neighboring countries. Stabilization was helped by FDI flows (attracted by stability-oriented policies) but also by the repatriation of capital held abroad.

Croatia combines a very high degree of currency substitution with relatively tight controls on portfolio flows, particularly for short-term cross-border capital transactions. Croatia experimented with Chilean-type capital restrictions on short-term capital inflows from 1998. These were initially successful but were lifted relatively quickly when fortune turned against emerging economies and the inflows dried up anyway. Although some relaxation is envisaged in 2003, it is likely that controls will remain in place until EU accession. Vujčić, who pointedly compares FDI flows to good cholesterol and short-term capital to bad cholesterol, argues that controls on short-term capital inflows are particularly relevant for countries with a high degree of currency substitution as they cannot develop a wide range of indirect monetary policy instruments which could be used to counter the inflationary impact of such inflows.

Croatia has experimented with national currency reserve requirements for banks on foreign currency-denominated deposits as an instrument to stabilize foreign exchange markets in a highly euroized economy. However, the inherent mismatch in banks' balance sheets seems only acceptable under supervisory guidance, for instance by limiting the net foreign currency exposure of banks in order to diminish the mismatch risk. Vujčić discusses the pros and cons of an early euro adoption which by eliminating the exchange rate risk would help diminish sudden reversals in capital flows and bring down interest rate risk premia. An important precondition would be increased flexibility of the economy as the exchange rate can no longer be used as an adjustment mechanism.

Hungary provides an interesting example of a country which has been particularly well aware of the risks of a premature liberalization of the capital account. It followed a process of gradual liberalization, both with respect to pace and sequencing, although the final goal of full liberalization was always clear. Supported by macroeconomic and structural policies it has been very successful in attracting FDI. In his contribution, Roger Nord (Chapter 10) argues that the relatively tight controls on short-term capital flows combined with a narrow-band exchange rate regime may have been instrumental in shielding Hungary from contagion effects from international financial crises in the second half of the 1990s. As nonresidents could only unwind long positions (mainly government bonds), but could not speculate against the currency by borrowing forint and going short, speculation against the currency was discouraged.

An important element in the case of Hungary was the crawling narrow-band exchange rate arrangement. Sterilized intervention helped shield domestic interest rates from external pressure, thus maintaining some measure of monetary independence. Nord considers that 'second-best' arguments in favor of controls on short-term flows in the case of Hungary apparently did not distract FDI flows. Insofar as these controls enhanced macroeconomic stability they may even have been conducive to attracting capital. More importantly, steady legal and regulatory reform enhanced the attractiveness of Hungary for foreign investors.

In Hungary, liberalization went together with the widening of the exchange rate band and the introduction of inflation targetting. Nord argues that the decision to liberalize therefore was more the consequence of conscious domestic policy choices (where investors needed the opportunity to hedge currency risk), as the benefits of liberalization began to become outweighed by the costs. The eventual abolition of all remaining controls on short-term capital flows in 2001 can be regarded as a sign of strength, Hungary being in the vanguard of the EU accession countries.

Moldova provides an example of a country where relatively decisive action on financial sector reform and the opening-up of the capital account has failed to deliver the hoped-for benefits. Veronica Bacalu (Chapter 11) ascribes this dismal performance to the very fragile macroeconomic and political environment, where reforms take a stop–go character. Initial successes were marred in the aftermath of the Russian crisis, which provoked a severe exchange crisis. Eventually, the national currency depreciated by more than 40 per cent and the local economy became increasingly dollarized, as noted above. There are no controls on inflows in an attempt to attract FDI, but dire economic circumstances have kept these extremely low. Barring marketable domestic financial instruments, portfolio inflows have been negligible. As the benefits of liberalization of capital outflows are not clear to the authorities, a cautious, gradual approach is being followed. Controls aim at keeping the limited financial resources at home and assist in avoiding tax evasion and fighting corruption. As actual requests for legally permitted outflows are very low, controls in all likelihood are more efficient as a tax enforcement instrument than as an instrument to regulate outflows of capital.

Poland's attitude towards capital liberalization has been cautious and the opening-up of the capital account has been subordinated to the overriding aim of getting inflation under control and stabilizing the economy, as Ewa Sadowska-Cieslak describes in Chapter 12. As in other Central European countries, application for OECD membership has speeded up the reform process. Capital liberalization was well sequenced in line with monetary developments. Poland first liberalized long-term (FDI) inflows, but kept controls on short-term inflows and outflows intact. The prospect of EU membership provoked relatively large capital inflows, attracted as well by the high real interest rates needed to stabilize inflationary expectations. The central bank tried to sterilize part of the inflows and allowed for some real appreciation of the exchange rate to take the heat off. Eventually a move towards greater exchange rate variability was more effective to discourage short-term inflows. An initial commitment to the OECD to abolish all capital restrictions by the end of 1999 was rescinded in view of the still prevailing imbalances in the Polish economy.

The change in the exchange regime from a fixed to a fully floating exchange rate took over a decade. Monetary policy strategies have switched in tandem from money targetting to inflation targetting. Thus, a macroeconomic environment has been created which should be conducive for Poland to reap the benefits from financial integration. A further strengthening of the financial sector and the supervisory regime may be well advised before the capital account is fully liberalized.

1.7 CONCLUDING REMARKS

The country studies discussed above illustrate that the direction towards capital account liberalization is clear in transition countries. It is also clear that these countries are being gradually integrated into world capital markets – with the likely EU accession countries leading the way. As was the case for industrialized countries in earlier decades, however, the liberalization paths chosen vary widely between countries. Clearly, there are many possible ways of successfully opening the capital account – if there is a 'best' way, it is yet to be discovered. Nevertheless, the importance of getting the institutional and macroeconomic framework right continues to be crucial for two reasons. First, to ensure that the risks associated with liberalization (for the financial system and exchange rate regime) are minimized. Second, the institutional framework helps determine whether the desired international capital flows will be forthcoming, and whether they will be productively used. The country experiences described in the following chapters make these links clear.

Our hope is that this book provides a useful overview of transition countries' liberalization experiences to date and makes a contribution to the ongoing search by policy makers for insights into the challenges they face.

NOTES

1. The chapter discussing Hungary is the exception and is written by the then IMF resident representative, in close consultation with national authorities. At the time of writing, Veronica Bacalu was Deputy Governor of the National Bank of Moldova and Armine Khachatryan was Head of the Monetary Policy Department at the Central Bank of Armenia.
2. Alternatively, controls have at times been used as a shield to delay necessary macroeconomic adjustment (see Bakker, this book). This raises the related concern that the reimposition of controls can signal a wavering of the commitment to reform in other areas of economic policy. The reimposition of controls is often presented as a temporary measure to allow for fundamental reforms to occur in an orderly manner. In practice, it has often been the case that controls have been long-lasting and have allowed the postponement of reforms.
3. See, for example, Eichengreen and Mussa (1998).
4. For example, Quirk and Evans (1995).
5. To its credit, the IMF acknowledges that prior to the Asian crisis, it could have placed more emphasis on the need for reforms to support capital account liberalization before controls were removed (see Rogoff, 2002).
6. See also Ishii et al. (2002).
7. Article VIII of the IMF Articles of Association refers to convertibility of the currency for current account (trade in goods and services) purposes.
8. In contrast, some countries (e.g., Moldova) have experienced an increase in the proportion of foreign currency deposits as doubts persist about the domestic currency.

PART ONE

Policy Issues and Earlier Experiences

2. Advanced country experiences with capital account liberalization

Age Bakker

2.1 INTRODUCTION

It is nowadays taken for granted that capital movements are fully liberalized among industrial countries. This is in striking contrast to the state of affairs only two decades ago when most countries still maintained restrictive capital regimes. Why did these industrial countries hang on to capital control regimes for such a long time? And what caused the remarkable shift in appreciation of the pros and cons of capital controls among policy makers? Which approaches for capital liberalization have been followed? And are there lessons to be learned from successes and failures?

It should be realized that capital controls have not been a generalized phenomenon in the industrial world. Not all advanced countries have made extensive use of capital controls. In particular, the two major post-war reserve currency countries, the United States and Germany, traditionally have adopted liberal policies, commensurate to the key role their currencies played in the international financial system. A brief episode at the end of the Bretton Woods system, when both countries tried to stem so-called 'hot money' flows, was the exception. Canada and Switzerland also generally adhered to a liberal regime.

There were also a few countries, including Belgium and Luxembourg, which did not apply direct credit controls, but operated a multiple exchange market instead, in the Belgian/Luxembourg case until 1990. Although in these countries there were no outright restrictions on capital flows, the administrative apparatus was still needed to distinguish capital transactions from current transactions, in order to decide in which exchange market they would be settled. Whereas trade and services flows were settled at the official managed exchange rate, capital transactions were settled in the market at a so-called 'financial exchange rate', which was a floating rate that typically carried a discount.

However, these were exceptions. For much of the post-war period, capital controls were seen as an essential part of economic policy in industrial countries. In the face of the so-called 'incompatible triangle' of simultaneously achieving an autonomous monetary policy, exchange rate stability and free capital movements, capital controls were considered to be the lesser evil of the available choices.

Controls on cross-border payments had been a widespread phenomenon immediately after the Second World War, in view of the prevailing foreign exchange scarcity. A first priority was to restore trade relations and thus allow for the generation of foreign exchange. For most industrial countries, trade in goods and services had been liberalized and current account convertibility had been restored around 1958. Thereafter, in the 1960s, most countries began to dismantle controls on capital movements as well. However, this shift towards a more liberal regime was stalled and subsequently reversed when problems emerged in the Bretton Woods system of fixed exchange rates in the late 1960s. In the 1970s and the 1980s economic performance diverged considerably among countries, particularly with respect to inflation, and the authorities aimed at limiting the impact of variable capital flows which reflected these divergences. Although the attitude *vis-à-vis* capital controls was clearly influenced by actions in neighboring countries or by peer pressure in a multilateral context, particularly emanating from OECD (Organisation for Economic Co-operation and Development) and European Community membership, advanced countries typically took restrictive action or liberalized at different points in time, depending on their individual circumstances.

Capital controls were applied in different ways by advanced countries. Because of this historical setting, countries took different approaches to liberalization and did so for different reasons. That makes it difficult to provide an overall picture of the liberalization process. On the other hand, it also illustrates that there is no single 'right way' to liberalize. Therefore the history of capital liberalization in part is a history of case studies. But there are also common threads and common denominators. By focussing on the experiences of a few representative countries, some lessons can be drawn that seem to be common to advanced countries.

The chapter continues in Section 2.2 with a discussion of the various motives for capital controls. In discussing liberalization, we make a distinction between countries that liberalized gradually and those that went through a more rapid process. Of those countries that liberalized gradually, Japan and France provide interesting examples and are covered in Section 2.3. The discussion of the French experience also provides the backdrop for a broader discussion of liberalization in Europe. The United Kingdom provides an interesting and leading example of a country undertaking a rapid liberalization (Section 2.4). Section 2.5 concludes with the key lessons from advanced country experiences.

2.2 MOTIVES FOR CAPITAL CONTROLS

The main motives for maintaining capital controls were to limit exchange rate movements and to preserve a degree of independent monetary policy (and thereby to increase economic policy autonomy more generally). In some cases, these motives were linked to a desire to protect and stimulate domestic industry or to taxation considerations. At the risk of oversimplification, countries using capital controls can be split into two broad groups. Some wished to maintain exchange rate stability while maintaining looser monetary conditions than those in other countries – these countries tended to use controls on outflows. Others wished to maintain relatively tight domestic monetary conditions without causing an exchange rate appreciation and consequent loss of competitiveness – these countries used controls on inflows.

In practice, in quite a number of cases controls were applied to both capital outflows and inflows. A prime example is provided by the experience of Japan. During the 1970s, Japan frequently tightened and loosened controls on both portfolio inflows and portfolio outflows in order to offset exchange rate movements. Figure 2.1 shows that the yen appreciated strongly between mid-1971 and late 1973 (to allow for inflation differentials the real effective exchange rate is depicted). The authorities responded by tightening controls on inflows and relaxing controls on outflows. As the exchange rate depreciated from 1973 to 1976, the pattern was reversed: outflows were restricted and inflows encouraged. The pattern was again reversed in 1977– 78 as the yen appreciated and finally, after another reversal of fortune for the yen following the second oil crisis in 1979, when the yen depreciated.

Most changes in controls were applied to portfolio flows only – for example reserve requirements on nonresident yen accounts were altered as were rules on the purchase of foreign securities by Japanese institutional investors. In contrast to the active management of portfolio flows, there were few formal changes to controls on direct investment. This could be because these flows were more easily influenced by administrative measures, such as varying the length of time taken to process the formal approvals that were required. In this informal way, net foreign direct investment flows were manipulated as well.

Were these measures successful? As Figure 2.1 shows, the controls were not able to prevent quite sizeable exchange rate movements during the decade. Whether these would have been bigger in the absence of controls is

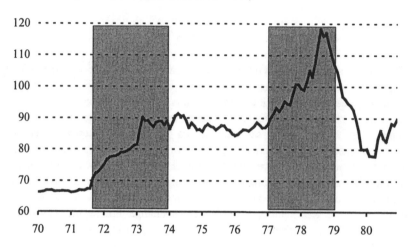

Figure 2.1 Japan: real effective exchange rate
(monthly averages, index 1990 = 100)

Source : International Monetary Fund.

an open question. Still, a number of authors have concluded that the controls were at least partly effective in insulating Japanese financial markets from world markets.[1] Even if the controls were unable to alter the basic trend of exchange rate movements (which were generally in line with economic fundamentals), they may have dampened volatility around that trend. The fact that the domestic financial system was heavily regulated during this period would also have helped limit the evasion of the controls.

Another example of a country which at a certain time used controls on both inflows and outflows was the Netherlands. The Dutch central bank policy in the immediate post-war period sought to limit domestic monetary expansion through direct credit controls. Short-term inflows were restricted as a supplementary measure, in order to prevent credit ceilings from being circumvented by borrowing abroad. At the same time controls on long-term outflows were imposed to ensure that foreign borrowers did not seek to take advantage of the low Dutch interest rates. However, as the economy opened up, the effectiveness of these controls diminished. One notorious loophole in the Netherlands was the use of intra-company credits between different branches of multinational companies. They were removed in the 1980s when monetary policy switched to market-oriented indirect instruments.

Controls on Outflows

Controls on outflows were typically imposed by countries operating a looser monetary policy than those countries with whom they were seeking to maintain stable exchange rates. Their main aim was to maintain room for maneuver for domestic policies while safeguarding the exchange rate. Especially countries which tried to maintain a measure of intra-European exchange rate stability after the demise of the Bretton Woods system had recourse to capital controls. Figure 2.2 illustrates that such controls were not particularly effective in the cases of France and Italy in maintaining exchange rate stability versus Germany. This is not surprising, considering that the French inflation rate averaged two to three times the German rate between the early 1970s and early 1980s, and the Italian inflation rate was even higher. Other countries, including the United Kingdom and New Zealand, also experienced exchange rate crises as capital controls proved unable to stem sizeable capital flows in the face of unsustainable macroeconomic policy settings.

Figure 2.2 French franc and Italian lire versus German mark
(monthly averages, index Q1 1970 = 100)

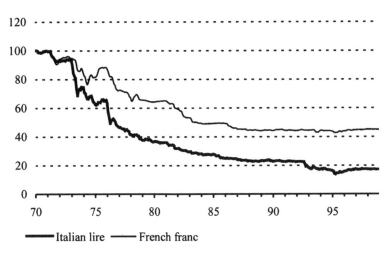

Source: Bundesbank.

To be fair, there were some temporary successes and controls sometimes provided short-term respite when imposed to offset speculative attacks. Controls introduced as part of a more wide-ranging package of measures designed to restore confidence were generally more effective than controls introduced without supporting policies.

On the other hand, capital controls were less effective when repeatedly used, especially when they proved unable to prevent exchange rate devaluations. More generally, the effectiveness of capital controls tended to erode over time, as financial innovations blurred the traditional distinctions between market segments. The European experience also illustrated that systems where restrictions can be reintroduced have the disadvantage that foreign investors anticipate these moves. Such currencies were perceived as 'mousetrap' currencies, where investors could bring assets in, but found it difficult to legally withdraw them. There is anecdotal evidence that foreign direct investment flows were negatively affected, but it is not possible to draw firm conclusions from existing data. However, capital controls did hamper substitutability between, for instance, German and French financial assets. Portfolio shifts triggered by expectations of an appreciation of the German mark *vis-à-vis* the US dollar therefore invariably prompted intra-European exchange rate tensions, since inflows into French franc assets were considered to run into a 'mousetrap'.

Controls on Inflows

While financial market participants often viewed outflow controls as a sign of weakness, this was not always the case with inflow controls. Controls on short-term capital inflows became a feature of the late 1960s and early 1970s in Europe, when strains in the Bretton Woods system of fixed exchange rates resulted in sizeable capital flows to low inflation countries such as Germany, the Netherlands and Switzerland, threatening domestic monetary stability. Controls in these countries generally included the prohibition of interest payments on nonresident accounts.

The case of Germany is typical of these experiences. Germany experimented with market-conforming indirect measures to discourage inflows. In 1972 the *Bardepot* was introduced, involving a non-interest-bearing deposit at the central bank of part of the proceeds of credits taken up by residents abroad (similar to the controls subsequently introduced in Chile). Higher domestic interest rates for monetary policy purposes continued to attract capital flight out of the United States and the flows were diverted to other financial instruments that were not subject to the *Bardepot*. In order to close loopholes, direct measures to control cross-border inflows eventually had to be introduced. Restrictions on inflows were to a large extent dismantled when the first oil crisis (1973) changed the fortunes of European currencies, including the German mark.

What are the lessons? First, controls do not deter speculation during times of currency unrest. Controls were circumvented on a large scale and enforcement was insufficient. Banks actively advised clients to use loopholes. Second, the effectiveness of market-oriented controls tended to erode over time. Therefore direct controls were also needed, including outright prohibition of certain capital transactions. Third, imposition of unremunerated minimum cash reserve requirements tended to dislocate financial activity to other financial centers and to other non-bank financial institutions. In sum, the effectiveness of capital controls tended to be relatively low in more developed financial systems such as Germany.

The case for controls on inflows may be stronger for less-advanced economies with a less sophisticated domestic financial system. Large-scale inflows have been a special problem in countries which were catching up with more advanced-countries. Good examples here are Spain and Portugal, which, after becoming members of the European Community in 1986, were confronted with very substantial capital inflows. These inflows threatened to undermine monetary stability and temporary controls on short-term capital inflows were introduced to dampen upward pressures on the exchange rate. On the whole, their effectiveness was mixed.[2] Although spreads between domestic and euromarket interest rates increased, suggesting some effect, the controls were evaded by substitution of regulated items of the capital account to non-restricted items. In addition, both countries were confronted with sales of securities by international fund managers who were unable to cover their positions. The negative repercussions for long-term capital flows were costly, given the dependence on external finance in the catching-up process. In view of these negative confidence factors, the restrictions were soon abolished in both countries.

2.3 EXPERIENCES WITH GRADUAL LIBERALIZATION

As the authorities over time became increasingly disappointed about the effectiveness of capital controls, their abolition became an attractive alternative policy option. Perhaps the most obvious difference between country experiences concerns the speed of liberalization and deregulation. Most countries followed a cautious approach so as not to jeopardize exchange rate and monetary stability. In addition, gradual liberalization was linked to reform in other policy areas, both domestically (such as the deregulation of the domestic financial sector and changes to the monetary policy strategy) and externally (with respect to the exchange rate regime). Japan provides a good example of the gradual approach, as does the European experience, albeit in a different political setting.

Japan

Japan took a very gradual approach towards opening up. The heavily regulated domestic financial system, including the ability of the authorities to exercise moral suasion, enhanced the effectiveness of controls. As noted earlier, controls on portfolio flows were actively used during the 1970s in an attempt to offset exchange rate pressures.

This approach was abandoned in 1979 and Japan embarked on a very gradual liberalization process. As regards direct investment flows, a key step was the change to a positive exchange control system in 1980 in which all flows were permitted unless expressly prohibited. However, a prior approval system remained in place for direct inward investment and the varying time taken to gain permission could be used to influence investment flows. Moreover, the high level of domestic savings also reduced the extent to which inflows were required to finance domestic industrial development. From 1992, prior approval was only required for investment in four industries although inflows remained very low, suggesting that explicit or implicit capital controls on inflows remained in place for a longer period. In contrast, outflows increased rapidly in the mid-1980s. In part this is likely to be a response to the high value of the yen, which made it more attractive to open manufacturing plants in other countries. Pressure from the United States regarding the bilateral trade deficit is also likely to have been a factor in encouraging Japanese companies to move production to facilities offshore. As Figure 2.3 illustrates, inflows remained low until the late 1990s, probably reflecting a combination of high domestic savings and limited reform of the domestic economy.

Liberalization of portfolio investment was also influenced by US pressure, which culminated in the so-called yen–dollar agreement in 1984. A number of liberalization moves had already taken place prior to 1984, including the abolition of restrictions on purchase by nonresidents of Japanese bonds, the removal of convertibility restrictions on nonresident yen accounts and the liberalization of euro–yen lending by Japanese banks. Following the yen–dollar agreement, liberalization moves gathered pace.

As a result, portfolio investment flows grew rapidly from the mid-1980s. The Japanese approach to portfolio flows initially involved allowing capital liberalization in offshore markets, preferably without disturbing the domestic financial system, which remained highly regulated. However, arbitrage between the various markets was possible (Ito, 1992), leading to sizeable capital flows when the exchange rate was considered to be misaligned.

The problems which emerged at a later stage in the Japanese banking sector following the asset price bubble do not appear to have been directly related to capital account liberalization *per se*. Instead, the problems are more likely to have been rooted in the gradual and partial approach taken to domestic financial market deregulation.[3] In addition, supervisory policies and risk management practices by the banks did not keep pace with the increased risk appetite when financial repression ended.

Figure 2.3 Japan: foreign direct investment (% GDP)

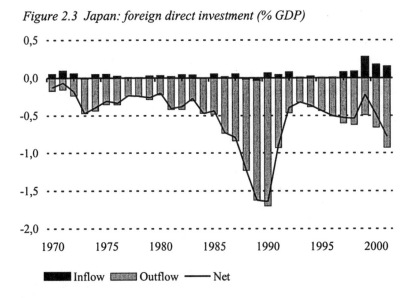

Source: International Monetary Fund.

A more forceful domestic deregulation prior to capital account liberalization would have reduced some of the pressures on the banking system. Domestic deregulation would also have facilitated greater direct investment inflows and would therefore have stimulated competition and innovation in product markets. Controls should probably have been abolished a decade earlier, in line with most other advanced economies.

Europe

European liberalization proceeded in fits and starts until the 1980s.[4] The liberalization in many European countries since then can only really be understood in the context of the quest for greater economic and monetary integration. In particular, the desire to preserve exchange rate stability in order to enhance the functioning of the internal market was important. The European Monetary System (EMS) was established in 1979 among European countries, precisely with a view to restoring exchange rate stability in Europe and thus giving a new impetus to regional economic integration. The first four years of its operation were at best a mixed success with repeated speculative attacks, large-scale interventions and, eventually, sizeable realignments. These were clearly linked to differences in economic fundamentals. From 1981 to 1983 capital controls were tightened considerably, including in France and Italy. These were the last attempts to control speculative outflows by capital restrictions.

Given the varying inflation performance between countries, it is not surprising that countries were unable to maintain stable bilateral exchange rates. The liberalization process (called 'active gradualism') started in 1985, when EU member states agreed on the Single Act aimed at removing all remaining obstacles for the internal market by 1992. 'Active gradualism' is an apt description as it conjures up both the notion of a careful and measured process, but also one where there is some pressure to reach the final goal of complete liberalization.

The willingness to further liberalize was regularly tested. After repeated realignments had underlined the difficulty of maintaining bilateral exchange rates with increasingly high capital mobility, the operating mechanisms of the EMS were strengthened in the so-called Basel/Nyborg agreement of 1987. This agreement constituted one of the distinct turning points in the history of capital account liberalization in Europe. It comprised changes aimed at deterring speculation by showing that speculation was both costly (due to high interest rates) and unrewarding (the full use of the fluctuation band in combination with small realignments implied only limited changes in actual exchange rates after a realignment). Importantly, these technical changes were supported by increased policy attention to economic fundamentals, resulting in a considerable decrease in the number and size of realignments and marking the beginning of a long period of quasi-exchange rate stability.

Nevertheless, countries did liberalize at different times and speeds, as Figure 2.4 on the reservations to the OECD liberalization codes shows. It is also clear that some of the countries which undertook a rapid liberalization, such as the United Kingdom, had previously had a more extensive control system than the countries which adopted a gradual approach. The dates of liberalization of some European countries also illustrate that point. The switch to a positive capital control system, implying that all capital flows were allowed unless explicitly prohibited, in many cases was a clear indication of a move towards a more liberal stance (see Table 2.1). Other countries maintained a negative system, implying that all capital transactions were prohibited unless expressly allowed, for a much longer time.

Within Europe, the French experience is an example of a relatively successful gradual liberalization process. After the severe exchange crises from 1981 until 1983, which occurred despite a sharp tightening of capital

Figure 2.4 Reservations to OECD liberalization codes in Europe (%)

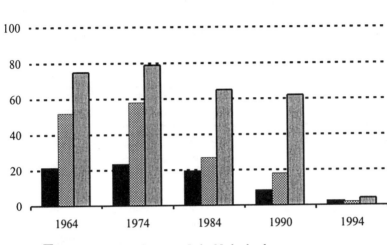

■ Belgium, France, Germany, Italy, Netherlands
▨ Denmark, Ireland, United Kingdom
▢ Greece, Portugal, Spain

Source: Bakker (1996).

controls, there was general disillusionment regarding the effectiveness of capital controls. This provided the political backdrop for a turnaround in French policies. The reorientation of France's economic strategy in 1983 included a major deregulation of the financial sector in stages, abolition of the quantitative credit control mechanism (1985), and reforms in the money and capital markets. In France there was thus a well-thought-out sequencing order, in which first deregulation of the financial sector, restoration of positive real interest rates, and more market-oriented ways of monetary control were implemented while still using capital controls. At the same time, macroeconomic policies were aimed at decreasing inflation and restoring balance of payments equilibrium.

When the French macroeconomic situation strengthened and the financial sector was considered able to withstand foreign competition, capital controls were gradually withdrawn over the second half of the 1980s. This made it possible to actively pursue a hard-currency policy which restored confidence in the financial markets. Periods of exchange rate tension were countered by decisive action by the monetary authorities. All in all, the French experience shows that full capital mobility can go hand in hand with greater exchange rate stability, provided that the authorities are prepared to adopt supporting policies. Unrest in exchange markets in April 1986 and January 1987 led to devaluations of the French franc of 6 per cent and 3 per cent relative to the German mark. However, these were smaller than the devaluations of the 1981–83 period and the liberalization process was not disrupted.

Table 2.1 Switch to positive regimes and full liberalization

	Positive regime	Full liberalization
Germany	1961	1981
Netherlands	1977	1986
United Kingdom	1979	1979
Denmark	1988	1988
Italy	1988	1990
France	1989	1989
Spain	1992	1992

Source: Bakker (1996).

The generally favorable sentiment in Europe changed abruptly when doubts arose over whether all EU member states would participate in monetary union. Market attention again shifted to the differences in macroeconomic policies between countries, resulting in the EMS crises of 1992 and 1993. After repeated speculative attacks, the fluctuation bands were widened from 2.25 to 15 per cent in 1993, creating a two-way risk in the market. Although the French franc came under severe downward pressure in the 1992–93 EMS crises, the central rate was not adjusted. But other countries suffered badly and the United Kingdom had to withdraw from the EMS. These crises demonstrate that even if the fundamentals are more or less correct and exchange rate targets are supported by stability-oriented policies, the exchange rate can still be forcefully tested by the markets. However, there was no backtracking on the earlier capital liberalization efforts.

2.4 RAPID LIBERALIZATION

As is the case with gradual liberalization, experiences of rapid liberalization vary widely. However, rapid capital account liberalization has generally occurred around the same time as, or immediately following, deregulation of the domestic financial system. Reforms often coincided with a period of strong economic growth, boosted by the increased availability of credit. In a number of countries, the associated boom in asset prices and bank lending led to a financial sector crisis when the economic boom ended.

The trend for rapid liberalization has been set by the United Kingdom, which in the post-war period operated one of the most extensive systems of capital controls alongside tight domestic financial regulation. The UK became a member of the European Community in 1973. Normally that would have required steps to liberalize those capital flows that were already liberalized by the founding members. However, the UK was permitted a temporary exemption and actually tightened controls following the sterling crisis in November 1976. Nevertheless, the UK continued to suffer frequent exchange rate crises, despite extensive controls. In 1979 that all changed. Capital controls were partially eased from June and in October remaining controls were abolished in one step. At the same time, the UK embarked on a major reorientation of economic policies.

The turnaround in economic policy coincided with the discovery of oil reserves in early 1979, which, combined with high nominal interest rates, put upward pressure on the exchange rate. The nominal exchange rate rose around 12 per cent over a six-month period, raising concerns about competitiveness. The removal of capital controls was expected to lead to welcome downward pressure on sterling as domestic institutional investors had indicated a desire to diversify their portfolios by increasing their holdings of foreign assets. The circumstances for the removal of controls were therefore favorable.

Economic growth did improve during the 1980s and inflation fell. This last factor was critical as it represented the end of the spiral of devaluations and inflation which had prompted crises in the past. Nevertheless, there were transitional costs, including a period of industrial unrest, and an asset price bubble developed towards the end of the 1980s. Exchange rate volatility was also problematic at times, although this was viewed as less costly than attempting to use capital controls to limit that volatility. The liberalized financial system helped mitigate the adverse impact of exchange rate volatility on the real economy by offering hedging opportunities to industry. The British example of rapid liberalization has been followed in particular by industrial countries which also had a history of relatively tight regulation, such as some of the Nordic countries and Australia and New Zealand.

The transition costs of liberalization and deregulation in some of these cases were greater than expected, especially when reform of labor and product markets lagged behind reforms in other areas of the economy. This was certainly the case in New Zealand, for example, where significant labor market reform and reform in some product markets did not occur for a number of years following capital account liberalization. These delays may have contributed to the build-up of imbalances in the New Zealand economy between the traded and non-traded sectors, and to the rapid rise in asset prices and the subsequent stress in the financial sector as asset prices fell back sharply.

In fact a number of countries experienced an asset price boom following rapid capital account liberalization, causing financial sector problems when asset prices subsequently collapsed.[5] However, determining why this developed into a financial crisis in some countries is not straightforward. Two key points emerge. First, given the increased risks that are present in a deregulated environment, and the loss of economic rents that financial institutions may previously have enjoyed, it is important to ensure that prudential practices and standards are strengthened to meet the challenges of the new environment. Both supervisory authorities and financial institutions need to enhance their risk management ability. Denmark, for example significantly increased required capital ratios in the early 1980s, applying more stringent requirements than those adopted by the Basle committee in 1993. There are also some suggestions that Danish supervision was more vigilant than in other Nordic countries during the 1980s, with earlier recognition of loan losses (Edey and Hviding, 1995). This may have contributed to their ability to avoid the financial crises which hit other Nordic countries at the end of the 1980s. Clarity regarding responsibilities is important where several institutions have responsibility for supervision to prevent financial institutions seeking the least costly regulation. Applying different prudential standards to different parts of financial conglomerates, as in Sweden in the 1980s, can also encourage regulatory arbitrage and increase the risk of financial sector problems developing.

Second, macroeconomic policy must be credible and sustainable – particularly with respect to the exchange rate regime. In comparison with some Nordic countries where an exchange rate peg was maintained at the time of rapid liberalization, countries such as the United Kingdom, New Zealand and Australia, which moved to a floating exchange rate around the time of capital account liberalization, experienced relatively minor financial sector difficulties. Although it can lead to greater exchange rate volatility in the short term, a floating regime also encourages hedging against exchange rate risk. In contrast, a fixed regime may encourage borrowers to accumulate unhedged foreign currency debt where offshore interest rates are lower. If an exchange rate adjustment is eventually required, as was the case in Finland, Norway and Sweden, the value of foreign currency debt increases, adding to financial and corporate stress.

2.5 KEY LESSONS FROM EXPERIENCES IN ADVANCED COUNTRIES

Policy makers in industrial countries have regarded capital controls as an integral part of economic policy until the 1980s. Various motives have played a role, such as the wish to limit exchange rate variability and preserve a degree of monetary autonomy, as well as a desire to protect domestic industrial sectors and avoid tax evasion. The effectiveness of these controls has varied considerably and has tended to erode over time as markets adjusted to them. At times, capital controls were able to have some stabilizing effect, depending on the economic circumstances and the financial structure of the country concerned. Controls were more effective when the domestic financial sector was heavily regulated and/or largely owned by the government. Capital controls therefore may have tended to prolong periods of relative exchange rate stability particularly in countries with dirigistic economic policies, such as Japan and France. However, when underlying tensions, emanating from inflation differentials or fiscal policy imbalances, were building up, eventually sharp exchange rate corrections could not be avoided. In circumstances of severe exchange rate tensions, intensification of capital controls generally provided only temporary respite when they were imposed to offset speculative attacks. They were usually not able to prevent an eventual exchange rate adjustment. As controls lost their effectiveness in response to market innovation, the authorities often sought to close emerging loopholes rather than reform the entire system. Therefore, controls tended to remain in place for longer than originally intended.

Why did countries hang on to capital controls for such a long time? Political economy considerations may provide part of the answer. Although the second-best character of capital controls was generally understood and their effectiveness was considered to be doubtful, the imposition of controls in the face of strong speculative pressures has at times helped to calm markets, thus providing a breathing space during which to adjust policies. The authorities' desire to have controls available if necessary may help to explain their longevity. Dismantling the administrative apparatus would have made the reimposition of controls difficult due to the loss of operational experience. Moreover, the economic costs of controls, particularly when financial markets were not yet well developed, were not easily visible. Even when evidence as to their limited effectiveness increased, as markets became more sophisticated and loopholes were actively exploited, the attraction of capital controls for authorities in the face of speculative capital movements can be understood. The authorities were seen as acting against exchange rate pressures. This was important, as devaluations could have serious repercussions for the lifespan of the government when political prestige had been attached to maintaining the level of the exchange rate.

Therefore, in may countries there was considerable reluctance to give up capital controls. Usually it was at the central bank, which was responsible for the execution of capital controls, that doubts as to their effectiveness first began to surface. The staff involved with their administration had trouble in applying the rules which usually left quite a degree of discretion. The central bank was also the first to notice the circumvention of the rules by the commercial banks and the limited effectiveness in the exchange markets. Enforcement of compliance with the rules was cumbersome and, in most countries, prosecution for non-compliance was rare.

Eventually, countries came to the view that the balance of costs and benefits of capital controls had shifted. The increasing size of international financial markets and the growing sophistication of financial products made it increasingly difficult to maintain effective controls. Over time, the growing importance of financial markets in the economy meant that real economic costs of controls tended to become more evident. Controls hindered financial sector development (an important consideration for France) and restricted companies' ability to fully diversify in search of profitable opportunities.

Increasingly the advantages of opening up became more apparent as more and more countries liberalized. These advantages included a considerable financial deepening through increased competition and innovation, a beneficial impact on developing and maintaining a financial center and, possibly, relevant effects on economic growth, partly by disciplining macro-economic policies and partly by increased financial intermediation opportunities. At the same time the experience of industrial countries shows the importance of a sound constellation of regulatory, legal and economic institutions in order to reap the alleged benefits of capital liberalization. In effect, institutional differences may provide the single most important explanation for a differing impact of capital liberalization on economic well-being between industrial and non-industrial countries.

What, then, can we learn from these experiences? First, it should be acknowledged that the financial environment has changed drastically since many advanced countries liberalized. Partly because of the process of liberalization and deregulation, financial markets react more swiftly to changed circumstances, the range of financial instruments has increased and, more generally, financial markets have become more complex and extensive. One example is the magnitude of capital flows, both in absolute terms and relative to current account flows. The increase in cross-border capital flows over the last decade is simply enormous, as noted in Chapter 1. Liberalizing in the current environment is rather different from liberalizing in the mid-1980s. Second, liberalization in many continental European countries has to be understood in the context of the EU integration process and the move towards monetary union (Bakker, 1996).

Another difference is that in the past in industrial countries' holdings of foreign currency deposits by residents generally were severely restricted. They were often among the last items to be liberalized. This is in sharp contrast to many emerging and developing countries nowadays, where dollarization or euroization of the deposit base is a common phenomenon, affecting the effectiveness of remaining capital controls.

However, some lessons from the previous analysis of advanced country experiences with capital controls are likely to continue to apply (Box 2.1). First, capital controls could, at best, only postpone exchange rate adjustment where that was required by macroeconomic fundamentals. The regular currency crises experienced by many advanced countries illustrate this clearly. Second, controls tend to become less effective over time as innovation occurs and loopholes are exploited. Third, there is no single 'right' way to approach liberalization. Sequencing has varied, although most countries have liberalized long-term flows ahead of short-term flows.

Box 2.1 Key Lessons From Advanced Country Experiences

Effectiveness

- Capital controls have been more effective in relatively calm periods than in times of market pressures or speculative flows.
- Controls have been more effective when they formed part of a more comprehensive set of regulations, including controls on domestic financial markets.
- The effectiveness of capital controls erodes over time and is thus inversely linked to their duration.
- The effectiveness of capital controls is enhanced through strict enforcement procedures and cooperation by the banking system.
- Partial systems of capital control that seek to discriminate between types of flows or destinations provide incentives for circumvention and are vulnerable to diversion of capital flows to unregulated financial markets.
- Where capital controls can be switched on and off, there is a risk that long-term capital flows will be adversely affected.

Relationship to policy goals

- Capital controls have not been particularly helpful in supporting exchange rate or monetary policy objectives over prolonged periods.

- Capital controls have been helpful in avoiding short-term fluctuations of the exchange rate and providing some room for maneuver for monetary policy, provided the exchange rate moves broadly in line with fundamentals.
- Capital controls cannot act as a substitute for macroeconomic policy, and, more generally, controls have tended to delay macroeconomic adjustment.
- When there have been clear misalignments, the maintenance of capital controls has resulted in distorting exchange rate corrections once controls have become ineffective.
- Capital account liberalization (particularly when combined with deregulation of domestic financial markets) may alter the monetary policy transmission mechanism.

Links to financial stability
- Domestic financial market deregulation renders capital controls less effective.
- A liberalized financial system helps mitigate the adverse impact of volatility on the real economy by offering hedging opportunities to industry.
- Controls on inflows have generally been regarded more favorably than controls on outflows.
- It is important to improve risk management and prudential supervision prior to reforms.
- Achieving macroeconomic stability prior to reforms may reduce the risk of financial crises, particularly when the exchange rate is fixed.

Source: Bakker and Chapple (2002).

From the experiences of industrial countries a number of factors can be distilled which can minimize the risk of financial instability following liberalization. Macroeconomic policies need to be stability oriented and credible. It is no surprise that the decision to liberalize has often coincided with an increased emphasis on price stability – either via direct inflation targetting as in the cases of the United Kingdom and Australia or money supply targetting in the cases of Germany and France. Other countries adopted exchange rate targets. The tools used to implement monetary policy also altered with a move away from direct credit controls to a more market-oriented focus on interest rates that were consistent with the development of a more competitive financial system. Relatedly, it is critical that macroeconomic policies are consistent with the exchange rate regime as the choice of the exchange regime has important policy implications. A floating exchange rate may be particularly important when liberalization is rapid and maintaining macroeconomic stability is more challenging. It increases the incentives to hedge foreign currency exposures, which provides some protection against exchange rate volatility.

If a fixed exchange rate is chosen, the European experience suggests that markets will, at times, test the willingness of authorities to defend the exchange rate at a particular level, regardless of macroeconomic fundamentals. This illustrates that while macroeconomic stability is a necessary condition for successful capital account liberalization, it is not always sufficient to ensure exchange rate stability.

Liberalization creates opportunities for risk diversification, and also leads to significant new risks for banks, particularly when combined with the deregulation of domestic financial markets. In several Nordic countries asset price bubbles, enhanced by excessive bank lending, resulted in financial crises. Competition between financial institutions increases, creating incentives for institutions to lend more aggressively to maintain or increase market share. At the same time, liberalization increases access to new sources of funding and provides new lending opportunities in which domestic institutions may have limited experience. Such factors increase the importance of institutional strengthening (particularly of prudential policies) prior to liberalizing capital flows.

What can be said about the speed of capital account liberalization? As the examples suggest, the pace of capital account liberalization varied considerably between countries, ranging from a considerable number of years in France and Japan to a matter of months for the United Kingdom and New Zealand. Experiences indicate that a successful liberalization critically depends on the accompanying macroeconomic policies and domestic reforms. Although a gradual approach generally allows changes to be made in an orderly manner, this approach runs the risk of being delayed by interest group lobbying, backtracking on previous reforms or losing (political) momentum. On the other hand, a rapid approach requires a strong institutional framework and, in particular, sound financial sector supervision, in order to avoid excessive risk taking by financial market participants as economic rents are eliminated. In practice, political feasibility may well determine the approach taken. In the EU, this political dimension is evident as capital account liberalization was part of the process towards economic and monetary integration.

Countries maintaining a fixed or managed exchange rate generally have opted for a more gradual approach. The French experience in the 1980s indicates that a gradual process of capital account liberalization can actually enhance exchange rate stability within a multilateral system when combined with supporting macroeconomic policies. Also some smaller open economies with fixed exchange rates, like Austria, Belgium and the Netherlands, avoided financial sector difficulties when opening up. On the other hand, in countries such as Italy, Spain and Portugal, where macroeconomic stabilization was only relatively recent, had a bumpier ride.

Although liberalization has brought considerable gains and often been a catalyst for further economic reform, the process has not been without its difficulties and costs. Some countries probably took too long to liberalize, and in recent years insufficient attention has sometimes been paid to the need to strengthen the prudential environment to avoid the risk of a financial crisis. In general, it is not so much capital liberalization *per se* which has caused financial sector instability, but rather domestic financial market deregulation without accompanying supervisory and prudential strengthening.

Overall, however, capital liberalization can be judged to have been generally successful in advanced countries. Despite the costs which liberalization has imposed at times, countries have not sought to reintroduce controls in recent years. This illustrates their view that they have made the right choice.

NOTES

1. See, for example, Argy (1987) and Fukao (1990).
2. See, for instance, Bacchetta (1996).
3. See Takeda and Turner (1992) and Hoshi (2000).
4. See Bakker (1996) for a detailed discussion of European capital account liberalization.
5. See, for example, Drees and Pazarbasioglu (1998) for a discussion of Nordic bank crises.

3. Sequencing capital account liberalization and financial sector stability

Stefan Ingves[1]

3.1 INTRODUCTION

Maintaining financial sector stability in an environment with high capital mobility requires sound macroeconomic and financial policies, as well as a financial sector that is resilient to capital movements. Countries liberalizing their capital accounts need to address existing vulnerabilities in their financial sectors and adapt their macroeconomic and financial sector policy frameworks to a more liberalized environment. Proper sequencing and coordination of measures to liberalize the capital account with macroeconomic policies and financial sector reform could help reduce the risks of financial sector instability. A simple rule for sequencing, however, does not exist. The design of an operational plan for sequencing and coordinating capital account liberalization with other policies must be based on a thorough assessment of individual countries' circumstances, and will inevitably require judgment, discretion and flexibility. The general principles for sequencing and coordinating capital account liberalization with other policies presented below, which have been derived from country experiences, could guide the design of a particular operational plan for liberalizing barriers for the cross-border movement of capital.

3.2 HOW CAN CAPITAL MOBILITY STRENGTHEN OR WEAKEN FINANCIAL SECTOR STABILITY?

Capital mobility has potential benefits that could strengthen and risks that could weaken financial sector stability. The net benefit from having access to more resources depends on how well these are used.

Benefits of Capital Mobility that May Strengthen Financial Sector Stability

Capital account liberalization has many potential benefits. It expands the opportunities for greater investment, smoothing consumption over time and sharing risk. It also allows investors in lending countries to obtain higher rates of return and borrowers in creditor countries to obtain less-expensive access to finance, as rates of return with similar risk characteristics tend to converge. Capital mobility could expand domestic financial activity as domestic financial systems usually play the role of intermediaries between foreign lenders and domestic residents because foreign lenders may rely on the monitoring capacity of domestic financial institutions that have close relations with domestic borrowers. Greater capital mobility may also introduce foreign competition that induces the financial system to become more efficient (Sundararajan et al., 2002).

Capital mobility could in principle promote financial stability by its beneficial impact on economic growth, investment, technology transfers and financial market depth. The relationship between capital flows and economic growth, however, is not well established, with some authors finding a positive relation and others finding a negative or no statistically significant link (see IMF, 2001). Three other facts, however, have been clearly established: capital inflows raise investment in physical capital, portfolio flows deepen financial markets, and foreign direct investment promotes spillovers from technology transfer. For example, direct investment by strong foreign-owned banks could help develop the financial system by introducing new financial methods and risk management techniques. These banks also could increase the stability of the financial system by providing secure international settlement services and by enjoying lender-of-last-resort facilities from their home banks.

Risks of Capital Mobility that May Weaken Financial Sector Stability

The liberalization of the capital account also entails risks. It has been associated with financial crises (banking, currency, debt) in several countries where sudden large capital outflows took place after a period of large capital inflows. Large capital outflows can disrupt both financial sector and macroeconomic stability. Depending on the exchange arrangement, large outflows could give rise to a liquidity shortage, raising interest rates or generating a sharp currency depreciation. They also may disrupt macroeconomic activity. These events could lead to a deterioration in the financial condition of banks and may even trigger a banking crisis. The banking crisis could then further exacerbate macroeconomic instability, and the macroeconomic and financial weaknesses could continue to reinforce each other.

Large inflows expose borrowing countries to economy-wide exchange rate risk. Most developing countries borrow from abroad in foreign currencies, typically the US dollar, euro-legacy currencies, or the Japanese yen. When external borrowing is intermediated through the banking system, banks may limit their net open foreign exchange positions by on-lending the foreign currency to their customers. However, if customers do not have a reliable source of foreign exchange receipts, they will be exposed to exchange rate risk. A sharp depreciation following a reversal in capital flows would then impair loan portfolio quality. Large inflows may also be associated with asset price bubbles, including in real estate and stock prices, and may bring about a sharp real exchange rate appreciation that could impair a country's external competitiveness and make it more difficult to service external debt.

Capital account liberalization also introduces new dimensions of financial risk. In writing financial contracts with individuals operating in different countries, private market participants deal with a number of different financial problems, including: (i) financial systems subject to diverse regulatory and supervisory standards, (ii) accounting standards, (iii) payment systems, (iv) legal and institutional frameworks, (v) mechanisms for the settlement of disputes and (vi) exchange regulations. For example, the risk that the conditions of international financial contracts will not be honored as agreed upon (credit risk) would increase if changes in exchange regulations impede residents from repaying financial obligations (transfer risk).

Capital mobility also may expand opportunities for financial abuse. For example, in countries with a weak prudential and supervisory framework, unsound banks may take advantage of capital inflows to disguise their weak financial condition, increase their risk exposure, and ultimately the size of their negative net worth. Foreign competition may lower banks' franchise value, encouraging some institutions to take excessive risks to increase their returns. The scope for financial crimes including fraud, embezzlement and money laundering could very well increase if these incidences were to occur.

3.3 MACROECONOMIC AND STRUCTURAL REFORM POLICIES THAT PROMOTE FINANCIAL SECTOR STABILITY

The large size of capital inflows raises the question of whether financial institutions and corporations truly understand the risks involved and whether the incentives for risk taking are appropriate. Financial institutions could take excessive risks unwittingly, for instance as a result of the inability of their management to operate safely in a more complex liberalized financial environment. They may also take excessive risks if they do not adequately understand the macroeconomic environment or the government's policy intentions, which could reflect lack of transparency in fiscal, monetary and exchange rate policies, or inadequate statistical information. Perverse incentives encouraging excessive risk taking, or moral hazard, may be associated, for instance, with poorly designed safety nets, which could possibly provide full deposit insurance and unconditional bailouts.

Well-designed macroeconomic and financial sector frameworks and policies could reduce the volatility of capital flows and might improve financial sector resilience. Meanwhile, macroeconomic policies should reduce uncertainty and financial sector policies should establish an incentive structure that encourages financial institutions to take only the risks they can understand and manage.

Macroeconomic Policies that Promote Financial Sector Stability

Macroeconomic policies can reduce, but cannot prevent, the risk of sudden reversals in capital flows. Prudent fiscal policies and appropriate debt management lessen the likelihood of debt-servicing difficulties by the government that could result in currency depreciation or eventually default. They avoid the volatility that might take place when investors perceive that increasing debt burdens associated with large fiscal deficits cannot be serviced as originally agreed. Good strategies for the management of public sector external debt can also reduce the potential volatility of capital flows, for instance, by increasing the duration of the debt portfolio and avoiding put options and covenants that could be called during a crisis.

The choice of the exchange rate regime can play a very important role in influencing capital flows, and such regimes determine the currency risk exposure of domestic investments. In an extreme case, abandoning the domestic currency, as Ecuador and El Salvador did in 2000, completely eliminates such risk. Permanently fixing the exchange rate has the same effect, but there is no guarantee that the exchange rate would not be changed eventually. Even in currency board arrangements, where a law sets the exchange rate, governments can choose to depreciate the currency by changing the law, if considered necessary. Other fixed regimes may be less credibly sustainable. In such cases, large short-term capital inflows may take advantage of interest rate differentials only while the implicit exchange rate guarantee is credible. Shifts in market sentiment would involve large outflows and trigger a currency crisis (the crisis Thailand experienced in 1997 provides an example). Fully flexible exchange regimes entail currency risk, but the range of daily fluctuations is much lower than those associated with a successful speculative attack on a fixed-but-adjustable exchange regime. Moreover, currency risk discourages speculative flows and encourages the efficient allocation of exchange rate risk.

In moving towards more flexible exchange regimes, countries will generally find it useful to rely on markets for price discovery, foreign exchange and credit allocation. Countries will also need an alternative nominal anchor, preferably based on variables that are market determined. To this end, interest and exchange rates would need to be liberalized; and the central bank should develop the ability to manage liquidity using indirect (i.e., price-based rather than volume-based) instruments of monetary policy. Such market-based monetary arrangements and associated central banking reforms in turn enhance monetary control and foster market development. Well-functioning monetary arrangements are also essential to managing the risks from short-term capital flows (Alexander et al., 1995). Central bank independence, established by clear objectives and mandated by law, should isolate monetary policy from political pressures.

A lack of transparency in monetary and exchange rate policies and objectives could increase capital flow volatility. For example, in the absence of clearly communicated policy intentions, foreign investors may fear the imposition of exchange controls that limit the transferability of their funds, if the recipient country has used capital controls as a policy instrument to curtail foreign exchange pressures. Transparency in monetary and financial policies, objectives and operational procedures can help to reduce uncertainty and thus lower capital flow volatility. To this end, the International Monetary Fund (IMF) has developed the Code of Good Practices on Transparency in Monetary and Financial Policies and the Code of Good Practices on Fiscal Transparency. In addition, it has established standards and systems for the disclosure of economic and financial data (Special Data Dissemination Standards and General Data Dissemination System).

Structural Reforms that Promote Financial Sector Stability

Financial policies that promote prudent risk management increase financial sector stability. Such policies may be supported on four pillars: (i) a strong capital base, (ii) adequate risk management, (iii) financial sector discipline and (iv) well-designed schemes for systemic liquidity management and support.

A strong capital base provides a cushion to absorb temporary losses and provides incentives to owners to limit their risks. Enforcing minimum capital requirements for financial institutions requires adequate accounting and auditing standards, especially for asset valuation, loan classification, provisioning and depreciation, since capital is a residual claim. It also requires close analysis of loan portfolio quality through on-site supervision.

Financial institutions should be prepared to manage risk associated with cross-border financial transactions. Prudential regulation can encourage adequate risk management not only by owners, but also by the management of financial institutions. In many countries, prudential regulations directly reduce risk exposure by limiting the positions financial institutions are permitted to take (for example, net open foreign exchange position limits, expressed as a fraction of the institution's capital). Other countries do not impose limits as such, but require additional capital when market risk increases. Supervisory authorities in countries with more sophisticated financial systems are adopting value-at-risk techniques and stress tests to measure the degree of exposure of financial institutions to market risks. To curtail credit risk, supervisory authorities may impose strict provisioning requirements based not only on the stock of past due loans, but also on forward-looking indicators of economic activity that consider all available information. While supervisors are considering value-at-risk methodologies to assess credit risk, most do not yet consider these methods sufficiently reliable.

Financial sector and corporate discipline contribute to the avoidance of excessive risk taking. Timely corrective actions mandated by the supervisory authority, appropriate bank exit policies and policies for financial disclosure are key elements of such discipline. Corrective actions include, for example, bank intervention and management replacement when the supervisory authority detects unsound financial practices. Putting adequate bank exit policies in place may sometimes require a thorough modification of the legal framework for the financial sector. Insolvent institutions may divert resources away from their most productive uses and engage in risky activities that may increase the magnitude of accumulated losses. Therefore, unsound institutions should be restructured, when possible, or otherwise liquidated. Authorities in charge of financial sector policies should put together the institutional infrastructure for bank liquidation and insist on the adequacy of bank and corporate bankruptcy laws. Mechanisms for loan recovery and adequate creditor rights must also be in place. Corporate discipline requires policies for corporate governance, insolvency and the systemic restructuring of nonfinancial institutions. Financial sector disclosure could also help impose financial discipline. Domestic depositors and foreign investors could penalize financial institutions engaging in riskier financial activities by moving their funds to institutions with better risk management, forcing wayward institutions to modify their behavior or close.

Liquidity support could avoid financial crises that may arise from bank runs. This may take the form of lender-of-last-resort facilities and deposit insurance. Lender-of-last-resort facilities should provide only temporary assistance to illiquid financial institutions. Insolvent institutions should not receive lender-of-last-resort support and the central bank should grant that credit only for very short terms and against collateral. Deposit-insurance design should factor in the existence of asymmetric information, which could foster moral hazard. To avoid incentive problems, deposit insurance should cover only a fraction of small-to-medium deposits and if individual institutions collapse, payments to insured depositors must take place quickly. In a systemic crisis, however, the government may have to offer a comprehensive guarantee for bank depositors and creditors to avoid a bank run that could exacerbate capital outflows. The authorities should clearly establish that the full guarantee is only a temporary measure.

Liquidity support, however, could create problems in a regime with limited exchange rate flexibility because the domestic liquidity provided by the monetary authority could be used to take positions in foreign currency and finance a speculative attack. The lack of a lender of last resort, however, could allow bank runs which subsequently squeeze liquidity out of the banking system and could cause institutions to become insolvent. A currency board would face this problem unless it maintains large excess reserves. These observations support the argument favoring flexible exchange rate regimes for financial sector stability in economies with capital mobility (Chang and Velasco, 1997).[2]

3.4 SEQUENCING AND COORDINATION TO SAFEGUARD FINANCIAL SECTOR STABILITY

The sequencing and coordination of capital account liberalization with other policies must be adapted to individual country circumstances. Countries may benefit from adopting a plan that carefully sequences and coordinates capital account liberalization measures with other reforms. A customized plan is necessary because countries differ in how well prepared they are to operate in an environment of internationally mobile capital and in how quickly the necessary reforms can be adopted. The plan should take full account of the characteristics of the economy being liberalized, and in particular of the risks and vulnerabilities in the financial system and in the financial structure of nonfinancial institutions.

In devising an operational plan for liberalizing the capital account, countries could benefit from the experiences of other countries. Rather than replicating the measures adopted by countries that have successfully liberalized their capital accounts, countries should prepare their operational plans taking into consideration a set of principles for sequencing and coordinating reforms that capture the lessons learned from diverse country experiences. Because preparing an operational plan for capital account liberalization could be a demanding exercise, countries may benefit from external assistance. Fund members may count on the IMF for technical assistance in designing such operational plans for opening the capital account and in the design and implementation of adequate macroeconomic and financial policies.

Country Experiences

Many countries have sequenced the liberalization of their capital accounts in different ways – in the speed with which liberalization has taken place and in the order in which different types of international financial transactions have been permitted. Some countries lifted a large number of capital controls in a very short period, in what has been called a 'big bang' (e.g., Argentina, Estonia, Kenya, Latvia, Peru and the United Kingdom). Others have liberalized more gradually (e.g., Austria, China, India, Korea and Sweden). While countries typically started by liberalizing foreign direct investment inflows (Colombia, Hungary, India, Indonesia, Mexico, Poland, Russia, Turkey and Thailand), they refrained from permitting foreign direct investment in all sectors of the economy. Several countries discouraged short-term inflows (e.g., Brazil, Chile, Colombia, Malaysia and Thailand). Some countries permitted certain types of short-term transactions, such as trade finance, while maintaining tight controls on most other short-term capital inflows (e.g., in Indonesia in 1991–96, Thailand in 1996 and South Africa until early 1997). Other countries may have unwittingly encouraged such short-term transactions through biasses in their regulatory frameworks that favored inflows intermediated through their banking systems, while restricting other types of short-term inflows (e.g., Korea, Russia, and Thailand in 1992–95) (Ariyoshi et al., 2000, and Ishii et al., 2002).

Some of these countries experienced financial crises, while others did not. The review of country experiences reveals that financial crises cannot be associated with particular patterns in the pace, timing and sequencing of capital account liberalization. For instance, countries have suffered financial crises when macroeconomic and financial policies encouraged excessive risk taking increasing the vulnerability of the financial sector. In Mexico, for example, the capital outflows followed growing macroeconomic imbalances that were inconsistent with the tightly managed exchange rate regime during a period of political turmoil. They had an adverse impact on the banking system because banks had relied heavily on short-term foreign borrowing to finance rapid credit growth. In Sweden, banks took excessive risks and macroeconomic policies were expansionary. An unsustainable credit and asset price boom developed, reinforced by excessive external borrowing facilitated by capital account liberalization and encouraged by the fixed exchange rate policy. The collapse of the bubble in late 1992 led to a crisis. In Korea, capital account regulations created a bias towards short-term external borrowing, sharply increasing the country's external vulnerability. The regulations favored borrowing by companies with poor corporate governance and financial institutions subject to government interference, lax prudential regulation, fragmented supervision and inadequate capital.

Countries that avoided crises pursued prudent macroeconomic and financial policies. For example, Austria maintained macroeconomic stability and ensured that its financial sector was well supervised before fully liberalizing its capital account, taking account of differences in the capacity of banks, corporations and households to manage the risks involved. Hungary privatized several banks and strengthened prudential regulation and banking supervision before liberalizing short-term flows. South Africa followed sound macroeconomic policies and strengthened its financial infrastructure before liberalizing virtually all restrictions on nonresidents' capital flows.

General Principles for Sequencing and Coordinating Capital Account Liberalization with Other Reforms

Based on a review of country experiences and theory, the IMF has developed general principles for sequencing and coordinating capital account liberalization with other policies that could guide countries in planning the timing of their reforms (Box 3.1).[3] Most of these principles are self-explanatory, but some require elaboration. The political aspect of the reform, for example, should recognize that liberalization could affect vested interests and that the authorities must be committed to and have ownership of the reform strategy. Liberalization that is more rapid can help to sweep away vested interests, but may increase the risk of a financial crisis if the supporting macroeconomic and financial reforms are not in place. Indeed, such a crisis may lead to a reversal of the liberalization process. Political considerations may preclude a first-best program of financial sector reform; and country authorities need to weigh carefully the benefits and risks of moving ahead with less than a critical mass of reforms. Regional associations or unions for economic and financial integration, such as the Organisation for Economic Cooperation and Development (OECD), also may affect the sequencing, pace and timing of liberalization.

Because sequencing should take into consideration the capacity to manage risks, it may be prudent to liberalize long-term flows before short-term flows, because longer-term flows may be less volatile, making it easier to manage the associated risks. However, banking flows, which are usually short term, may be liberalized first if banks are better prepared than households and corporations to manage the risks associated with certain international capital flows.

Box 3.1 General Principles for Sequencing

1. Lifting controls on international capital flows, and financial liberalization more generally, is best undertaken against a background of sound and sustainable macroeconomic policies.
2. Specific financial sector reforms that support and reinforce macroeconomic stabilization should be given priority in implementation.
3. The pace, timing and sequencing of liberalization need to take account of political considerations.
4. The liberalization of capital flows by instruments or sectors should be sequenced to take into account the capacity to manage the concomitant risks.
5. Reforms that require substantial lead time for adequate technical preparations and capacity building should be started early.
6. Financial sector reforms that are operationally linked and mutually reinforcing should be implemented together.
7. Prudential regulation and supervision and financial restructuring policies should be phased in gradually to complement other financial reforms aimed at enhancing competitive efficiency and market development, in order to help manage risks in liberalization and foster financial sector stability.
8. The pace of reforms should take into account the conditions relating to the financial structure of nonfinancial corporations and other entities (e.g., debt–equity ratios, foreign currency exposure) and their effects on the quality of the loan portfolios and the capital base of financial institutions.
9. The operational and institutional arrangements for policy transparency and data disclosure, including monetary and financial policy transparency, should be adapted to support capital account opening.
10. Reforms need to take into account the effectiveness of the controls on capital flows currently in place. Ineffective enforcement of controls may argue for accelerating their removal.

Source: Ishii et al. (2002).

The principles recognize that some reforms may take longer than others. Systemic bank restructuring, for example, may take a long time, but many capital flows could, nonetheless, be liberalized if adequate prudential and financial safeguards have been put in place. Reforms of accounting practices and standards also typically require substantial time because such practices are a basic and often deeply ingrained feature of a country's business practices and legal and regulatory institutions. Identifying unsound financial institutions requires the enforcement of adequate accounting and auditing standards and appropriate loan classification and provisioning requirements.

The principles also recognize the possible interaction among reform measures. For example, measures to introduce market-based instruments of monetary and exchange rate policy go hand in hand with measures to develop money and exchange markets, with reforms of payments and settlements systems, and with improved public debt management (Baliño et al., 1994 and Sundararajan et al., 1997). Increased flexibility in interest rates and exchange rates requires prudential norms that address the associated market and liquidity risks, which should be tailored to the level of market development. The integration of money and exchange markets typically requires some liberalization of capital flows through the inter-bank market, subject to adequate prudential safeguards.

These principles are consistent with various speeds of capital account liberalization and they do not imply that liberalization should be unduly delayed. Countries may want to proceed with both capital account liberalization and financial sector development, and to reform in accordance with these principles as quickly as they can develop the ability to manage effectively the risks associated with international capital flows.

Preparing an Operational Plan for Capital Account Liberalization

Preparing an operational plan for capital account liberalization involves several stages. First, the necessary macroeconomic, financial and other supporting reforms need to be identified. A broad reform strategy should then group, sort in order of priority, and phase in reforms according to feasibility, taking account of the principles set out in the previous section. Finally, a detailed plan should work out, schedule and implement each reform. These plans will, of course, need to be revised and updated from time to time in light of developments.

Analysis
The first stage involves a thorough analysis of the financial sector, the macroeconomic policy framework and the effective degree of capital account liberalization. The analysis of the financial sector should assess soundness

and identify vulnerabilities in the financial sector. In particular, the analysis ought to gauge the resilience of the financial sector to shocks that could trigger capital movements. It would then identify the reforms in financial policies and market infrastructure that are required to operate safely in a more liberalized environment and ascertain how these reforms are interrelated. These reforms should strengthen the four pillars that support and encourage sound financial practices, namely a strong capital base, adequate risk management, financial sector discipline and well-designed schemes for systemic liquidity management and support.

The analysis of the macroeconomic policy framework involves assessing whether the current set of monetary, exchange rate and fiscal policies are consistent with an open capital account and the sources of macroeconomic and external vulnerability that could result in large shifts in capital flows. It should identify the potential shocks to the macroeconomic environment given current policies and measure their potential impact on financial sector stability with stress tests. The analysis should also cover the depth and liquidity of foreign exchange and money markets and the transmission of monetary and exchange rate policies. Finally, the analysis should identify the necessary reforms to monetary, exchange and fiscal policy frameworks and markets, and determine their political feasibility.

Determining the actual degree of capital account liberalization involves assessing the extent and effectiveness of capital controls. Assessing the extent of controls involves compiling an inventory of existing capital controls by examining laws, regulations and administrative practices. Assessing the effectiveness of capital controls requires an understanding of the incentives and modalities for circumventing the controls; the administrative and enforcement capacity of the authorities; and the authorities' practices and capacity in applying and enforcing the controls. This work will require considerable judgment and will remain subject to a large margin of uncertainty, as it is often impossible to distinguish the effects of capital controls from the effects of other variables.

Design and implementation of detailed plans
The broad reform strategy for sequencing and coordinating capital account liberalization with other policies must establish priorities among the identified reforms and organize them along a time line. Figure 3.1 depicts such a strategy for a hypothetical case. The pace of reforms depends on the financial sector infrastructure already in place and on the speed with which a critical mass of reforms can be achieved at each stage. In economies with a very weak financial infrastructure, it may take a long time to put in place basic policies and institutions. This may slow the pace of capital account liberalization. Once the process of developing an efficient and robust

financial system is well under way in economies, subsequent steps towards capital account liberalization may be accelerated. By contrast, in economies with an already well-established financial infrastructure, and therefore a greater capacity to manage the risks associated with international capital flows, liberalization can proceed more quickly. The experience of some countries (e.g., the United Kingdom) shows that under the right macroeconomic and financial conditions, rapid liberalization of all capital controls can be undertaken without undue risk.

Figure 3.1 A stylized representation of sequencing

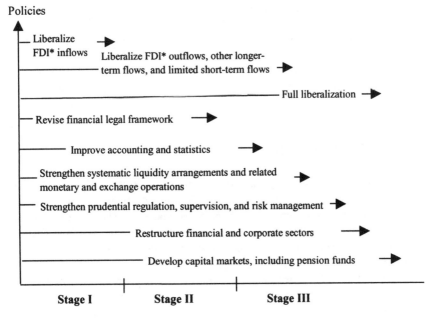

Note :* FDI is foreign direct investment.

Source : Ishii et al. (2002).

A detailed operational plan based on the broad strategy will set out the specific actions in each policy area and the timing for their implementation. This stage may require the development of deeper expertise in the design and implementation of the particular policies, and may benefit from technical assistance. (For an example, see Ishii et al., 2002.)

The broad reform strategy and detailed operational plans provide a reference point, but the overall strategy and plans must be flexible and adapted to changing macroeconomic conditions or emerging signs of vulnerabilities. Sometimes, it would therefore be appropriate to delay further capital account liberalization until conditions become more favorable.

The Role of the International Monetary Fund

The IMF may assist countries in liberalizing their capital accounts in several ways. The Fund stands ready to provide technical assistance to assist authorities in devising a liberalization strategy and formulating the detailed operational plans for sequencing and coordinating capital account liberalization and associated reforms. Under the Financial Sector Assessment Program (FSAP), the Fund and the World Bank already perform a thorough analysis of the financial sectors of interested member countries, identifying vulnerability areas and measures that would increase financial sector resiliency, among others, to external shocks. The IMF could also provide technical assistance for individual financial reforms, such as enhancements in prudential regulation and banking supervision. Finally, during Article IV consultations, the Fund is uniquely positioned to provide advice on macroeconomic and financial policies that are consistent with capital mobility.

3.5 CONCLUSIONS

Proper sequencing and coordination of policies is crucial for orderly capital account liberalization, but a simple rule for sequencing does not exist. Countries can learn from the experiences of others, but should be aware that the pace, timing and ordering of policies in countries that have successfully liberalized reflects each individual country's specific financial and economic structures. The ten general principles elaborated by the IMF in a recent review of country experiences and the economic literature emphasize the importance of macroeconomic stability to orderly liberalization and give priority to financial sector reforms that support it. They highlight the importance of coordinating different financial policies, taking into consideration the initial condition of institutions and their capacity to manage the risks associated with international capital flows. The principles point to the desirability of liberalizing long-term flows ahead of short-term flows. At a minimum, any partial early liberalization of short-term flows needs to be accompanied by adequate prudential measures. A gradual approach to capital account liberalization may often be required, but the pace of liberalization is not as important as the consistency of the measures.

NOTES

1. I am grateful for comments and inputs received from Messrs Jorge Canales-Kriljenko, Karl Habermeier and Shogo Ishii. The views expressed in this chapter are mine and do not necessarily reflect the views of national authorities or International Monetary Fund (IMF) Executive Directors.
2. Lender-of-last-resort facilities in foreign currency are feasible, but are limited by the stock of reserves and by the nature of the exchange rate regime.
3. See Ishii et al. (2002).

4. Managing capital account liberalization: Indonesia, Malaysia, Korea and Thailand

Yung Chul Park and Chi-Young Song

4.1 INTRODUCTION

For the five years following the financial crisis that broke out in July 1997 in Thailand and subsequently spread to other East Asian countries, the four crisis countries – Indonesia, Malaysia, Korea and Thailand – have managed an impressive recovery from the financial market turbulence. Of the four countries, Indonesia, Korea and Thailand sought International Monetary Fund (IMF) rescue financing and agreed to a wide range of structural and institutional reforms. Malaysia, on the other hand, decided to go its own way in dealing with the crisis by pegging its exchange rate to the US dollar and imposing various capital controls on both capital inflows and outflows. This is in sharp contrast to Korea, for instance, which has followed the IMF program and liberalized substantially the capital account regime. The experiences of Malaysia and Korea therefore provide an interesting case study of the effects of both capital controls and liberalization on the recovery from a crisis in emerging market economies.

The purpose of this chapter is to analyze the background to and economic consequences of capital account liberalization in Indonesia, Korea, and Thailand and capital controls in Malaysia. Sections 4.2 and 4.3 discuss the extent and scope of capital account liberalization before and after the 1997 crisis. Section 4.4 focuses on macroeconomic developments in Malaysia and Korea since the eruption of the crisis to examine whether and how the two opposite types of capital account management have contributed to the ongoing recovery in the two countries. Section 4.5 discusses some of the reasons why East Asia's policy makers have been reluctant to liberalize the capital account. Concluding remarks are found in a final section.

4.2. THE CAPITAL ACCOUNT MANAGEMENT IN EAST ASIA: BEFORE THE CRISIS

Overview

Following the approach developed by Johnston et al. (1999), we have estimated indices measuring the degree of capital account control for the four East Asian crisis countries since 1995.[1] They use disaggregated classifications of capital account transactions compiled by the IMF in its *Annual Report on Exchange Arrangements and Restrictions* for the measure. We are not able to calculate the indices for the earlier years in the 1990s and beyond, because these data do not exist before 1995.

According to our estimates presented in Table 4.1, Indonesia had been leading the other crisis countries in removing capital controls before the crisis in 1997. Since then Korea has been most aggressive in liberalizing capital movements, whereas Malaysia has reversed its liberalization policy to return to a tightly controlled capital account regime. Both Indonesia and Thailand have made some progress in opening their capital markets, but they still maintain a relatively large number of restrictions on capital mobility compared to Korea and other emerging market economies. Therefore, the experiences of Korea and Malaysia provide an interesting case study of the capital account management in East Asia in the 1990s: one country has accelerated liberalization of capital market opening, whereas the other one has reinstated many control measures it had previously removed. This section discusses developments in capital account liberalization in the four East Asian crisis countries, namely Indonesia, Korea, Malaysia and Thailand before the 1997 crisis.

*Table 4.1 Degree of capital control**

	Indonesia	Korea	Malaysia	Thailand
1995	0.53	0.68	0.71	0.72
1996	0.53	0.67	0.71	0.72
1997	0.51	0.58	0.71	0.70
1998	0.48	0.48	0.76	0.70
1999	0.49	0.42	0.76	0.70

*Note :** Higher values indicate a higher degree of capital controls. See endnote 1 for a description of the methodology.

Source : Authors' calculations following Johnston et al. (1999).

Korea

During much of the period preceding the 1997 crisis, Korea had been characterized as one of the most hard-line interventionist regimes in East Asia. Beginning in the mid-1980s, however, Korea undertook a series of reforms that would transform it into a more market-oriented economy. With a large increase in current account surpluses over the 1986–89 period, the Korean government found room in which a progressive liberalization of imports and deregulation of both current and capital account transactions could be carried out without disrupting the economy. The removal of restrictions on capital outflows was therefore given a higher priority than liberalizing inflows. In fact, the Korean authorities were compelled to impose various restrictions on capital inflows to mitigate the expansionary effects of the large current account surpluses in a managed floating system. For the first time, Korean institutional investors were allowed to undertake direct investment, to purchase real estate abroad and to invest in selected foreign securities. The limit on the amount that domestic pension funds could invest in overseas securities was abolished and domestic residents were allowed to hold overseas deposit accounts for the first time.

The favorable current account position did not last very long, however. By 1990 the current account recorded a significant deficit with little prospect for an early turnaround. In order to deal with the weakening current account, some of the earlier restrictions on capital inflows were lifted. Inbound foreign direct investment (FDI) was further liberalized, banks were allowed to borrow from abroad and the limits on the amounts of foreign exchange that could be brought in for lending to local banks were also raised.

As a result of these reform efforts in deregulating both current and capital account transactions, Korea had developed a relatively liberalized capital account by 1992. Nevertheless, Korea was severely criticized by the US, European countries and international financial institutions for being too restrictive in regulating the capital account relative to the Organisation for Economic Co-operation and Development (OECD) standard at a time when Korea was exploring the possibility of joining the OECD.

The critics pointed out that the rigid controls undermined the efficiency of the financial system, and also acted as a constraint on sustaining rapid growth because they kept domestic interest rates higher than interest rates in international financial markets (trading partners as well as export competitors). In response to these complaints, and to foreign pressure for further deregulation, the government began a gradual liberalization that was to be implemented over a five-year period in three stages, with the actual speed of liberalization to be adjusted to the state of the economy. A focal point of the reform was the adoption of a negative list system in regulating capital flows.[2]

At the initial stage of liberalization, there was considerable concern that a sudden deregulation of portfolio capital flows could destabilize the economy, while efficiency gains to the economy from the liberalization would be too small to justify such instability. Many skeptics of liberalization argued that the gains might even be insignificant and that they would only be realized over the long run. Also at that time there was no way of really knowing how a small, semi-open economy such as Korea, where domestic interest rates were twice as high as those in the international financial markets, would move to a new equilibrium if the restrictions on capital flows were removed suddenly and completely, when the market-supporting infrastructure and financial supervision were not sufficiently well established to curb speculative activities in the foreign exchange and other financial markets. These concerns and the debate on the speed and extent of liberalization delayed the actual implementation of the plan. Only after accepting IMF financial support did the Korean government begin to undertake most of the reform measures they had promised four years earlier.

Thailand, Malaysia, and Indonesia

In the early 1990s, Thailand, Malaysia and Indonesia maintained a more open capital account than Korea with regard to both FDI and portfolio capital inflows. According to Lane et al. (1999, p.73), 'in Indonesia the capital account had been liberalized well before the crisis and the free foreign exchange system had been a pillar of economic policy for the past 30 years'. Because of their relatively low saving rates, these countries needed large amounts of foreign capital to sustain rapid growth, and for this reason they actively deregulated inbound FDI and cross-border financial transactions, beginning in the early 1980s when capital inflows decreased sharply as a result of the Latin American debt crisis in 1982.

Foreign direct investment

Thailand had lifted many restrictions on FDI inflows in the 1970s, mainly through the Alien Business Law of 1972 and the Investment Promotion Act of 1977. These two acts basically introduced a negative list system of control. Most of the restrictions on FDI inflows in import-substituting industries had been lifted in the 1970s. In the latter half of the 1980s, the Thai government broadened and accelerated the liberalization process by deregulating FDI inflows to export industries in order to support the launching of an export-led development strategy. In 1991, for example, foreign investors were allowed to own 100 per cent of domestic firms that export all of their output. Additional incentives for FDI in export industries, such as tax breaks or exemptions, were introduced. With the help of these deregulatory measures, annual FDI inflows to Thailand increased from a mere US$0.4 billion in 1987 to US$2.4 billion in 1990.

In Malaysia, much of the liberalization of FDI inflows took place during the 1985–87 period. In 1985, as an incentive to encourage the transfer of advanced foreign technology to domestic industries, the Malaysian government permitted nonresidents to own more than half of the capital of companies which were considered 'high-tech'. The Investment Promotion Act of 1986 provided various incentives for foreign investment in manufacturing, agriculture and tourism. These included simplifying the investment process and raising the limit on the percentage holdings of joint ventures that nonresidents could own.

Since 1987, nonresidents have been allowed to wholly own companies that export at least 80 per cent of their output and to purchase domestic real estate for business purposes with funds brought in from abroad. In 1989, nonresident firms were allowed to issue corporate bonds in the domestic securities market, and legislation was passed to protect the copyright of nonresidents for 25 years. These measures helped increase annual FDI inflows from US$0.7 billion in 1988 to US$2.3 billion in 1990, and to US$6.1 billion in 1994.

In Indonesia, from the early 1970s until the mid-1980s, the bulk of FDI inflows were concentrated in the oil and gas industries. The upshot of this was that the economy became increasingly dependent on these two industries. In an effort to develop a more balanced industrial structure and promote exports of manufactured products, Indonesia began to liberalize FDI inflows in industries other than oil and gas. In 1985 the approval process for FDI inflows was greatly simplified, and the following year nonresidents were allowed to establish joint ventures in non-oil/gas export industries. Initially the maximum limit on nonresident ownership of joint ventures that export all of their products was 80 per cent. The limit was raised to 95 per cent in 1987. More importantly, a negative list system was adopted in managing FDI inflows in 1989. The minimum limit on FDI for a specific project was gradually reduced from US$1 million and then entirely abolished in 1994.

In 1994, FDI was allowed in previously restricted industries such as telecommunications, ports, railways and nuclear power generation. During the early 1990s, most of the remaining restrictions on foreign ownership were removed so that by 1994, 100 per cent ownership was possible in most industries. The total volume of FDI inflows increased from US$0.6 billion in 1987, to US$1.5 billion in 1991 and to US$2.1 billion in 1994.

Portfolio and other investment

Along with the deregulation of FDI, the three countries also accelerated the liberalization of cross-border financial transactions throughout the 1980s and early 1990s for the purpose of supporting high levels of domestic investment, diversifying their sources of foreign capital and improving the efficiency of their domestic financial markets.

Thailand undertook a major effort in accelerating liberalization of cross-border financial transactions during the 1985–97 period. The government created two funds for foreign investors in Thai securities, the Bangkok Fund in 1985 and the Thailand Fund in 1986, and allowed ten more funds to be launched between 1987 and 1990. In 1987, because the foreign-ownership limit has been reached by so many companies, the Stock Exchange of Thailand established an Alien Board where foreign investors can trade such stocks among themselves. In general, foreign investors were permitted to hold up to 49 per cent of the outstanding shares of any listed Thai company, except for in some industries, such as the banking sector, where a 25 per cent limit was applied.

During the period under consideration, the Thai government also introduced various measures of liberalization to promote further capital inflows including portfolio capital such as tax incentives to foreign mutual funds, reduction of taxes on dividends remitted abroad, and the lifting of all restrictions on the repatriation of loan repayments, interest payments, and investment funds by foreign investors (Johnston et al., 1997). When it became an Article VIII country in 1990, Thailand also began to ease restrictions on trading in and cross-border transfer of foreign exchange and the use of nonresident baht accounts and resident foreign currency accounts.

The Bangkok International Banking Facility (BIBF) was launched in March 1993 with the purpose of expanding access to low-cost foreign borrowing and developing Thailand as a regional financial center. BIBF was Thailand's version of an offshore financial market, in which commercial banks with BIBF licenses were allowed to conduct lending (in–out) and engage in other international and investment banking operations as well as traditional offshore banking (out–out). In 1993, 47 commercial banks were granted BIBF licenses. These included 32 foreign banks, 12 that had been operating in Thailand and 20 newcomers (Tivakul and Svetarundra, 1993; and Vichyanond, 1994). Three years later, the Provincial International Banking Facility (PIBF) was created which allowed loans to be made in both local and foreign currencies with funds raised from abroad.

Malaysia became an Article VIII country in 1968 and adopted a flexible exchange rate system in 1973.[3] Malaysia was a highly open economy and followed a development strategy that espoused liberalization of capital movements (Johnston et al., 1999). Before the crisis Malaysia had undertaken a major capital account liberalization on two occasions: 1986–87 and 1994–96. Before capital controls were reimposed in 1998, there were few restrictions on cross-border transactions in ringgit and financial transactions with nonresidents.

Malaysia permitted foreign investors to participate directly in the domestic stock market from 1973 when the Kuala Lumpur Stock Exchange was established. The Malaysian authorities allowed offshore over-the-counter (OTC) trading in Malaysian equities and bonds and the development of an offshore market in ringgit in Singapore. Malaysian banks were freely able to engage in arbitrage between the domestic and offshore markets by providing forward cover against ringgit to nonresidents. Foreign investors were relatively free to invest in all types of Malaysian financial assets, including bank deposits. As for portfolio outflows, domestic corporations were subject to relatively few limitations in remitting funds for overseas investments. Authorized dealers and tier-1 merchant banks were unrestricted in their borrowing from abroad and lending in foreign exchange to both residents and nonresidents, although foreign currency borrowing by residents was subject to limits.

Up until the mid-1980s, Indonesia maintained a highly regulated regime with regard to portfolio capital inflows, although it had the most liberal policy for outflows among the four countries under consideration. Nonresidents were not allowed to purchase equity in the domestic stock market and selective limits on foreign borrowings were in effect. It was not until 1985 when Indonesia became an Article VIII country that it took measures to liberalize payments and transfers for current international transactions and to develop the foreign exchange market. In the same year, nonresidents were allowed to establish joint-venture securities firms. Foreign banks were permitted to establish joint ventures with domestic banks.

While only one joint venture existed in 1988, there were 30 by the end of 1994. Altogether, during the same period, the number of branches of foreign banks and joint-venture banks increased from 21 to 83. In 1992, the purchase of bank shares by nonresidents, initially banned, was raised to 49 per cent, while domestic firms were permitted to list up to 30 per cent of their equity on foreign stock exchanges. A year later, quantitative limits on banks' borrowing from abroad were lifted. Foreign investors were allowed to acquire up to 49 per cent of the ownership of listed stock.

With the removal of restrictions on capital account liberalization, a large amount of foreign capital began to flow in. Table 4.2 shows that net capital inflows in Indonesia and Thailand amounted to 4.1 per cent and 9.1 per cent of GNP, respectively, on average during 1992–96, while the corresponding figures are 1.9 per cent and 7.2 per cent in Korea and Malaysia. Concerned about the difficulties this inflow could create for macroeconomic

Table 4.2 Net capital flows to East Asia (% GNP)

	1990	1992	1993	1994	1995	1996	1997	1998	1999
Indonesia	3.0	4.4	3.7	2.2	5.2	4.9	1.2	-4.1	-3.4
Foreign direct investment	1.0	1.3	1.1	0.9	1.9	2.5	2.1	-0.4	-2.1
Portfolio investment	0.3	-0.1	1.2	2.3	2.1	2.3	-1.3	-2.0	-1.4
Loans	1.7	3.1	1.4	-0.9	1.2	0.1	0.3	-1.7	0.0
Korea	0.4	1.5	0.2	2.2	2.3	3.4	-2.4	0.4	1.9
Foreign direct investment	0.3	-0.1	-0.2	-0.4	-0.4	-0.5	-0.3	0.2	1.3
Portfolio investment	0.3	1.9	2.9	1.6	2.4	2.9	3.0	-0.4	2.3
Loans	-0.2	-0.3	-2.5	1.1	0.3	0.9	-5.1	0.5	-1.6
Malaysia	2.5	7.3	8.6	6.5	7.8	5.6	7.2	4.0	4.5
Foreign direct investment	1.9	9.2	7.7	6.1	4.9	5.3	5.4	3.2	2.1
Portfolio investment	1.6	-2.0	-1.1	-2.3	-0.5	-0.3	-0.3	0.4	1.1
Loans	-1.0	0.1	1.8	2.7	3.4	0.6	2.0	0.4	1.3
Thailand	5.2	7.0	9.5	8.4	12.8	7.8	6.4	-2.9	-4.8
Foreign direct investment	2.9	1.8	1.3	0.6	0.7	0.8	2.3	6.6	4.9
Portfolio investment	0.4	0.8	4.4	1.7	2.5	2.0	3.1	0.3	0.1
Loans	1.9	4.4	3.8	6.0	9.6	5.0	1.1	-9.9	-9.7

Source : International Monetary Fund.

management, the Indonesian government reimposed quantitative restrictions on borrowing from abroad by banks and state enterprises, which remained in place until 1996. Even during this period, however, Johnston et al. (1997) suggest that the Indonesian policy makers continued to liberalize FDI and portfolio investment from abroad through the stock market as part of their financial sector development.

During the first half of the 1990s, the three countries saw the need to slow down, and in some cases reverse, capital account liberalization. A number of measures were adopted to reduce the volume and volatility of short-term capital flows as governments became wary of the potentially destabilizing effects of massive and sudden flows of foreign capital (in either direction). As noted earlier, Malaysia and Indonesia imposed quantitative restrictions on capital inflows, while Thailand chose to liberalize outflows rather than to restrict inflows. By liberalizing foreign exchange controls in three stages from 1990 through 1994, most restrictions on outflows from Thailand were removed. Previously, the outflow of capital was tightly controlled and there was almost no restriction on inflows. The first round of the liberalization process in May 1990 focussed on deregulating current account transactions. The second (April 1991) and third rounds (February 1994) saw most controls on capital outflows lifted.

The Malaysian government, in 1991, made outstanding ringgit received through swap transactions with nonresidents subject to a reserve requirement. In 1992, the total maximum amount of borrowing in foreign currency from domestic banks by a resident was limited to US$1 million; previously there had been no maximum. In early 1994 the government also implemented administrative controls to discourage the inflow of foreign capital, especially speculative short-term capital, or 'hot money'. These controls included the prohibition of the sale of short-term money-market instruments to nonresidents, and a ban on commercial bank swaps and outright forward transactions on the bid side with foreign customers (unless trade related). These measures proved to be successful in curbing short-term capital inflows (Ariyoshi et al., 2000).

Indonesia adopted several measures in 1991 to discourage overseas borrowing. The Bank of Indonesia, the central bank, successfully reduced the volume of swap operations by lowering the limit for an individual bank from 25 per cent to 20 per cent of its capital, raising the swap premium by 5 percentage points, and announcing that future swap operations could be undertaken only on its initiative. Limits were imposed on offshore borrowing by government-owned enterprises and commercial banks and all public sector overseas commercial borrowing was subject to government approval. In the same year, a debt management team was organized to supervise foreign loan transactions.

4.3 CAPITAL ACCOUNT LIBERALIZATION: AFTER THE 1997 CRISIS

Korea

As part of the conditionality of the IMF rescue financing, the Korean government agreed immediately after the crisis broke out to shift to a freely floating exchange rate regime and to open up financial markets, including those for short-term securities. These liberalization measures were aimed at stabilizing domestic financial markets by inducing foreign capital inflows. The Korean government also agreed to liberalize further the foreign exchange system over a three-year period, divided into two phases beginning in April 1999. The basic plan for the liberalization was announced in June 1998 and was similar in coverage to the 1993 plan.

During the first phase, controls on capital account transactions were converted into a negative system, removing all restrictions except for those limited by law or decree. In order to promote overseas investment by private corporations and financial institutions, residents' purchases of overseas real estate were deregulated and their overseas borrowing and issuance of foreign currency-denominated bonds with maturity of less than one year were also allowed. At the same time, nonresidents were permitted to make deposits and open trust accounts denominated in Korean won with maturity of more than one year. The bona fide principle in forward and derivative transactions was abolished.

Beginning in January 2001, foreign exchange liberalization entered its second phase with further liberalization for individuals and the streamlining of remaining restrictions on corporations and financial institutions regarding their foreign exchange transactions.

Since the start of the second phase of the liberalization:

- restrictions on obligatory repatriation of external claims have been eased;
- ceilings on overseas payments and monetary possessions for residents when leaving the country have been eliminated;
- the US$20,000 ceiling on foreign currency purchase by residents has been lifted;
- the maturity restrictions on Korean won-denominated deposits or trusts via domestic financial institutions by nonresidents have been removed;
- overseas borrowings by individuals and non-profit organizations have been allowed, if they are notified to the Bank of Korea (central bank). However, short-term overseas borrowings by domestic firms with financially unsound structure are still restricted; and

- OTC securities transactions between residents and nonresidents have been deregulated.

Indonesia

On 29 August 1997, immediately after the crisis began, the Indonesian authorities imposed limits per customer on forward currency trading between nonresidents and banks and on each bank's outstanding position in the forward market (US$5 million) to restore stability in the foreign exchange market. However, the Indonesian government agreed to phase out these controls as soon as possible in its letter of intent to the IMF.[4] At the same time, the Indonesian authorities allowed foreign investors to purchase unlimited domestic shares (except for those in banks) as of 4 September 1997 to encourage inflows of foreign capital.

In 1998 many restrictions on foreign direct investment were eased in order to stimulate domestic investment. Some of the deregulation measures include:

- the removal of all formal and informal barriers to FDI in palm oil plantation;
- the lifting of restrictions on FDI in retail and wholesale trade; and
- reducing the number of activities closed to foreign investors in July 1998.

In the following year the Act on the Foreign Exchange Flows and Exchange System was promulgated, liberalizing in principle the ownership and use of foreign exchange. The Act also provided a legal basis for introducing prudential regulation on foreign exchange transactions. The Act gives the central bank authority to request information and data concerning foreign exchange transactions conducted by residents and to prescribe provisions for prudential regulations on various types of foreign exchange transactions conducted by banks.

Malaysia

When Malaysia came under speculative attacks in July 1997, it shifted to a tight monetary and fiscal policy to defend its currency. Unlike Thailand and Indonesia, Malaysia was able to weather the initial attack for almost a year after the Thai crisis erupted. By mid-1998, however, it was clear that the initial policy response was not working. Because of the expectation of a depreciation of the currency, interest rates in the offshore ringgit market rose relative to domestic interest rates. This increase triggered large capital outflows and led to an increase in domestic interest rates, which in turn accelerated contraction in the economy and exacerbated the corporate debt build-up and non-performing loan problems at financial institutions.

Faced with a rapidly deteriorating macroeconomic situation, Malaysia decided to fend for itself by taking radical measures of its own, rather than accepting an IMF rescue package. On 1 September 1998, the Malaysian government announced capital-control measures to halt the movement of short-term capital and restore monetary autonomy. The ringgit was pegged to the US dollar at the rate of M$3.80 the next day and monetary policy was further eased.

The capital controls were aimed at eliminating the offshore ringgit market and restricting the supply of ringgit to speculators. Some of the specific measures introduced on 1 September 1998 included:

- the prohibition of repatriation of portfolio investment held by nonresidents for 12 months;
- the mandatory repatriation of ringgit held offshore by the end of September;
- restrictions on the transfer of capital abroad by residents;
- the prohibition of granting ringgit credit facilities to nonresident corresponding banks and stockbroking companies by residents;
- the prohibition of obtaining ringgit credit and facilities from nonresidents by residents; and
- the approval of investment abroad by residents.

About six months later, however, some of these controls were relaxed. For example, the 12-month holding period restriction on the repatriation of portfolio capital was replaced with exit levies on the principal of capital investment made prior to 15 February 1999 and on the profits from investments made after that date.

Thailand

The deregulation of capital inflows, combined with rapid growth, brought in a large amount of foreign capital in excess of the absorptive capacity of the Thai economy. In 1995, restrictions on short-term capital inflows were introduced in the form of a 7 per cent reserve requirement on banks' nonresident baht accounts. These measures, however, did not slow down capital inflows. Subsequently, growing concerns about the rapid deterioration of the current account, an overvalued exchange rate and the insolvency of the financial system led to a sharp reversal of capital inflows and eventually touched off a major crisis.

In an effort to stave off speculative attacks against the baht, the Thai government introduced a number of capital controls in May 1997 that aimed at breaking the direct arbitrage link between the domestic and offshore baht markets and restricting holdings of baht by nonresidents. The control measures prohibited nonresidents from obtaining baht credit facilities through swap and forward transactions and from transferring baht abroad. Foreign equity investors were not allowed to repatriate their funds in baht. In addition, nonresidents were also required to use the onshore exchange rate rather than the offshore rate when they were repatriating their portfolio investment in foreign currency. These measures remained in effect until the end of January 1998.

Since then the Thai authorities have not taken any steps towards deregulating portfolio capital flows. Instead, their liberalization efforts have focussed on encouraging new inflows of foreign direct investment in service industries such as brokerage services, wholesale and retail trade and construction by converting the Alien Business Law into a new and more liberal foreign investment law.

In recent periods there have been indications that the Thai authorities have intervened in the foreign exchange market to limit the short-term volatility of the nominal exchange rate. For this intervention purpose, they have tightened foreign exchange reporting requirements, raising concerns that the tightening is a prelude to reintroducing some of the capital-control measures they phased out earlier.

4.4 CAPITAL ACCOUNT LIBERALIZATION AND ECONOMIC RECOVERY IN EAST ASIA

The economic recovery in the East Asian crisis countries has been impressive by any measure of performance. The recovery began approximately one year after the crisis erupted in July 1997 and accelerated through 2000. Indeed, following a year of robust growth in 1999 (except in Indonesia), the crisis countries recorded higher rates of growth than expected in 2000, ranging from 4.8 per cent in Indonesia to 8.8 per cent in Korea. The recent global economic downturn, however, has dealt a severe blow to the region's exporters, clouding the prospects for economic growth.

Despite the recent slowdown, the pace of recovery in East Asia has been much faster than other crisis episodes would predict (Park and Lee, 2001). What are the developments that are driving the rapid recovery in these crisis countries? To what extent has economic liberalization, in particular capital account liberalization, contributed to the recovery in these countries? Korea has succeeded in developing a capital account regime comparable to other

OECD member countries in terms of the degree of liberalization, whereas Malaysia has moved in the opposite direction. Although it is too early to make any definite judgment, the experiences of the two countries suggests that the degree of capital account liberalization is immaterial to macroeconomic performance. Indeed, judging from changes in macroeconomic indicators such as GDP growth, CPI inflation and current account balances, the performance of the Malaysian economy has been as impressive as that of Korea (see Table 4.3).

As for Korea, it would indeed be presumptuous to argue that capital account liberalization has produced substantial efficiency gains or promoted investment to drive the ongoing recovery, simply because the second and more important phase of capital account liberalization started only in 2001. In fact, a recent study (Park, 2001) shows that the removal of capital controls cannot be credited with the recovery and may not even have triggered the upswing. Instead, the easing of monetary and fiscal policy, openness, export orientation, and most important of all the changes in market perceptions that the crisis was not a permanent shock, have buttressed the ongoing recovery.

The capital account liberalization in Korea may not have supported the recovery process, but there is no evidence that it has interfered with the process. Then how could one explain the equally impressive recovery in Malaysia? Park (2001) argues that the Malaysian government's decision on 1 September 1998 to impose capital controls and to peg the ringgit to the US dollar, triggered the economy's fourth-quarter turnaround in 1998. Contrary to expectations, Malaysia's decision did not disrupt domestic or regional financial markets, but seems to have ignited the ongoing recovery.

Dornbusch (2001), on the other hand, shows that at the time of the imposition of capital controls, Malaysia was no more vulnerable than other crisis countries. In his view, therefore, it is incorrect to argue that capital controls contained a situation that otherwise would have been much worse. In fact, he points out that Malaysia had more favorable macroeconomic financial conditions than the other crisis countries. Moreover, the timing of controls coincided with the reversal of yen appreciation, the end of crises elsewhere in East Asia, and the interest rate cuts by the US Federal Reserve. Fischer (2001) makes a similar point: by the time Malaysia imposed capital controls, most of the turbulence of the first part of the East Asian crisis was over and regional exchange rates were already appreciating.

According to Jomo (2001) the effects of the capital controls were exaggerated, because when capital controls were imposed, the bulk of foreign funds had already fled the country. The controls therefore penalized the investors who had not left in the preceding 14 months. He also agrees with Fischer (2001) and Dornbusch (2001) that the external environment became favorable to Malaysia when the controls were imposed, while the bulk of short-term capital had already left the country so that in a very real sense, the control regime was never tested. For these reasons, he speculates that the capital-control imposition is likely to have slowed down recovery and acted to contain FDI inflows.

Table 4.3 Selected macroeconomic indicators

	1995	1996	1997	1998	1999	2000
GDP growth (%)						
Indonesia	8.2	7.8	4.7	-13.0	0.8	4.8
Korea	8.9	6.8	5.0	-6.7	10.9	8.8
Malaysia	9.8	10.0	7.3	-7.4	6.1	8.3
Thailand	8.9	5.9	-1.7	-10.2	4.2	4.4
Inflation (%)						
Indonesia	9.4	7.9	6.2	58.0	20.7	3.8
Korea	4.5	4.9	4.4	7.5	0.8	2.3
Malaysia	3.5	3.5	2.7	5.3	2.7	1.5
Thailand	5.7	5.8	5.6	8.1	0.3	1.9
Current account / GDP (%)						
Indonesia	-3.2	-3.4	-2.3	4.1	3.5	7.8
Korea	-1.7	-4.4	-1.7	12.6	6.0	2.4
Malaysia	-10.0	-4.4	-5.6	13.1	15.9	9.9
Thailand	-8.1	-8.1	-1.9	12.5	10.2	7.5
Investment / GDP (%)						
Indonesia	28.4	30.0	28.3	23.4	18.3	24.3
Korea	36.7	36.8	35.1	29.8	27.8	28.7
Malaysia	43.6	42.5	43.1	26.8	22.3	20.4
Thailand	41.0	41.1	33.3	22.2	21.0	21.3
Exports / GDP (%)						
Indonesia	26.3	25.8	27.9	53.7	35.3	38.5
Korea	30.2	29.5	34.7	49.7	42.3	45.0
Malaysia	94.1	91.6	93.2	114.4	121.7	125.5
Thailand	41.8	39.2	47.9	58.6	57.3	67.1
Nominal exchange rate [a]						
Indonesia	2,308.0	2,383.0	4,650.0	8,025.0	7,085.0	9,595.0
Korea	774.7	844.2	1,695.0	1,204.0	1,138.0	1,265.0
Malaysia	2.54	2.53	3.89	3.8	3.8	3.8
Thailand	25.19	25.61	47.25	36.69	37.47	42.27

	1995	1996	1997	1998	1999	2000
Real effective exchange rate [b]						
Indonesia	100.0	104.9	98.0	48.5	73.7	72.1
Korea	100.0	102.7	96.4	75.4	83.3	90.2
Malaysia	100.0	104.9	102.5	78.7	80.0	82.1
Thailand	100.0	103.8	97.6	85.2	89.1	89.8
Foreign reserves / GDP (%)						
Indonesia	7.5	10.6	9.6	23.0	16.2	15.0
Korea	6.5	6.5	4.2	16.2	17.8	21.0
Malaysia	25.8	26.7	20.8	35.0	37.7	32.6
Thailand	21.1	20.7	17.3	25.7	27.5	26.0
Short-term debt / total debt (%)						
Indonesia	20.9	25.0	24.1	13.3	13.3	–
Korea	54.3	57.5	39.3	20.2	26.8	–
Malaysia	21.2	27.9	31.6	19.3	16.4	–
Thailand	44.1	39.5	34.5	28.3	24.3	–

Notes:

a: Against US$, end of year data.

b: Indices 1995 = 100; higher values indicate appreciation of the domestic currency.

Sources: International Monetary Fund, World Bank, Bank of Indonesia, Bank of Korea, Bank of Thailand and Bank Negara Malaysia.

In a recent study of the Malaysian capital controls, Kaplan and Rodrik (2001) argue that a more fruitful analysis of the Malaysian experience requires a comparison of the economic performance of Malaysia after the imposition of capital controls on 1 September 1998, with that of Korea and Thailand when they were undergoing IMF programs, that is, after accepting the IMF rescue financing and conditionality (21 November 1997 for Korea and 28 July 1997 for Thailand). Such a counterfactual analysis, they claim, requires a time-shifted difference-in-difference approach. According to their empirical results, the Malaysian controls have indeed contributed to stabilizing financial markets and the economy as a whole: Malaysia suffered a smaller decline in the GDP growth rate, in employment in manufacturing and in stock prices, and experienced a larger decrease in interest rates and a smaller currency depreciation than Korea.

Haggard and Low (2001) and Hood (2001) reach a similar conclusion: the Malaysian capital controls were effective in revitalizing the stock market, lowering domestic interest rates and building up foreign exchange reserves, which in turn initiated and sustained Malaysia's recovery. The Malaysian control measures also provided breathing space in which the planning and implementation of economic reform (which entailed the substantial costs of restructuring ailing financial institutions and corporations) could be undertaken. The controls were not costless, of course: one of the major costs was that Malaysian banks and corporations had to pay a higher risk premium on their borrowing from abroad. Table 4.4 shows that Korea recovered its sovereign credibility more rapidly after the East Asian crisis than Malaysia.

In conclusion, the East Asian experiences with capital account liberalization do not provide any evidence as to whether capital controls or the application of an explicit IMF program resulted in better economic performance. This is because the costs and benefits of capital controls remain ambiguous.

Table 4.4 Portfolio investment risk

	Moody's	Standard & Poor's	Moody's	Standard & Poor's
	Indonesia		**Korea**	
Nov. 1996	Baa3	BBB	–	AA
Jan. 1998	Baa3	BBB	–	B+
Dec. 1998	BB	BB+	Ba1	BB+
Jan. 2000	B3	CCC+	Baa2	BBB
	Malaysia		**Thailand**	
Nov. 1996	A1	A+	A2	A
Jan. 1998	A1	A+	Baa3	BBB
Dec. 1998	Baa3	BBB	Ba1	BBB
Jan. 2000	Baa3	BBB	Ba1	BBB

Source: World Bank.

4.5 PROSPECTS FOR CAPITAL ACCOUNT LIBERALIZATION IN EAST ASIA

There is the widely held presumption that emerging market economies would want to liberalize the capital account and integrate into global capital markets because that is the course of development advanced countries have taken. Fischer (2001) and many others also argue that the potential benefits of integration into the global capital markets outweigh the costs.

Although the IMF supports liberalization of capital account as a matter of principle, it also recognizes that the use of market-based inflow controls may be necessary to gain monetary policy independence and to increase the long-term share in capital inflows, while controls on capital outflows can be used to help maintain a fixed exchange rate system. In the long run, the IMF believes that capital controls lose their effectiveness and efficiency and should therefore be removed, at least gradually.

As noted earlier, Korea is the only country that has managed a substantial degree of capital account liberalization in East Asia after the 1997 crisis. Thailand and Indonesia have done very little in deregulating further capital flows. Most of the other ASEAN (Association of South-East Asian Nations) countries and China have shown little enthusiasm for speeding up the liberalization of capital account transactions. In fact, there are indications that some of these countries may reinstate various capital controls as a means of stabilizing the nominal exchange rate. Why do these countries have so little confidence in the efficiency of an open capital account regime and place so little value on the benefits of integration into global capital markets? One simple answer may be that they believe, as does Bhagwati (1998), that the costs of liberalization are greater than the benefits. The rest of this section discusses some of the important reasons why East Asian policy makers are as averse as they have been to liberalizing the capital account.

Sustainability of Capital Controls

A number of studies have shown that capital controls on either inflows or outflows tend to lose their effectiveness and efficiency over time. Only in the short run may capital controls be effective in strengthening monetary independence with pegged exchange rates and in influencing the composition of capital inflows. The celebrated case of the Chilean controls had, according to Edwards (2000), outlasted their effectiveness by 1998.[5] If the long-term effectiveness of capital control is indeed at best doubtful, then one can make a strong case for capital account liberalization in emerging market economies: these countries would be better off by removing capital controls gradually over time, regardless of and despite the short-run costs.

In a review of recent studies on the Chilean capital controls, Williamson (2000, p.29) shows that the literature on the Chilean controls has exaggerated their ineffectiveness and that 'capital controls can be a useful complement to macroeconomic policies designed to limit counterproductive movements in the exchange rate'. The controversy on the effectiveness of capital controls is not likely to be resolved soon. Unless more reliable pieces of evidence on the long-term ineffectiveness of capital controls are presented, East Asian policy makers are not likely to be persuaded to take further steps in deregulating the capital account transactions.

Benefits of Capital Account Liberalization

There is a large body of empirical literature analyzing the effects of capital account liberalization. Despite the voluminous literature, recent empirical studies have failed to produce convincing evidence that the benefits of capital account liberalization are indeed greater than the costs. Rodrik (1998) does not find any evidence that capital account liberalization leads to a higher ratio of investment to GDP in a cross-section study that includes 100 developing and advanced countries. Edwards (2001) and Arteta et al. (2001) also find no strong causal effects of capital account liberalization on economic growth in developing economies.[6]

It is often argued that capital market opening speeds up the growth and sophistication of the domestic financial system, thereby improving the allocative efficiency of domestic financial markets. Except for OECD members, there is no empirical evidence supporting financial deepening brought about by capital account liberalization in emerging market economies (Kraay, 1998). Klein and Olivei (1999) find that capital account liberalization contributes to financial development in a cross-section study of 93 developed and developing countries. However, when 20 Latin American countries, which maintain a relatively free capital account, are separated out for a similar study they do not find any positive effects of capital account liberalization on financial deepening. Among the four East Asian countries under consideration, there is no evidence that open capital accounts have been associated with financial development. According to various financial indices shown in Table 4.5, it seems that the degree of financial deepening just before the East Asian crisis was highest in Malaysia, whereas it was lowest in Indonesia. However, as can be seen in Table 4.1, Indonesia had the most liberalized capital account regime during that period, while Malaysia was behind the other countries in removing the restrictions on capital account transactions.

There is also the argument that an open capital account regime can help facilitate not only the financing of current account deficits but also the efficient allocation of surpluses. However, as we discuss below, this benefit depends on the size of deficits, because practically all emerging market economies are subject to credit rationing in their offshore borrowing. Since all four East Asian crisis-hit countries have produced large current account surpluses since 1997, the East Asian experiences do not shed much light on the question of whether capital account liberalization increases access to international financial markets in emerging market economies.

Could free capital mobility provide strong incentives for policy makers to adhere to a rational and responsible policy regime, so that bad policies, such as maintaining an overvalued exchange rate for an extended period of time, are avoided to minimize the risk of provoking an outflow of foreign capital that may complicate macroeconomic management? All four East Asian countries had achieved a relatively high degree of capital account liberalization before the crisis compared to many other emerging market economies, but according to a large number of studies on the East Asian crisis, capital account reform does not appear to have prevented authorities from going astray in policy making. Instead, the disorderly and hurried liberalization invited speculative attacks and precipitated a major crisis.

Table 4.5 Financial deepening of East Asian countries before the crisis (% GDP)

	Money stock (M3)		Domestic bank credit		Stock market capitalization	
	1990	1996	1990	1996	1990	1996
Indonesia	40.4	52.5	45.5	54.6	7.1	40.3
Korea	54.6	84.0	65.7	74.5	43.8	28.6
Malaysia	64.4	121.5	75.7	131.9	110.4	309.6
Thailand	74.9	79.5	91.1	98.8	28.0	53.9

Source: World Bank.

Sequencing of Liberalization

An accepted norm of the sequencing of liberalization in emerging market economies is that capital account liberalization should be carried out at the end of the reform process, that is after completing trade liberalization, FDI liberalization and domestic financial deregulation (McKinnon 1973, 1993). Cooper (1999) also argues that emerging market economies could gain little and most likely suffer from financial instability, if liberalization of the capital account is prematurely undertaken when domestic financial markets are underdeveloped, soundness and safety of banks and other financial institutions are not assured, an effective system of prudential regulation of financial institution is not established, and many trade restrictions remain.

Fischer (2001, p.5) also points to a number of preconditions for capital controls (on outflows) saying that 'they would need to be removed gradually … as the necessary infrastructure – in the form of strong and efficient domestic financial institutions and markets, a market-based monetary policy, an effective foreign exchange market, and the information base necessary for the markets to operate efficiently – is put in place'. Judging by this set of sequencing criteria, most of the East Asian economies, except for Singapore,

Hong Kong and Japan, have not reached a stage where they could safely open their capital markets. Indeed, a number of recent studies on the East Asian crisis show that the misguided financial market opening in the absence of an effective system of prudential regulation and supervision of financial institutions was one of the most critical factors that triggered and deepened the crisis; it allowed the unsustainable build-up of unhedged short-term foreign currency debts by both financial institutions and corporations (Furman and Stiglitz, 1998 and Krugman 1999).

Globalization Without Global Governance

There is growing apprehension in East Asia that the rapid process of financial globalization has not been accompanied by the development of an effective system of global financial governance that can support the emergence of a stable and efficient global financial system. In theory, the viability of the global financial system requires a global lender of last resort and global regulatory authorities. Since it is politically unrealistic to establish these global public goods, the establishment and enforcement of various international economic and financial standards have been put forward as a second-best alternative to the creation of global institutions.

From the perspectives of emerging market economies, integration into global financial markets means considerable erosion of their policy autonomy, in particular monetary policy, and hence raises the need to coordinate their macroeconomic and other policies with those of developed countries (G7 in particular). Although the advocates of common international standards claim that the universal acceptance of the standards will help stabilize international financial markets and reduce the frequency of financial crises, there is no evidence to support such an argument. On the contrary, as Pistor (2000) notes, harmonization may produce perverse results.

A group of advanced economies dominated by the G7 has been developing various common financial standards. This group intends to ask other countries to accept and to authorize international financial institutions such as the IMF to enforce compliance with common standards and codes. In doing so, these countries attempt to provide quasi-governance of international finance as they are developing a de facto global legal architecture for international financial markets through legal harmonization. Therefore, East Asian countries which are largely left out of this standard-setting process may justifiably ask whether this group of countries promoting the universal standards is also prepared to provide public goods such as the services of lender of last resort. This question arises because there is no guarantee that those emerging market economies which faithfully comply with the common standards will become less vulnerable to financial crises. If a financial crisis broke out, and spreads to other countries, emerging market and developing economies may expect that the group of countries providing quasi-governance will assist them with unconditional liquidity support so that they do not fall victim to contagion. However, at this stage of development, these advanced countries promoting the adoption of common standards have not shown any indication that they would collectively provide these global public goods.

Capital Mobility, Free Floating and Inflation Targetting: A Workable Macroeconomic Policy Framework?

Finally, it is often argued that capital account liberalization would be more successful if combined with a freely floating or at least more flexible nominal exchange rate. Once a country begins to float, it has to choose a basis for monetary policy and many countries have adopted inflation targetting as a nominal anchor. That is, these emerging market economies contemplating capital account liberalization may find it necessary to rely on a macroeconomic policy framework which embraces free floating, free capital mobility and inflation targetting. One such framework, which the IMF and many experts have recommended to emerging market economies open to international capital flows is a variant of the Mundell–Fleming model with a Phillips curve.[7] East Asian policy makers do not appear convinced that such a framework would be operable and effective in ensuring price stability while sustaining robust growth and avoiding large current account imbalances. This lack of confidence in the new macroeconomic system has raised the question of whether an alternative framework, such as an intermediate exchange rate regime with capital controls, may be more appropriate to many East Asian emerging market economies (Williamson, 2000).

With the deregulation of capital account transactions, capital flows have increasingly dominated changes in the nominal exchange rate in many emerging market economies: mobile capital in and out of these economies has largely determined the direction and scope of fluctuations and has often resulted in an overshooting of nominal exchange rates. Under these circumstances, if the interest rate parity condition holds in real terms, there is no reason to believe that an equilibrium real exchange that satisfies the arbitrage relation for a given domestic real interest rate and expected real exchange rate will also be the rate that could maintain export competitiveness. Nor would it necessarily be the rate that will balance the current account.

In models of free floating and capital mobility with inflation targetting, such as the one developed by Svensson (2000), the current account is immaterial and does not raise any policy problems because current account imbalances are adjusted through lending to or borrowing from the international financial markets. This assumption on the current account adjustment may be incorrect and unrealistic. It may be incorrect because the current account is also driven by exports and an import demand so that not only do capital movements affect the current account through their effects on the exchange rate, but they also affect income levels. It may be unrealistic because most emerging market economies integrating into international financial markets cannot go on borrowing indefinitely: in reality, most are subject to borrowing constraints.

To elaborate further on the current account issue, consider an exogenous increase in the foreign interest rate.[8] In the Mundell–Fleming model with a Phillips curve that assumes free floating and capital mobility and introduces inflation targeting, this change induces an increase in capital outflows. This outflow subsequently causes, other things being equal, a depreciation of the currency, which in turns builds up inflationary pressure, a gain of export competitiveness and an incipient surplus on the current account that was initially balanced. The expansionary effects of the depreciation result in an increase in output and domestic interest rates. Depending on the strength of the inflationary pressure, policy authorities may move to tighten money market conditions by further raising interest rates to meet a predetermined inflation target. These changes are likely to prevent any further weakening of the currency, but have ambiguous effects on the current account. If the initial capital outflows and the subsequent changes in output and interest rate create expectations of a further currency depreciation, then current account surpluses may continue.

Conversely, an increase in capital inflows triggered by a fall in the foreign interest rate may cause an appreciation of the currency with a subsequent current account deterioration. The increase in capital inflows would therefore exert downward pressure on the interest rate and the level of output. Inflation targetting may then require an easing of monetary policy. As in the case of the increase in the foreign interest rate, however, these changes may not dissipate the pressure for appreciation and hence may not restore balance in the current account. As we discuss below in this subsection, if the deficit is large and expected to grow, foreign investors and lenders may view the imbalance as a sign of serious structural weaknesses and withdraw their investments. When the withdrawal is combined with the herd behavior in the international financial markets, it precipitates a major crisis. To the extent that maintaining a current account imbalance at a manageable level is an important policy objective, as it is in many emerging market and developing economies, the open economy model with free floating, free capital mobility and inflation targetting is not a useful policy framework.

Fischer (2001) proposes using fiscal policy as an instrument to manage the current account when there is a large deficit as a result of a real exchange rate appreciation. When monetary policy is locked in for inflation targetting, this means that fiscal policy is reserved for achieving either the current account or employment objective. However, it is rather obvious that such a target-instrument approach could destabilize the Mundell–Fleming model with inflation targetting in the short run.[9] Consider an increase in the foreign interest rate. Other things being equal, this will induce an outflow of capital, thereby depreciating the currency. The weakened currency generates a surplus on the current account, while it builds up inflationary pressure through the increase in both the prices of imports and nontradables. Monetary policy will be tightened to reduce the inflationary pressure. On the other hand, fiscal policy will have to be expansionary to reduce the incipient current account surplus. Therefore, policy makers may find themselves in an unsustainable situation where they pursue contractionary monetary policy and expansionary fiscal policy at the same time.

There is also another adjustment problem in the Mundell–Fleming model with inflation targetting. In a world of free capital mobility, the freely floating exchange rate system could exacerbate rather than temper the boom-and-bust cycle associated with procyclical capital flows: the system may not be able to guard against speculative disturbances as effectively as is claimed. For example, consider a large increase in capital inflows in an emerging market economy attracted by the prospect of a boom (a higher expected rate of return on capital). The increase initially creates pressure for currency appreciation. However, the initial appreciation may not deter or reverse the inflows if it does not create expectations of depreciation, particularly when foreign investors' perception of economic expansion does not change.

So long as this perception of a continuing boom persists, both domestic and foreign investors are likely to believe that asset prices will continue to increase.[10] This expectation will in turn attract further foreign capital inflows. In the absence of central bank intervention, the inflows will then lead to a monetary expansion and subsequently to increases in equity, property and other asset prices. The asset price increase keeps the currency strong, but the booming asset markets and domestic demand expansion do not generate any expectation of a depreciation, hence resulting in further inflows, which in turn feed the speculation in the asset market.[11]

The currency appreciation will undermine export competitiveness and shift resources to the nontradable sector; eventually it will slow down export earnings and bring about a current account deterioration. It may take some time to observe such effects. Only when the current account begins to show signs of a large deterioration would currency depreciation expectations set in. Once the current account deficit is perceived to be too large to be sustainable, market expectations may shift and foreign portfolio investors and lenders may pull out their investments simultaneously. Such an exodus of foreign investors could easily provoke a major financial crisis, as it did in Thailand in 1997.[12]

4.6 CONCLUDING REMARKS

While the case for open trade is hardly disputed, the case for integrated international capital markets remains controversial. In theory, financial globalization leads to a more efficient resource allocation, diversification of opportunities, and the equalization of risk-adjusted returns. The controversy on the desirability of open capital markets rages on largely because there is no evidence that countries with open capital accounts grow faster or develop a deeper and more sophisticated financial system whereas there is a large empirical literature on the costs of trade restrictions.

In this study we have examined the experiences of two countries which moved to opposite ends of the spectrum of capital account management during a major financial crisis: Korea accepted and implemented an IMF policy reform program that required a capital account opening; Malaysia took recourse to capital controls instead of seeking an IMF rescue financing. The two different approaches to capital account management, however, have not resulted in different outcomes as far as recovery is concerned: both countries have engineered an impressive recovery from the crisis, leading us to wonder whether an open capital market matters at all.

Despite the conflicting evidence on the costs of capital controls, one can still make a strong case for integrated international financial markets. As Fischer (2001) notes, all developed countries have open capital accounts and given this universal feature of advanced countries, one could assume that emerging market and developing economies would want to open their capital markets in the course of their development. The issue concerning capital account liberalization in emerging market economies is therefore not whether they should open their capital markets, but how they should go about doing it. In this regard, many important questions as to the sequence of market opening and the preconditions for capital account liberalization remain unanswered.

Finally, at this stage of development, there is no evidence that global financial markets and accompanying international standards, regulation and supervision will do a better job at allocating capital and preventing financial crises than individual country markets. As long as these doubts are not properly addressed, many emerging market economies, including those in East Asia, will be skeptical of the benefits of opening their capital accounts and will continue to waver on this issue.

NOTES

1. Following Johnson et al. (1999), the degree of capital control is defined as CC_i/N, where N denotes the number of types of capital controls listed in the IMF's annual publication 'Exchange Arrangements and Exchange Restrictions'. CC_i is the number of controls which country i actually imposes on capital movements. Capital controls refer to prohibitions, quantitative limits, approval and registration requirements and restrictions on investors' opportunities.
2. A negative system is here defined as meaning a system in which all transactions are permitted unless explicitly prohibited.
3. The discussion of capital account liberalization in Malaysia draws on Johnston et al., (1999, p.4–6).
4. Letter of Intent and Memorandum of Economic and Financial Policies, 31 October 1997.
5. See also Valdes-Prieto and Soto (1998), Simone and Sorsa (1999) and Laurens and Cardoso (1998) on the ineffectiveness of the Chilean capital controls.
6. However, empirical results from Kim et al. (2002) suggest that capital account liberalization in the 1990s induced a greater inflow of foreign capital to Korea, leading to consumption and investment boom, and consequently increase in output.
7. See Svensson (1997, 2000) and McCallum (1997).
8. See Dooley et al. (2001) for an extension of the Svensson model with a capital account.
9. In the long run, it is reasonable to assume that the capitalized value of present and future current account imbalances approaches a constant level, if not zero. However, it is not clear how and whether the international financial markets could ensure such a long-run equilibrium in the absence of policy intervention.
10. For the sake of simplicity, it is assumed that the domestic bond market is underdeveloped and closed to foreign investors, as is the case in many emerging market economies.
11. In a floating regime, there is a tendency for changes in the spot rate to lead to an almost identical change in the forward rate (Svensson, 1992). Williamson (2000) argues that this implies a lack of a market expectation that the exchange rate may return to an equilibrium level within any time horizon relevant to market participants. Given this exchange rate behavior, the expected future exchange rate may simply appreciate as the spot rate appreciates.
12. For a similar argument, see Furman and Stiglitz (1998).

5. Recent codes-based liberalization in the OECD

Eva Thiel

5.1 INTRODUCTION[1]

The establishment of the Organisation for Economic Cooperation and Development (OECD) in 1961 testified to the need felt by its members for a balanced framework within which they could pursue gradual progress towards capital account liberalization. Although the mood in the early 1960s was not in favor of the immediate and total abolition of controls on all forms of capital flows, there was consensus that joint work towards reaping the economic benefits of freer capital movements should be pursued, as is clearly set out in the objectives of the OECD Convention.[2]

The commitment to the philosophy of free and open markets is expressed in the two OECD codes of liberalization: the Code of Liberalization of Capital Movements, which also covers direct investment and commercial establishment, and the OECD Code of Liberalization of Current Invisible Operations which covers cross-border services. The *modus operandi* designed for implementing the codes also reflects members' search for a balanced and orderly process where liberalization could be pursued in a safe manner. The codes provide a dynamic and ongoing process of analysis, consultation and peer pressure, jointly developed by members over the OECD's 40-year history to respect individual countries' specific needs and preferred pace of liberalization. In the case of capital movements, the codes safeguard a degree of autonomy for monetary and exchange rate policy by preserving the flexibility to restrict those capital flows deemed to be of a destabilizing nature in situations of economic disturbance.

This chapter continues with a discussion of the scope and function of the OECD codes of liberalization, before analyzing the recent liberalization experiences of six new OECD members in the context of the codes. Section 5.4 concludes.

5.2 THE OECD CODES OF LIBERALIZATION: STRUCTURE AND IMPLEMENTATION

Clearly, the quantum shift in major industrial countries' attitude towards liberalization in recent decades cannot be credited to the progressive implementation of the OECD Capital Movements Code alone. While this code remains the only multilateral instrument under which obligations of liberalizing capital movements are agreed and enforced (supported since 1988 by the European Union (EU) directive on capital liberalization), its main function has been to consolidate liberalization gains made possible by policy shifts in member countries. Together with the code concerning the invisibles trade, it has served to entrench the capital account opening process via irreversible undertakings by members and to push the process forward on a broad multilateral and non-discriminatory basis. Thus, the codes can be viewed as complementing and reinforcing a number of other instruments and processes for the promotion of a liberal international economic environment, managed by the World Trade Organization and the International Monetary Fund (IMF), as well as via regional and bilateral undertakings.

The OECD codes of liberalization are legal instruments, agreed unanimously by the members, which establish rules of conduct for the governments of OECD member countries. While legally binding on member governments, the instruments are not a treaty or international agreement in the sense of international law and therefore carry no sanctions. Under the codes, members are obliged to maintain – as a minimum – the existing degree of freedom for international capital movements and current invisible operations and to pursue further liberalization in both areas. The compliance review process relies exclusively on consultation, discussion and peer pressure.

The examination of measures implemented by the members occurs within the Committee on Capital Movements and Invisible Transactions (CMIT). This peer review process has proved to be quite a powerful tool for driving liberalization forward, even though it does not involve direct negotiations and sanctions. Peer pressure in a multilateral setting can provide strong incentives for authorities to undertake necessary policy adjustments. By benchmarking regulations and administrative procedures against those adopted and enforced by peer members in the OECD, countries are encouraged to take further liberalization measures once a critical mass of liberalization and deregulation has been reached. This form of guidance for capital account opening, supported by adequate standards of governance and supervision, can assist countries to become better integrated into the global financial system, with the benefits that this entails.

The key objective is set out in the first article of each code: members subscribe to the general aim of eliminating restrictions on capital movements and invisible transactions between one another. The remaining provisions describe the framework under which member countries shall work towards reaching this goal, while annexed liberalization lists specify the operations to which the obligations apply. Today, the Capital Movements Code applies to all long- and short-term capital movements between residents of OECD countries. Coverage of cross-border trade in services by the Current Invisibles Code is large, but not quite as comprehensive. The obligation to liberalize goes beyond the requirement that transfers of funds to and from abroad should be free of exchange control restrictions. There is also a requirement that the underlying transactions themselves should not be frustrated by laws, regulations or administrative approval processes.

The main provisions of the codes can be summarized as:

- the right to proceed gradually towards liberalization through a process of lodging and maintaining reservations;
- the obligation not to discriminate among OECD members;
- exceptions for reasons of public order and security;
- derogations for short-term operations in the case of temporary economic difficulties;
- provisions to ensure compatibility with regional arrangements such as the European Union and its special processes; and
- a system of notification, examination and consultation administered by the CMIT.

The first tenet – usually referred to as the 'rollback principle' – allows member countries to achieve liberalization gradually, according to their individual situation. If and when a member country has decided to maintain restrictions to the free circulation of capital and services, its situation is examined periodically. The other member countries will be informed about the reasons why a restriction is considered necessary and may suggest alternative ways in which the concerns can be addressed.

Members unable to liberalize immediately are permitted to lodge a full or limited reservation against specific operations or items on the codes' liberalization lists. If a country has not lodged a reservation to a particular item, the transactions covered by this particular item are expected to be fully liberalized. A full reservation means that the transaction to which it refers cannot be undertaken at all. A limited reservation means that the transaction may be permitted, subject to certain restrictions. Members are required to notify all measures which affect any of the transactions covered by the codes. Reservations are drafted so as to reflect as precisely as possible the restrictions still imposed. This facilitates transparency as well as the review process which aims to turn full into limited reservations and at further limiting, or deleting altogether, limited reservations. Transparency is also enhanced by publishing updated lists defining each country's current commitments on the OECD public website (as well as in regular hard-copy publications of the codes, together with country positions).[3] Any country's individual position at a given moment can thus be understood through reading the lists of reservations annexed to each code. Market participants can be confident that there are no restrictions aside from those appearing in the reservation lists.

OECD member countries have accepted under the codes that they may not introduce new barriers. Reservations to the obligations of the codes can only be reduced or deleted, but not added to or extended. This applies across the board and to all transactions under the coverage of the codes. The only exceptions are for new obligations, for some specific items in the Capital Movements Code,[4] and for a special derogation procedure designed to take account of temporary economic and financial difficulties. Once a restriction has been abolished, it cannot be reintroduced. This is usually referred to as the 'standstill obligation'. In order to achieve standstill as efficiently as possible, governments are expected to word their reservations very precisely so that they reflect only restrictions that actually exist. The regulatory status quo is thus locked in and can only evolve in the direction of further liberalization, the so-called 'ratchet-effect'.

The obligation of non-discrimination means that OECD members are expected to grant the benefit of open markets to residents of all other member countries alike, without reciprocity requirements or any other discrimination. Where restrictions have been lifted, this must be applied to everybody in the same way, including members experiencing economic difficulties and who are themselves currently unable to liberalize. The only exception permitted under the codes to the non-discrimination principle concerns liberalization measures adopted under a special system of regional integration, such as the EU, which do not have to be automatically extended to all OECD members.[5]

While the legal commitments under the codes only apply to the OECD area, member governments have agreed to use their best efforts to extend the benefits of liberalization to all members of the IMF. Thus, non-member countries can reap the advantages of free market access in OECD countries to the same extent as OECD members can. Indeed, surveys have shown that there is an overwhelming trend among OECD governments to adopt liberalization measures without discriminating against non-OECD countries.

The reimposition of controls in cases of acute economic stress is covered by a derogation procedure, under which members gain dispensation from their obligations to preserve the freedom of operations on a temporary basis. Resort to derogation must be based on a clearly demonstrated deterioration in the balance of payments situation or some other serious economic and financial disturbance resulting from liberalization.

In common with other multilateral agreements affecting the international operations of financial institutions, the codes recognize the potential stresses and risks for the domestic financial sectors of the liberalizing economies brought by capital account opening. The fundamental importance of adequate prudential regulation and supervision as a *sine qua non* for financial sector liberalization is thus reflected in the codes, although they do not contain any specific prudential carve-out chapter or section. There are many references to the need for investor protection and preventing evasion of national regulation in separate remarks or supplementary explanations to the individual sections and items. Limitations on banks' foreign exchange exposure as well as the mandatory maintenance of certain crucial ratios in their balance sheets are thus not viewed as restrictions, and nor are reporting requirements necessary to enable authorities to monitor risks inherent in institutions' assets and liabilities on an ongoing basis. However, in line with the codes' principles, such regulations should not discriminate against nonresident market participants.

In past examination processes it has sometimes become clear that prudential as well as other regulations have the potential to compromise competition and condone entry barriers, restrictive practices and other anti-competitive mechanisms. The tendency has nevertheless been to steer away from any in-depth questioning of prudential regulatory arrangements. Only outright bans on different types of transactions or forms of establishment have been viewed as restrictions under the codes, even where these have been considered to be justified on prudential grounds by the authorities concerned.

Overall, the codes and their implementation structure have provided a multilateral framework to support, in a cooperative spirit, the individual paths towards liberalization pursued by OECD countries over the last 40 years. They have also created an environment in which member countries with less-developed economies, or those going through temporary economic difficulties, have benefitted from consultation and frank discussion with their peers.

5.3 THE LIBERALIZATION EXPERIENCES OF NEW OECD MEMBERS, 1994–2000

The OECD membership constituency remained unchanged for 20 years, following the accession of New Zealand in 1973.[6] During the 1994–2000 period six new members joined the OECD. Mexico was the first to join (May 1994), with the Czech Republic (December 1995), Hungary (May 1996),

Poland (November 1996) and Korea (December 1996) following suit in quick succession. The Slovak Republic joined in December 2000.

From the beginning, the codes of liberalization played an important role for the new members joining the OECD. For the new Central and Eastern European (CEE) members, still in the early stage of transition to market-based economic systems, the codes formed a central part of their overall of economic and financial opening. For Korea and Mexico, accepting the codes' obligations meant adhering to a set of permanent liberalization standards, confirming their commitment to an open markets policy on a non-discriminatory basis. For all accession countries, the codes have served as a tool to measure readiness to share their peers' philosophy concerning international economic relations.

Following a brief overview of the policy context in the 1990s, this section summarizes the liberalization approach of the six new members under the OECD codes, focussing in particular on the CEE countries. In accordance with the structure of the committee review process, the account is organized by major categories of capital account operations. The focus is on the policy concerns expressed and the motivations given for maintaining controls in certain cases, with an attempt to distill the essence of the discussion during the examinations.

Policy Context

The accession to the OECD of the six new members took place during a period marked by a fundamental shift towards a liberal economic system in the 1980s and into the 1990s, as the former socialist economies of Central and Eastern Europe, Russia and the remainder of the former Soviet Union began their transition from command to market-based economies. This process was also under way in China, Vietnam and other Asian economies, where central planning and other forms of detailed state intervention were being abandoned in favor of more market-based principles of economic management. That the increased capital account openness, which formed part of this general shift, implied significant macroeconomic and structural policy challenges, was clearly demonstrated by the severe financial crises which affected Mexico in 1994–95 and South Korea in 1997. Important indirect effects of the 1997 Asian financial crisis spread to the new CEE members, reinforced by contagion from the Russian financial crisis of August 1998. These developments focussed world attention on the issue of how to achieve desirable capital account liberalization without incurring destabilizing effects in the domestic financial sectors of the liberalizing countries.

The fact that Mexico and Korea experienced deep and harmful financial crises following their OECD accession led to some questioning of the liberalization impetus embodied in the accession process. Questions were raised regarding whether adherence to the OECD codes of liberalization had contributed to a premature opening up of their economies to destabilizing short-term flows. In many instances, such questioning of the OECD role in the liberalization process arose from a lack of understanding of both the process which guides new OECD members in assuming the liberalization obligations under the codes and the policy background which shaped the approach of the six new members to liberalization. While each application for membership in the OECD is judged on its own merits, all candidate countries are expected to meet, *inter alia*, the following standards based on the guiding principles of the Code of Capital Movements:

- no restrictions on payments and transfers in connection with permitted international transactions;
- an open and transparent regime for foreign direct investment;
- liberalization of other long-term capital transactions; and
- an indication of a timetable for further liberalization.

While these standards chart a prudent path towards the eventual goal of full capital account openness, they cannot in themselves represent a guarantee that external pressures and vulnerabilities will not occur.

The specific economic policy context and degree of institutional development of the new members were of paramount importance for their respective liberalization experiences. Because of the fundamental system shift of their economies from central planning to market-based economic management, the approach by the four CEE countries to capital account liberalization differs fundamentally from that taken by the advanced economies during the 1980s and prior to the collapse of the Bretton Woods system in the early 1970s. As a consequence of this system shift, market-oriented monetary and exchange rate policies were adopted and important sectors of the economies were deregulated over a much shorter time span than in the advanced economies in Europe and elsewhere. While capital account liberalization in the latter economies tended to be a protracted process, accompanied or preceded by the gradual development of market-based, indirect monetary policy instruments and the progressive deregulation of financial sectors, the CEE economies compressed this process into a much swifter transition, synchronized on many fronts. This is not to say that capital account liberalization was undertaken in one big-bang exercise, but to emphasize that there was less time for experimenting and allowing policies to evolve slowly. That stresses and imbalances arose within such a large undertaking of institution-building and policy development is hardly surprising.

In summary, all six new members faced pressures arising from the need to build or adjust institutional and regulatory structures to the increased degree of integration with the global economy made possible by accession to the OECD. It is also true that for all of the six, the OECD accession had a very significant impact on the degree and form of capital liberalization undertaken. Without the impetus provided by the need to adopt a position *vis-à-vis* the codes of liberalization, involving detailed discussions and justification of the various exceptions and dispensations they proposed, there would probably have been less progress in dismantling exchange controls. However, this momentum was not gained in a context heedless of the stresses that capital account opening brought.

A review of the discussions held during the accession examinations of the six recent members produces numerous references to the need for institution-building and for addressing financial sector fragility through improved regulation and oversight. In fact, these discussions probably also encouraged reforms necessary to promote financial robustness and improve management practices in both the financial and the corporate sectors. Domestic political constraints, as well as inertia in the legislative process, prevented the new entrants from introducing the full range of improvements to corporate and public governance practices and to the predictability and transparency of rules and regulations recommended by the CMIT. However, it is significant that liberalization of exchange controls proceeded largely according to the agreed time schedule both in Mexico and in Korea following the crisis experience, allowing for certain delays connected to the extent of the overall administrative burden of pursuing financial sector reform in the wake of the crisis. None of the new members sought recourse to new control measures under the derogation procedure and several explicitly stated in post-accession examinations that reverting to controls had never been considered a viable option.

It should also be noted that the four new CEE members had a special policy agenda in that they were looking towards EU accession and eventual monetary union. They had all signed separate association agreements with the EU before joining the OECD, imposing time limits for certain liberalization measures, and the prospective date of entry to the Union naturally set a cut-off point for all restrictions on capital movements. To the extent that this prospect influenced their monetary and exchange rate policies as well as the development of their financial frameworks, it could reasonably be expected to have reinforced their commitment to the OECD process.

Pattern of Liberalization by Major Categories of Flow

Direct investment flows: considerations of industrial policy and foreign ownership of domestic resources

In the more protracted liberalization processes of the advanced economies of Europe and elsewhere, controls on long-term capital flows in the form of direct and portfolio investment (motivated by industrial policy concerns) sought to curtail both outflows and inflows for two principal reasons. Restrictions on outflows were based on the developmental objective of keeping scarce capital resources from flowing to better investment opportunities abroad. Restrictions on inflows were maintained in order to discourage or prohibit foreign ownership in different sectors of domestic industry. For some of the six new members, it is mainly the latter form of policy concern that has prevailed, with resort to outright exclusion from certain strategic sectors of industry, maximum shares of overall foreign ownership in the sector concerned or joint-venture requirements with domestic investors. In a few cases, non-transparent privatization procedures as well as cumbersome administrative authorization processes and operational requirements have also been applied with the aim of limiting foreign participation in certain sectors. As to outward foreign direct investment (FDI), none of the six new members (except Korea) imposed any restrictions. Moreover, none of the countries imposed any controls on the liquidation of permitted direct investments and acquisitions of real estate, or any limitations on the repatriation of proceeds from such liquidation, including capital gains.

The absence of any general screening mechanism for new 'greenfield' investments or for the takeover of, or participation in, existing enterprises established in the domestic economy was specifically noted in the case of the Czech Republic, Hungary and Poland. In the case of the Slovak Republic a number of features limiting the access of foreign investors, especially in relation to the privatization process, were noted in the first examination in 1996. Generally, the four CEE members entered the OECD with very few sectoral restrictions on inward FDI. FDI inflows were encouraged across the board in order to stimulate domestic industrial development and enhance access to new technology and management techniques (although in the case of the Slovak Republic, this was only after political changes in 1999). With the exception of air and water transport – and in a few cases broadcasting and telecommunications – there were no significant concerns raised regarding the protection of the competitive position of domestic producers.[7] On the whole, these four CEE countries have achieved a level of FDI openness comparable to, and sometimes exceeding, that of older OECD members.

The attitude adopted towards foreign ownership of land and certain other natural resources constituted a special case, due in particular to the political complications of restitution rights to assets confiscated during the communist regimes and geo-political considerations dating from the Second World War. All four countries were therefore reluctant to liberalize fully the acquisition of land by foreign investors and lodged reservations accordingly, although the purchase of real estate necessary for business establishments was generally permitted. These restrictions are expected to be progressively lifted in the context of the EU accession, leaving certain categories of land and real estate subject to a transitional period. High political sensitivity to nonresident ownership of land other than that directly related to the establishment of production facilities is not unique to the CEE members. It has also found an expression in similar restrictions by established OECD members such as the Nordic countries, Spain and Switzerland.

Poland and Hungary both restricted the form of establishment of foreign investors via branches, requiring full incorporation, but these restrictions were lifted within three years of accession. As a result of shared legislation in the past, the Czech and Slovak Republics also imposed restrictions on FDI in the energy sector, as well as on foreign participation in lotteries and casino operations (the latter have been addressed by amendments to the respective laws).

Given the important role of the state as owner of productive assets in all of the CEE countries, the CMIT carefully examined the strategies and procedures for the ongoing privatization process. In particular, the committee wished to ensure that foreign investors were given the same access as domestic investors in all phases of the process. In the cases of Hungary and Poland, the committee also recommended that the number of strategic enterprises designated to remain under state control in draft privatization legislation be limited as far as possible. During the first examination of the Slovak Republic, the committee expressed concerns regarding delays in the privatization process as well as the evident lack of transparency, predictability and consistency in the implementation of privatization rules.

Foreign participation in the financial sector – developmental benefits versus domestic control

The CEE members had very few restrictions regarding nonresident acquisition and establishment in their financial sectors at the time of OECD accession. An exception was the Czech Republic, which maintained a special approval requirement covering foreign equity participation in Czech banks. This restriction was only lifted in 1998, in connection with a thorough revision of the Banking Law, after the extent of non-performing assets in the state-owned banks and related governance problems had become clear.[8] Limitations on foreign ownership in companies listed on the Prague Stock Exchange were also maintained until 1998.[9]

For both the Czech and Slovak Republics, the extensive state ownership of financial institutions, the slow pace of privatization and the lack of transparency regarding cross-ownership of interests in the banking and the corporate sectors were subjects of repeated discussion in accession and post-accession examinations. Concern was expressed not only regarding the substantial overhang of bad loans resulting from the large state involvement and related moral hazard issues, but also about the interconnections between banks and non-financial corporations and the attendant forms of crony capitalism. The latter also had significant adverse effects on the development of the securities markets in the two countries, as the absence of sanctions on non-transparent (and even fraudulent) securities operations caused a loss of confidence on the part of investors in the stock market as an institution.

The CMIT recommended that privatization plans for the major state-owned banks be accelerated and carried out on the basis of transparent rules and procedures. Although the Czech banking sector is now largely privatized with substantial foreign participation, the restructuring process was lengthy and complicated by repeated state bailouts of distressed banks. Recurring political intervention in the sector initially depressed foreign investor interest.

By the time of the second examination of the Slovak Republic in 2000, the conditions in its banking sector had deteriorated into a crisis situation, requiring urgent action by the government to recapitalize the state-owned institutions in preparation for imminent privatization. Hence, no significant restrictions on foreign participation in the financial sector were maintained, as policy direction had shifted towards encouraging foreign acquisitions of Slovak banks and other financial institutions. Nevertheless, in view of the fragility in the financial sector, the committee encouraged the Slovak authorities to vigorously pursue structural reforms, including completion of the rehabilitation and privatization process under way for the three major banks.

With respect to the Hungarian financial sector, the committee welcomed the successful privatization and large participation by foreign financial institutions which had resulted from Hungary's policy of selling controlling shares in state-owned banks to foreign strategic investors. This raised the skill content in the sector and introduced more sophisticated credit evaluation and risk management techniques at an early stage. Earlier problems of insolvency in the Hungarian banking sector had been addressed prior to its accession to the OECD and a bank consolidation program initiated in 1994 paved the way for privatization of the major banks that was completed in 1996. At the present time, the Hungarian banking sector ranks among the healthiest in Central and Eastern Europe, with foreign participation exceeding 60 per cent of the capital of the sector, the share of non-performing loans standing at low levels and capital adequacy ratios well above levels required by international standards.[10]

Poland's comprehensive measures for dealing with bad debt problems in financial institutions were undertaken prior to OECD accession, based on the Financial Enterprises and Bank Restructuring Act of 1993. This consisted of a bank-led enterprise restructuring program based on a variety of instruments, including debt–equity swaps through which banks acquired ownership stakes in their financially impaired clients. The program provided ample room for foreign participation and significant foreign strategic investment was attracted to the sector in the second half of the 1990s. Overall, privatization had proceeded rapidly, banking supervision had been well developed and foreign participation in the sector was already substantial upon accession. Thus the committee raised no special concerns regarding risk management and solidity. The only restriction requiring a reservation was an incorporation requirement for foreign financial institutions. This requirement was lifted on 1 January 1998, one year ahead of the accession commitment, and was welcomed by the committee.

Other capital account operations[11] – considerations of monetary and exchange rate policies, investor protection, excess volatility

All six new members maintained restrictions on certain securities markets operations as well as on operations in short-term debt, derivative instruments and deposit accounts at the time of their accession. Restrictions were maintained in order to influence the speed of convergence of domestic interest rate levels with those prevailing in international markets and to shield the domestic economy from the impact of short-term flows on the exchange rate. Investor protection concerns were also voiced in the accession reviews, as several new members considered that domestic investors lacked the sophistication required to operate in international markets.

In considering the pattern of liberalization of portfolio flows and, in particular of those flows considered more volatile, it is useful to briefly review the monetary and exchange rate policy settings of the six new members (Box 5.1). To varying degrees, the monetary authorities in all six new entrants faced the same central challenges of completing and consolidating disinflation (and securing financial stability) during an ongoing process of major structural change in the real economy. Financial markets were (to some extent) underdeveloped and there were open or latent vulnerabilities in financial institutions. These factors limited the range of available policy choices for preserving monetary stability and made monetary transmission mechanisms less predictable. By committing to progressive liberalization of capital movements through joining the OECD, the option of trying to preserve the full autonomy of monetary and exchange rate policies via extensive capital controls was no longer available.

Box 5.1   Exchange Rate and Monetary Policy Regimes

Exchange rate regime

Czech Republic	Pegged to a basket of currencies since 1990. Simplified to 35 per cent US$, 65 per cent DM from May 1993. Fluctuation band 1992–97 with ± 0.5 per cent band until February 1992, then ± 7.5 per cent. Managed float from May 1997.
Hungary	Central parity crawling peg with fluctuation band of ± 2.25 per cent. Band widened to ± 15 per cent in May 2001.
Korea	Daily fluctuation bands until end 1997 then free float.
Mexico	In 1989 crawling-peg exchange rate based on a pre-announced rate of devaluation (following a short period of completely fixed rate). From 1991 creation of a widening fluctuation band. From 1995 floating exchange rate.
Poland	Fluctuation band mechanism around crawling peg, abandoned in May 2000.
Slovak Republic	Peg to US$ / DM basket 1993–98, then free float.

Official intervention

Czech Republic	Occasional intervention to smooth large swings.
Hungary	Interventions at edges of band.
Korea	Some intervention.
Mexico	Until 1995 sterilized intervention to prevent capital inflows from fueling base money growth and inflation. From 1995 interventions only under exceptional circumstances.
Poland	No intervention since April 2000.
Slovak Republic	Occasional intervention, at times with sterilization, to restrain appreciation of exchange rate.

Monetary policy goal

Czech Republic	Exchange rate peg served as anchor until 1997, since then pre-announced inflation targets.
Hungary	Announced declining target for headline inflation.

Korea	Monetary aggregates.
Mexico	Until 1995 base money as a nominal anchor. From 1996 gradual transition towards inflation targetting.
Poland	Exchange rate anchor since 1991, via pegged band mechanism until 2000. Monetary aggregates targetted until 1998, since then announced headline inflation targets.
Slovak Republic	Exchange rate peg until 1998, then inflation benchmarks for core and headline inflation.

Source: OECD.

Having decided to liberalize, countries had to choose the most appropriate monetary policy and exchange rate regimes – and specific anchors – that would help to sustain growth and reduce financial instability in the context of increased capital mobility. Naturally all countries expressed concerns during the accession process regarding exposure to volatile capital flows, particularly in combination with speculative attacks. Concerns as to whether certain categories of short-term flows should remain restricted and what safeguards, if any, needed to be kept during the liberalization process, were repeatedly voiced and also reflected in the drafting of new foreign exchange legislation (notably by the Czech Republic, Poland and Korea).

Box 5.1 sets out the exchange rate and monetary policy regimes in force in the four transition countries from 1994 to 2001. The box shows that pegs were considered useful in the early stages of disinflation by the CEE countries, but were successively abandoned. Exchange rate flexibility was found to be preferable for dealing with increased capital mobility and the associated need to minimize financial vulnerability. Inflation concerns also prompted the abandonment of the exchange peg, as the flexibility in wages and prices which had prevailed earlier in the transition process could no longer be relied upon for adjustment. Hungary retained its crawling peg but moved to a wider band in May 2001, reflecting a need for more maneuverability in the face of sizeable capital inflows. Free-floating regimes also replaced earlier exchange rate targetting efforts in Korea.[12] Floating exchange rate regimes are now maintained by all of the new OECD members (except Hungary) and monetary policy strategies are directed towards controlling inflation. Some degree of exchange rate volatility is regarded as acceptable as the corporate sector is generally able to hedge against exchange risk.

Box 5.2 gives an overview of the restrictions in place on major categories of portfolio flows. The new CEE members did not maintain restrictions on long-term portfolio inflows at the time of accession, other than those arising out of regulations on inward direct investment. Outward flows through purchase abroad by residents were only restricted by Hungary (although this

---

Box 5.2   Capital Account Restrictions other than on Foreign Direct Investment*

Restrictions at time of accession

Czech Republic	Outflows through issue by nonresidents on domestic market. Outward financial credits (other than banks). Outflows via residents' purchase of financial derivatives and operations with deposit accounts.
Hungary	Outflows through issue by nonresidents and purchase abroad by residents (removed for high-grade issuers, non-OTC from 1997). All operations with money market securities and financial derivatives (except banks). Financial credits (except banks).
Korea	Inflows through issue abroad by residents, purchase by nonresidents in Korea. Inward and outward financial credits (except banks). Operations in financial derivatives. Operation of deposit accounts.
Mexico	Inflows through issue by residents abroad (only peso) and purchase on domestic market by nonresidents (only peso). Outflows through issue by nonresidents on domestic market. Outflows through purchase by domestic securities firms of foreign securities. All short-term operations in domestic currency by nonresidents or in foreign markets by residents, financing operations in foreign currency from abroad by resident banks (but applied in a liberal manner).
Poland	Inflows through issue by residents abroad, long term and short term (except banks) and outflows through issue by nonresidents on Polish market, long term and short term, and through purchase of money market instruments and financial derivatives (except banks). Inward and outward short-term financial credits (except banks). Operations in deposit accounts (except banks). Repatriation requirement.

Slovak Republic Inflows via issue by residents abroad (only imposed on municipal debt and maturities below one year). Outflows via issue by nonresidents on domestic markets (restricted to high-grade issuers) and via purchase abroad by residents of money market instruments and financial derivatives. Inward and outward financial credits (except banks). Operation of deposit accounts. Repatriation requirement.

Restrictions as at 1 January 2002

Czech Republic No restrictions.

Hungary No restrictions.

Korea Outflows through issue by nonresidents of money market securities in Korea and via residents' purchase of won-denominated short-term securities abroad. Inward (screening) and outward (limits) on short-term financial credits. Certain limits on operations of deposit accounts.

Mexico Same as on accession, except: outflows through issue by nonresidents on domestic market (only debt securities). Operations of deposit accounts in foreign currency subject to minor restrictions.

Poland Inflows through issue abroad of short-term debt instruments and financial derivatives (except banks). Inward and outward short-term financial credits (except banks). Operations in deposit accounts (except banks).

Slovak Republic Operations in financial derivatives, operation of deposit accounts, repatriation requirement.

Note: * Restrictions presented are not a full description of all operations. For a more complete review consult annex B to the Capital Movements Code of the OECD.

Source: OECD.

---

restriction was relaxed from 1997 onwards). However, several of the new members still restrict the purchase and trading of over-the-counter (OTC) securities and only allow trade in securities listed on a regulated stock exchange. Outflows through issuance on domestic markets by foreign entities were initially restricted by all the new entrants, except for the Slovak Republic which had earlier liberalized this item. The other countries successively lifted or narrowed their restrictions on this form of capital outflow.

As a result of this progressive liberalization, no reservations of any significant scope apply at the present time to long-term portfolio flows in any of the new members. They can thus be considered as fully liberalized, with the exception of certain limitations on the portfolio allocation by institutional investors which have recently been included in the liberalization obligations under the codes. Considering operations with short-term money market securities and financial derivatives, all the new member countries applied some controls at the time of accession, generally restricting such operations to authorized banks and foreign exchange dealers. During the post-accession reviews, several of the new members reported the progressive relaxation of controls on this type of operation, allowing the corresponding reservations to be considerably narrowed.

Short-term financial credits were restricted by all the new entrants upon accession, including the Slovak Republic, as were operations in deposit accounts. While financial credits are now generally liberalized, several of the new members have retained reservations with respect to the opening of deposit accounts by residents with nonresident banks in domestic and foreign currency, which is considered a possible channel for volatile short-term flows. Similarly, the new members typically imposed repatriation (and in some cases surrender) requirements on foreign currency earnings, which necessitated reservations under the Capital Movements Code. The Czech Republic imposed a repatriation requirement since accession, which was abolished with effect from 1 January 2002, together with all remaining capital controls. The Slovak Republic had a surrender requirement until 1998, two years prior to accession.

5.4 CONCLUSIONS AND LESSONS

The recent OECD experience with liberalization of capital movements and financial services confirms the crucial role played by financial regulation and supervision in the process of establishing the conditions that will allow a full dismantling of restrictions and the free flow of funds on an international scale. It also brings into focus the important role played by international financial market developments and integration in driving liberalization of cross-border movements of capital and financial services and the continued interaction between these forces.

An important lesson from the incidence of financial and corporate sector strains connected with the adjustment to a liberated system concerns the need for international financial market confidence in the regulatory and supervisory framework of a counterparty economy. Unless its system of financial regulation and supervision is seen by international market participants as conforming to international standards, most forms of capital inflows are potentially volatile, with anticipation of signs of financial sector fragility heightened by recent crisis experience. This means that not only should high standards of regulation and oversight be instituted in a virtual sense, but they should be perceived as properly embedded in practices and attitudes in the domestic economy. It is also important that the regulations are seen to be vigorously enforced. It is evident from the above discussion that the task of developing and upgrading the systems of financial regulation and supervision in the six recent members of the OECD formed a crucial part of the liberalization process.

Another lesson deriving from the experience of international financial crises, and supported by evidence from the accession process of the recent OECD members, is that the regulation and supervision of financial markets need to be complemented by the provision of adequate financial disclosure as well as high-quality standards of governance in the corporate sector. These are necessary to strengthen the transparency and accountability furnished through financial accounts and audits. If there is insufficient high-quality data, then perceptions based on a mixture of news, rumors and sentiments, rather than economic fundamentals, will drive capital flows. In this context, an important factor is the maintenance by the governments of consistent messages to all market participants throughout the reform period, regarding authorities' intentions to adhere to an orderly process of capital account liberalization, based on pre-announced phases and coordinated with other supporting policies. Of the six new members, Hungary's strategy and signaling of policy intentions stand out as particularly successful.

It is clear that the construction of the various elements required to ensure good regulation, disclosure and governance takes time, especially in emerging markets where financial infrastructure and regulation may have to be built on relatively sparse foundations. Thus, the search for a satisfactory path towards full liberalization has come to the forefront, in order to allow sufficient time for crucial institution-building before opening markets fully. On the whole, the experience acquired with the codes and OECD member liberalization favors full freedom of direct investment flows and equity-related portfolio investment as a priority, followed by other long-term flows related to operations in debt securities. In most countries, controls on non-trade-related financial credits and deposit operations were among the last to be relaxed. Controls on derivative operations by non-bank entities are also often maintained, to guard against 'speculation'. This was also the case for the six recent members of the OECD, albeit with variations. However, it must be recognized that the strategy of initially welcoming longer-term, equity-related flows and discouraging, or at least avoiding a bias in favor of, more volatile flows undertaken for short-term portfolio adjustment purposes, works only in periods of relative stability in international financial markets. In addition, it can be difficult to distinguish in a meaningful way between long-term and short-term capital flows. Nowadays there are many avenues for altering the effective maturity of an investment, depending on the depth and liquidity of the particular marketplace. In periods of stress and generalized loss of confidence by international market participants, the floodgates can only be kept shut by taking draconian measures. Some countries recognize this reality by opting for rapid and full-scale liberalization of most or all flows, essentially relying on prudential supervision of financial institutions and improved transparency, and the associated availability and dissemination of relevant data to assess and limit risks relating to private capital flows.

Finally, a contrast between the experiences of new members discussed above and of earlier liberalization experiences is that countries increasingly shun the reimposition of controls. Of the six new members discussed above, none resorted to derogation procedures during periods of financial turbulence. An important reason is that such a policy is negatively perceived by international market participants. A country which reimposes controls on operations previously liberalized other than *in extremis* will not only find future access to international borrowing compromised, but also experience a potentially lasting setback in terms of the development and standing of its own financial marketplace and its links with other financial centers. The OECD codes, which incorporate a so-called 'ratchet' effect, are well suited to support this process.

In practice, it can be difficult to assemble the political coalitions necessary to undertake comprehensive reforms. Experiences in some countries seem to indicate that assembling the political support for broad reform needs to be preceded by a crisis that rules out the alternative of carrying on as before with outdated and over-regulated financial systems. However, this represents a passive, defeatist attitude. Rather than waiting for costly and destructive crises to occur, the reality may be that piecemeal reform is the best way forward, even though it is likely to engender strains and difficulties at one time or another.

NOTES

1. This chapter is adapted from OECD (2002).
2. See Article 2 (d) of the OECD Convention of December 1960: members will jointly 'pursue their efforts to reduce or abolish obstacles to the exchange of goods and services and current

payments *and maintain and extend the liberalisation of capital movements'* (emphasis added).

3. At www.oecd.org/daf/investment.
4. The code contains a so-called List B of operations with respect to which a member country can reintroduce restrictions, and lodge reservations accordingly, at any time. List B currently covers only short-term financial operations and nonresident acquisitions of real estate. The facility for member countries to reintroduce reservations under List B has proved in practice to be an effective way to ease liberalization in sensitive areas and to avoid precautionary reservations (i.e., maintained for the sole reason of leaving open the opportunity to reimpose restrictions without breaching the standstill provisions of the code).
5. Article 10 of the code stipulates that members forming part of a special customs or monetary system may liberalize more rapidly among themselves without extending the additional liberalization measures to other members; however, they may not raise new barriers to third countries.
6. The original 20 members of the OECD are Austria, Belgium, Canada, Denmark, France, Germany, Greece, Iceland, Ireland, Italy, Luxembourg, the Netherlands, Norway, Portugal, Spain, Sweden, Switzerland, Turkey, the United Kingdom and the United States. The following countries subsequently became members through accession on the dates indicated: Japan (1964), Finland (1969), Australia (1971) and New Zealand (1973). The Commission of the European Communities has taken part in the work of the OECD since its inception.
7. These sectors are also commonly protected by older OECD members.
8. The ultimate public cost of the government's clean-up of the banking sector is usually estimated to be between 15 and 20 per cent of GDP. The restructuring and privatization process started towards the end of the decade and had by the end of 2001 brought the foreign ownership share of total banking sector assets up to 94 per cent. The sale of the 60 per cent public sector stake in Komercni banka to Société Générale in mid-2001 provided a grand finale to the rapid introduction of strategic foreign investors into the sector.
9. This was also the case in the Slovak Republic (for the Bratislava Stock Exchange) due to the common legislation applying before the separation of the two countries. An amendment to the securities legislation in the Slovak Republic eliminated this restriction in November 2000.
10. The foreign-owned share of registered capital in the Hungarian banking sector at the end of 2001 stood at 78.4 per cent, of which 61.7 per cent was owned directly by foreign credit institutions.
11. Debt and equity securities, money market instruments, financial derivatives, financial credits and operations in deposit accounts.
12. Prior to December 1997, the exchange rate was 'allowed' to fluctuate in a band of ±2.25 per day, but in practice, the system functioned as a fixed but adjustable peg in view of intervention and capital market regulation (OECD Economic Survey of Korea, 1998).

6. Capital account liberalization and financial sector development in transition countries

Willem Buiter and Anita Taci

6.1 INTRODUCTION

The first decade of transition has seen remarkable progress in financial sector reform for the former-socialist countries of Central and Eastern Europe and the former Soviet Union, although this progress has been uneven across regions, countries and market segments. There have been significant achievements in the privatization and restructuring of state banks in most (but not all) of these countries; there has been exit by failing institutions and entry and development of new domestic and foreign banks; there has been improvement in the legal, supervisory and regulatory framework, which has supported enhanced competition in the provision of banking services.

However, even in the most advanced transition countries (including the eight likely early EU accession candidates from the region), the banking sector still lags behind best practice as regards the scale and scope of their provision of financial services. The level of bank intermediation between domestic savers and potential investors in the domestic real economy remains low. The menu of financial products and services offered by the banking sector remains restricted. Even in the most advanced countries of the region much more needs to be done in order to achieve a fully functioning and efficient banking sector (Fries and Taci, 2002). The relative underdevelopment of the banking sector in transition countries is not compensated for by a strong non-bank financial sector or by thriving capital markets. If anything, the degree of underdevelopment of capital markets and non-bank financial institutions is greater than that of the banking system (Claessens et al., 2001).

Enhancing financial stability and reducing the vulnerability of financial systems remain key challenges for all countries in transition. The importance of meeting this challenge, both from the point of view of savers looking for a superior risk–return trade-off and from the point of view of domestic enterprises looking for external sources of finance, cannot be over-emphasized. The integration into the international capital markets that has progressed significantly in some transition countries, especially in the EU accession candidates, reinforces the importance of building strong, stable and efficient domestic financial markets and institutions. The strengthening of the domestic financial sector, particularly the banking sector – the main vehicle for the intermediation of both domestic and international financial flows now and for the foreseeable future – is essential if these countries are to gain the benefits and withstand the risks associated with large, and potentially volatile, gross and net cross-border capital flows.

Without an efficient domestic banking sector and deeper and more liquid domestic financial markets, only the subsidiaries of well-capitalized and liquid foreign enterprises and a few domestic players in the oil and gas sectors could hope to attract significant amounts of external finance. In the more advanced transition countries, the role of the domestic financial sector in supporting domestic investment and stable growth becomes even more important with the EU accession process and the greatly increased financial integration this brings.

Without significant further enhancement of domestic financial intermediation, the superior access to foreign investment opportunities that will become available to domestic savers when accession candidates become full EU members could be at the expense of investment in domestic enterprises, especially in small and medium-sized domestic firms. The well-known risks associated with large and potentially volatile cross-border capital flows introduce an additional dimension and urgency to financial sector reform, especially in the period between EU accession and European Monetary Union (EMU) membership.

Remaining challenges for building a stable and efficient financial sector in transition countries include: (i) strengthening prudential supervision and regulation; (ii) improving risk management of both individual institutions and supervisory agencies; (iii) improving transparency and disclosure of financial activities and market discipline; and (iv) improving the effectiveness of the legal framework.

The chapter is organized as follows. The next section provides an overview of developments in capital market liberalization and cross-border capital flows in transition countries, and their benefits and costs for domestic financial sector development and stability. Section 6.3 discusses the main features of the development of the financial sector in the transition countries in the last decade, considering both banking sector and securities markets developments. This section compares the reform progress in the financial sector across the different regions/countries, drawing lessons from these regions'/countries' diverse experiences with different dimensions of reform such as privatization and policies towards foreign entry, and examining their implications for financial sector development. The fourth section examines ways of addressing likely future challenges to financial stability, through strategies to enhance the legal and supervisory framework and thus to strengthen the financial sector's ability to manage the risks inevitably associated with exposure to free cross-border capital flows. Section 6.5 concludes.

6.2 CAPITAL ACCOUNT LIBERALIZATION AND CAPITAL FLOWS IN TRANSITION COUNTRIES: BENEFITS AND RISKS

The policy towards capital account liberalization of transition countries has been cautious, despite some differences across the regions as regards the use of individual controls. Most of these countries abolished restrictions on foreign direct investment (FDI) inflows at the beginning of the transition. Since early in the transition process, most countries have also guaranteed the free repatriation of both profits (current account convertibility) and FDI capital. Individuals are allowed to hold and operate foreign exchange accounts at local banks and treatment of trade credits has also been liberal in most countries.

However, non-FDI-related transactions remained restricted in many countries. Only the Baltic states adopted a policy of a high degree of capital account openness at the beginning of the transition process. More severe restrictions were kept on short-term than on long-term transactions and only some advanced transition economies fully liberalized portfolio flows.

Capital controls have been progressively eased in recent years. In the Central European countries this progress in liberalization has been in part due to Organisation for Economic Co-operation and Development (OECD) membership requirements and EU accession commitments. Since 1995 there has been a gradual easing of restrictions on non-FDI-related capital movements, led by the Czech Republic and Hungary as part of their accession to the OECD. The liberalization of portfolio flows is still incomplete in most of the countries.

Figure 6.1 presents the state of liberalization for specific controls on capital account transactions for transition economies as of end 1999. It provides indices of liberalization for all categories of capital flows, calculated for each country and averaged over three regions: the Central and Eastern Europe and Baltic states (CEEB), South-Eastern Europe (SEE), and the Commonwealth of Independent States countries (CIS).[1] The indices can take

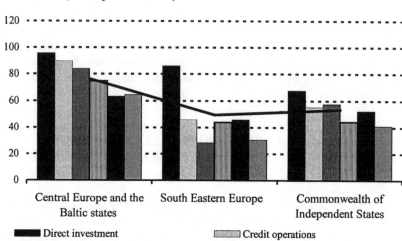

Figure 6.1 Progress in capital account liberalization, end 1999
(index of liberalization)

Note: * See text for description of index.

Source: International Monetary Fund.

values between 0 and 100, with 100 representing the maximum degree of liberalization.[2]

Figure 6.1 shows that capital flows have been liberalized most in the more advanced transition countries. In particular, liberalization in portfolio flows and in provisions specific to commercial banks and other credit institutions has lagged behind in SEE and the CIS, with the exception of Armenia and to some extent Georgia (not shown in Figure 6.1).[3] Within CEEB, the three Baltic states, the Czech Republic, Hungary and the Slovak Republic have now largely liberalized their capital accounts, while Poland and Slovenia continue to maintain some short-term capital controls mostly aimed at encouraging non-debt financing and at lengthening the maturity structure of external financing. Upon EU accession, at the latest, remaining controls will have to be removed, potentially stimulating further capital flows.

Evolution in Structure and Composition of Capital Flows

Over the past decade, transition countries have absorbed a growing share of total net capital flows to emerging markets and developing countries.

Capital flows to all three European Bank for Reconstruction and Development (EBRD) regions have followed a path similar to that followed by policies towards liberalization of capital controls. Countries of CEEB that have had more liberalized capital accounts have attracted more foreign capital. The level of (net) capital inflows has been affected, above all, by the degree of macroeconomic stability, the stage of and commitment to reform, and, especially in the CIS and in some of the SEE countries, by political instability and corruption. Reform achievement and efforts have been the most important determinants of private capital flows. The most advanced reformers, such as Hungary, Slovenia, Estonia and the Czech Republic have attracted large amounts of foreign savings (Figure 6.2).[4]

Early on in transition, the capital flows were mainly fiscally driven. They reflected the sharp decline in fiscal revenues and the lack of creditworthiness of some countries. These flows, which often came from bilateral and multilateral sources, made up about 45 per cent of total net flows for the first half of the decade. However, the share of official lending to transition countries declined very quickly. By 1993, private flows exceeded official flows, as transition countries resumed their access to international capital markets.

Central and Eastern Europe and Baltic states
During the second half of the 1990s official flows going to CEEB countries decreased significantly (Poland and Hungary also repaid some official financing). The cumulative amount of net official capital inflows in CEEB for the 1996–2001 period accounted for only 1 per cent of total net inflows. For these countries, the success of earlier reforms meant improved access to international capital markets.

Among the private flows, FDI accounted for a substantial part of net capital inflows in CEEB countries (Figure 6.3). Cumulatively over the 1996–2001 period, FDI accounted for about 64 per cent of total net flows in CEEB countries.

Some accession countries have at times faced a large and sudden surge in short-term capital inflows. In the Czech Republic, for example, net capital inflows in 1995 accounted for about 18 per cent of GDP. Of this, net short-term capital flows[5] reached about 8 per cent of GDP (and about 5 per cent of GDP during 1996–97). Eventually, and inevitably, the increase in the current account deficit and a rapid real exchange appreciation (the nominal exchange rate was fixed and about half the flows were sterilized by the central bank), fear of a devaluation caused the sudden and sharp reversal of short-term flows. The resulting financial distress led to a currency crisis in mid-1997 when the currency was devalued and left to float. During 1995–97, short-term liabilities also increased rapidly in the Slovak Republic.

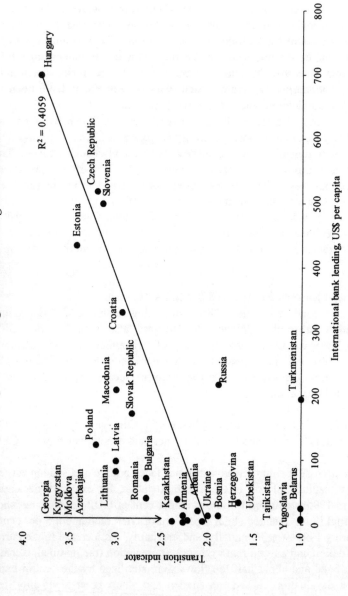

Figure 6.2 International bank lending to the banking sector and banking sector transition

Sources : Bank for International Settlements and the European Bank for Reconstruction and Development.

110

Total net capital inflows in CEEB countries decreased after the 1998 Russian crisis as foreign investors became more cautious about the region. However, both confidence and capital inflows appear to have recovered in 2001, despite the global slowdown. Debt-creating flows (loans and bonds) remain a key component of external financing in CEEB countries. Within these debt flows, international commercial banks are primary suppliers of capital. The domestic banking system has been the main channel for absorbing that lending. On average over 1996–2001, it accounts for about 47 per cent of lending by international commercial banks.

Figure 6.3 Net capital flows to Central-Eastern Europe and the Baltics (US$ bn)

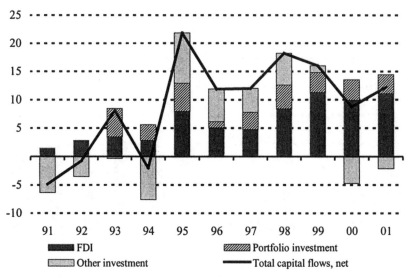

Notes:
a: FDI is foreign direct investment.
b: Figures for 2001 are estimates.

Sources: World Economic Outlook Database and European Bank for Reconstruction and Development.

South-Eastern Europe

The reduced reliance on official flows has been more marked in CEEB than in SEE countries and in the CIS. While FDI and portfolio flows were large in CEEB countries by 1991–92 (especially in Hungary and the Czech Republic), they only acquired significance for other transition countries after 1994.

Some SEE countries even experienced net private capital outflows (e.g., Bulgaria).

The composition of capital flows in and out of SEE countries has been strongly affected by the political instability in the Balkan region. Official flows, often concessional, continue to support government deficits and external deficits in SEE. Net private inflows have increased, driven by growing FDI as large-scale privatization progressed (Figure 6.4). However, private net inflows are mostly concentrated in Bulgaria and Romania which accounted for 80–85 per cent of total net FDI going to SEE during 1996–2000. This share has decreased over time and reached 66 per cent in 2001, as the other countries in the region are attracting more foreign investors (partly through the privatization of large companies).

Figure 6.4 Net capital flows to South-Eastern Europe (US$ bn)

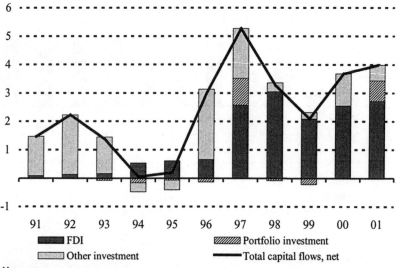

Notes:
a: FDI is foreign direct investment.
b: Figures for 2001 are estimates.

Sources: World Economic Outlook Database and European Bank for Reconstruction and Development.

Portfolio and other investments in the region are increasing with Bulgaria and Romania accounting for most of it. Both countries are gradually integrating into international capital markets with Romania successfully issuing two eurobonds in 2001. About 62 per cent of all non-FDI-related net inflows in SEE during 1996–2001 represent lending by international commercial banks, with the domestic banking sector intermediating about 43 per cent of this total.

Commonwealth of Independent States

Russia accounts for most of total net capital flows into the CIS (see Figure 6.5 and Figure 6A.1 in the Appendix). Ukraine and Kazakhstan were the other two CIS countries that attracted some capital inflows, albeit considerably less than Russia.

Figure 6.5 Net capital flows to the Commonwealth of Independent States (US$ bn)

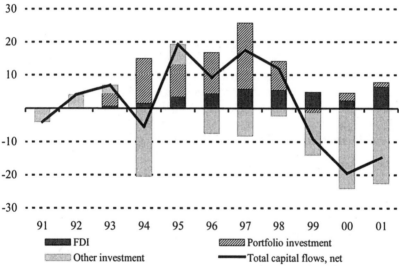

Notes:
a: FDI is foreign direct investment.
b: Figures for 2001 are estimates.

Sources: World Economic Outlook Database and European Bank for Reconstruction and Development.

The changes in the level and composition of capital flows throughout the CIS region are influenced significantly by developments in Russia. Russia saw increasing net portfolio inflows after 1993, reaching around US$17.8 billion in 1997, or 4.2 per cent of GDP. Most private capital flows into Russia took the form of foreign private investment in government Treasury bills (T-bills) (GKOs), attracted by high interest rates and oblivious to default risk. Portfolio outflows immediately before and after the August 1998 crisis implied a halving of net portfolio inflows in 1998 compared to 1997 and a net outflow in 1999. Since then there has been a slow recovery in inflows. Since 1997, Russia has experienced huge private capital outflows in the form of other investments, a large part of which (about 50 per cent in 2000) are commercial bank placements outside of the country. FDI has accounted for only a very small portion of capital inflows into Russia. FDI flows into other CIS countries (and private capital flows in general) have been mainly concentrated in the natural resource sectors, such as gold in Kyrgyzstan, oil in Kazakhstan and (mainly from Russia) oil refineries in Ukraine.

The record shows that over the past decade there has been an increase in the net short-term external liabilities of transition countries, reaching US$15 billion in 1997. There was a decline during 1998–2000, reflecting foreign investors' changing assessment of the region after the Russian crisis. However, after decreasing to US$7.3 billion in 2000, short-term liabilities increased to US$9.4 billion in 2001, with Russia accounting for almost 80 per cent of the total. The growth in net short-term inflows, although not large as a percentage of GDP, could be a source of concern for policy makers, as short-term flows could be associated with higher volatility and risk of sudden reversals. This may be particularly important for those countries that receive the greater share of these in short-term flows, that is, some CEEB countries, Russia and Kazakhstan – countries that can be expected to experience a steadily rising degree of global financial integration.

Benefits and Risks Associated with Capital Flows

There is general agreement among scholars and practitioners about the benefits and risks associated with cross-border capital flows for economic development in general and for financial sector stability in particular. The benefits include filling the saving–investment gap, allowing portfolio diversification directly and production diversification indirectly (through the more diversified domestic capital formation permitted by access to foreign finance in general and FDI in particular), lowering financing costs, setting and/or raising standards of business and corporate governance, raising the intensity of competition, and enhancing fiscal discipline through the restraining effect of the threat of capital flight. FDI is also supportive of structural reforms, which pay off in terms of a higher productivity growth regardless of the host country's initial conditions.

However, capital inflows can also have less desirable side-effects. In the context of incomplete structural reforms, international capital flows carry considerable risks and may magnify underlying macroeconomic and structural weaknesses. If capital inflows are in excess of the recipient economy's ability to absorb them productively, they can have a potentially negative impact on the financial sector and, ultimately, on the real economy. Large capital inflows have been associated with rapid credit expansion and riskier lending practices in many countries.

Large inflows can also lead to real exchange rate appreciation, resulting in a loss of competitiveness and a deterioration in the debt servicing capacity of clients in the internationally exposed sectors and thus in the quality of banks' balance sheets.

As the experience of the 1997–98 financial crises in South-East Asia and Russia in 1998 have shown, risks associated with capital inflows also include the sudden (unexpected and large-scale) reversal of some type of flows, particularly short-term inflows. Short-term inflows driven by speculative position-taking aimed at exploiting an interest rate differential or by views on the likely future direction of exchange rate movements can easily be reversed if fundamental or extraneous events cause expectations to change.

While there is general agreement about the nature of the benefits and costs of capital account liberalization, the balance of costs and benefits remains an open issue. There now is general agreement on the following two points. First, that the cost–benefit analysis of international financial integration is highly conditional on the nature and credibility of the exchange rate regime. A less than fully credible peg is a recipe for financial sector instability and economic dislocation.   Second, that the sequencing and coordination of capital account liberalization, macroeconomic stabilization and structural reforms aimed at strengthening the domestic financial sector is key. Capital account liberalization should follow domestic financial sector reform and macroeconomic stabilization. Liberalization of FDI should precede liberalization of portfolio investment and cross-border bank lending (for a recent analysis, see Ishii et al., 2002).

Unfortunately, the strategy of financial liberalization in several CIS countries has increased their vulnerability to financial crisis, without any commensurate economic benefits. Liberal policies towards the unregulated entry of (domestic) banks and the development of domestic debt markets, together with an opening of capital accounts (while macroeconomic conditions were dodgy), although not the primary cause of financial crises in countries like Russia or the Ukraine, sharply increased the vulnerability of these countries to crisis (Coricelli, 2001).[6]

Many economists dispute the effectiveness of capital controls in managing the risks associated with capital flows. An alternative approach to managing these risks is not to attempt to control the flows directly, but to limit the vulnerability of the economy to the risks associated with these flows (Johnston and Otker-Robe, 1999). Prudential policies applied to domestic financial institutions can play a significant role in reducing the risks associated with cross-border capital flows by influencing the risk–return trade-off faced by financial institutions and by improving the robustness of the financial system to external shocks. The past experience of financial crises in emerging countries (especially in Latin America and Asia), underscores the role that a weak financial sector plays in intensifying a crisis. A sound financial system can also provide a useful cushion against major market disturbances affecting the direction and magnitude of capital flows.

The risks associated with cross-border capital flows are greater for countries in transition where institutional development, particularly of the legal system and the financial sector, is still limited, as is the case in all countries of the CIS and SEE. By tackling these domestic institutional development issues now, transition countries stand to gain more of the benefits of financial market integration while at the same time enhancing their capacity to withstand the risks associated with greater financial integration and larger cross-border capital flows. This issue gains importance as these countries undergo increasing integration of their financial sectors into the global financial system.

6.3 FINANCIAL SECTOR DEVELOPMENT IN TRANSITION COUNTRIES

The development of a sound and stable, market-oriented financial sector is of fundamental importance to the post-communist transition. Banks in a market economy play a key role in the monetary payments mechanism, without which markets, financial and nonfinancial, can function only at high cost. Banks also play a key role in the mobilization, intermediation and allocation of capital. An efficient and prudent banking system facilitates the processes of saving and investment and thus promotes long-term growth.

After a decade of transition, maintaining (and in some cases achieving) financial stability and reducing the vulnerability of the financial system remain key challenges. The relative underdevelopment of the banking sector in transition countries is not compensated for by a strong non-bank financial sector or by thriving capital markets. If anything, the degree of underdevelopment of capital markets and non-bank financial institutions is greater than that of the banking system.

The initial conditions and the subsequent strategies and policies followed by different transition countries are important in explaining the level of development of the financial sector in transition countries. Most transition economies have followed the same broad paradigm for the transformation of their banking sector from the monobank system existing under central planning. The so-called Washington consensus on banking transition advocated the establishment of a two-tier banking system, the abolition of restrictions on the internal convertibility of money, liberalization of interest rates, restructuring and privatization of state banks and their enterprise borrowers, and the entry of new private banks. At the same time, the state had to take on the important new roles of providing effective prudential regulation and supervision of banks.

However, although most countries have followed this broad paradigm, the pace and sequencing of reforms have differed significantly.[7] In the countries of CEEB the state liberalized the market for banking services and developed its capacity for effective prudential supervision and regulation in step with the growing role of private banks in the system. Unfortunately, in the countries of SEE, the banking sector has remained a source of directed subsidized lending to politically well-connected, financially troubled enterprises. The continuation of such practices well into the second decade of transition constrains the pace of banking reform, including the implementation of prudential regulation and bank privatization. The explosion in the number of nonviable private banks in the CIS in the early 1990s created significant vested interests that favored a 'partial reform equilibrium' and were opposed to sound prudential regulation and mechanisms for the exit of these banks.

In addition, the success of financial market reform has been crucially dependent on progress in real sector adjustment, the establishment of market-sensitive mechanisms of corporate control for enterprises, and the degree of disengagement of the government from the private sector.

Banking Sector

Set against a difficult background of major structural shocks, macroeconomic reforms aiming to establish monetary and fiscal stability, and with no past experience in the sector for any of the key players, the establishment and functioning of efficient financial markets was inevitably subject to high risks. The response to this challenge and the subsequent performance of the financial sector differed significantly across countries. However, several common characteristics of financial sector development have emerged, a decade after the start of market reforms in transition countries.

The financial systems in these countries have developed more as 'bank-based' systems than as 'market-based' systems. Given the insufficient scope and effectiveness of legal contract enforcement and, frequently, with inappropriately or imprecisely defined property rights, transition countries had no alternative but to develop a relationship-based financial system, with banks as the main financiers. Banking sector assets in transition countries account for about 85 to 95 per cent of overall financial assets, compared to about 50 per cent in the United Kingdom. Banks therefore dominate the provision of financial services.

Nevertheless, the banking sector in transition countries remains small and underdeveloped compared to that of advanced industrial countries. Even in the most advanced transition countries (including the likely early EU accession candidates), the banking sector still lags behind best practice as regards the scale and scope of their provision of financial services. The level of bank intermediation between domestic and foreign savers and potential investors in the domestic real economy remains low. In addition, the menu of financial products and services offered by the banking sector is restricted. Despite the often large number of banks (especially in Russia and some of the other CIS countries), the transition economies remain 'underbanked' and the banking sector continues to be highly concentrated, with a few banks dominating the market. Bank efficiency remains low.

Marked differences are evident in the level of development of the financial sector between CEEB countries, on the one hand, and SEE and CIS countries, on the other. The level of bank intermediation, measured by the ratio of domestic credit to GDP, is low in all transition countries, compared to countries with the same level of development (as measured by GDP per capita.)

Figure 6.6 shows the ratio of the stock of domestic credit provided by banks to the private sector as a percentage of GDP for all transition economies, together with the estimated ratio of domestic credit to private sector relative to GDP for a market economy at a comparable level of development (EBRD, 1998).

Figure 6.6 indicates that in 2000 all transition economies lie below the market economy benchmark for the ratio of total domestic credit to GDP. However, some countries of CEEB (Croatia, Estonia, Hungary, Latvia, Poland, the Slovak Republic and Slovenia) are gradually converging towards the benchmark for middle-income developing countries and emerging markets. In the countries of SEE and the CIS there was no convergence towards the benchmark between 1994 and 2000, despite the expansion of domestic credit to the private sector in excess of output growth.

Factors that affected banking sector intermediation in transition countries include macroeconomic and fiscal performance, as well as bank-specific characteristics such as ownership, market power and capitalization (Fries and Taci, 2002). Legal enforcement has been another important factor that has deterred banking intermediation to the private sector in transition countries.

Figure 6.7 illustrates the positive relationship between banking credit to the private sector as a percentage of GDP, and progress in the effectiveness of legal reform as measured by the EBRD's legal transition indicator (EBRD Transition Report, various years). Besides concerns about borrowers' creditworthiness and government interference in lending to state-owned enterprises, the issues of creditor rights protection, slow bankruptcy procedures and low realization of collateral have caused banks to lend to 'safer' borrowers such as governments. As Figure 6.7 shows, the legal enforcement issue is more prevalent in CIS and SEE countries.

Figure 6.6   Ratio of private credit to GDP relative to market economy benchmark, 2000

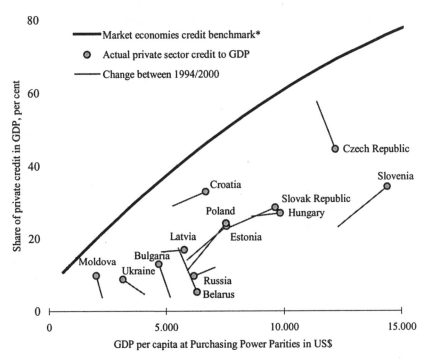

Note :   * See text for explanation.

Sources :   European Bank for Reconstruction and Development and World Bank.

Apart from the similarity in sector concentration ratios (the five largest banks control 50–90 per cent of the market), the banking systems in the three transition regions differ in other dimensions of their development, activity and performance. Table 6A.1 in the Appendix presents several commonly used indicators of banking sector development and performance. The share of non-performing loans in total loans, an indicator of inefficiency (or imprudence/lack of caution) in asset management by the banking sector, is high in almost all transition countries compared to EU countries. There are two reasons for this. First, the accession countries had to deal with the issue of the large amount of inherited non-performing loans from the past (the command economy). Second, new non-performing loans mounted up in the balance sheets of commercial banks due to a lack of experience, inappropriate regulation and supervision, government intervention and ill-designed privatization methods (often associated with connected lending).

Figure 6.7 Private sector credit and legal transition, 2000

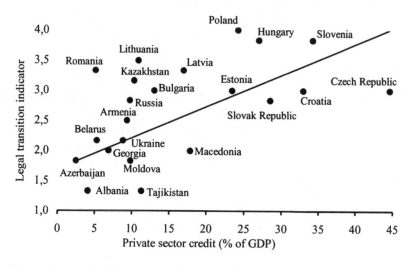

Source : European Bank for Reconstruction and Development.

In CEEB countries the amount of non-performing loans has decreased, both through the resolution of the problem of old non-performing loans and through an increase in quality of new loans. In SEE countries the amount of non-performing loans remains high due to the often difficult macroeconomic environment, government intervention through directed lending to loss-making state enterprises, and connected lending by banks to enterprises with which they have shared financial interests (Bosnia and Herzegovina, FYR (Former Yugoslav Republic) of Macedonia, Yugoslavia). The CIS countries always report a lower share of non-performing loans than CEEB and SEE countries. However, this probably reflects poor accounting and the continued presence of government-directed and guaranteed credit in CIS countries (e.g., Turkmenistan, Uzbekistan).

Table 6A.1 in the Appendix also shows that measured profitability (average return on assets) of banks in the countries of SEE and the CIS is on average higher than in the countries of CEEB. Net interest margins (also shown in the table) are an important determinant of high reported profitability. High profitability of banks in CIS countries can be partly explained by the high inflation which was reflected in higher spreads between borrowing and lending rates. However, the main reason behind the high profitability of banks is the crowding-out effect of high interest government T-bills on bank lending to the more risky and defaulting private sector (see Fries and Taci, 2001) A further factor behind the high reported profitability may be insufficient provisioning for non-performing loans.

Banking efficiency in all transition countries is lower than in EU countries (Figure 6.8). The high spread between lending and deposit rates indicates high inefficiency (as well as greater market power), or greater default risk. Even in the most advanced countries of the region much more needs to be done in order to create an efficient banking sector. Once more, a sharp contrast is evident between on the one hand CEE and Baltic countries, and SEE and CIS countries on the other. CEEB countries are characterized by an average spread not exceeding 10 per cent and are gradually converging to the EU average. In contrast, the spread remains significantly higher in CIS and SEE countries.

Figure 6.8 Differential between lending and deposit rates
(percentage point)

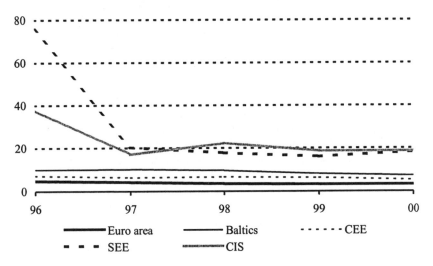

Source : European Bank for Reconstruction and Development.

Competition has, however, strengthened, as evidenced by declining intermediation spreads, a shift in bank portfolios from government securities to private sector lending, and declining bank profitability. The experience of CEEB countries has shown that the driving force for improving efficiency in the banking sector is strong competition achieved through privatization and through the entry of foreign banks.

Countries in transition chose very different strategies for the method and speed of privatization of state-owned enterprises, including banks. These strategies were different even within each of our three transition regions. Consider CEEB countries. While Hungary went for a quick sale of its banks to foreign direct investors, Poland combined public offerings with management buyouts and some placements with foreign strategic investors. The mass voucher privatization strategy of the Czech Republic and the resulting complex cross-ownership structure of banks and enterprises led to an increase in non-performing loans and persistent bank bailouts by the government. The state retained a significant ownership in banks, and only recently opted for their sale to foreign strategic investors.

The process of bank privatization has been slower in the SEE countries (Figure 6.9). However, good progress in bank privatization was made recently in some SEE countries, especially in Romania and Bulgaria where the remaining state-owned banks are in the process of being privatized. FYR of Macedonia has also made very good progress with bank sales to strategic investors. In the Federal Republic of Yugoslavia, which started the transition process only recently, the privatization process is now under way.

In the CIS, the state still maintains a high degree of control over the banking sector, with the exception of Armenia, Kazakhstan and Tajikistan (Figure 6.9). The issue of government-directed lending is pervasive in these countries. In addition, the mass voucher privatization in some CIS countries, including Russia, and the rapid creation of a large number of small banks established by nonfinancial enterprises create the twin problems of connected lending and excessive sectoral concentration of bank loans.

The entry of foreign banks has been an important factor that has raised the level of development in the sector. Foreign banks spur competition and innovation, often bring stronger corporate governance and management, and render the sector more efficient by introducing new skills, products and technology. The presence of foreign banks that have not just a local but a global reputation at stake may reduce the risk of capital flight or widespread deposit runs. The presence of foreign banks in the banking sector, as shown in Figure 6.10, has also supported reform in the sector.[8]

Political as well as economic considerations explain the different country experiences across the region regarding the scope and efficiency-enhancing implications of foreign entry in the banking sector. Foreigners control most of assets of the banking sector in CEEB countries, except Slovenia. Hungary was the first to open its banking sector to foreign participation. Foreigners now control more than 80 per cent of banking assets. The Czech Republic resisted foreign ownership of its larger banks until the failure of several of these banks in the 1996–98 period prompted the sale of all large banks to foreign strategic investors.

The Baltic countries sold their banking sector to foreign strategic investors, mainly from Scandinavian countries. Foreign entry in SEE countries was constrained by the slowness of the privatization process. In the CIS, the entry of foreign banks has been restricted, with liberalization a very recent phenomenon.

Figure 6.9 State ownership in the banking sector
(asset share of state-owned banks, %)

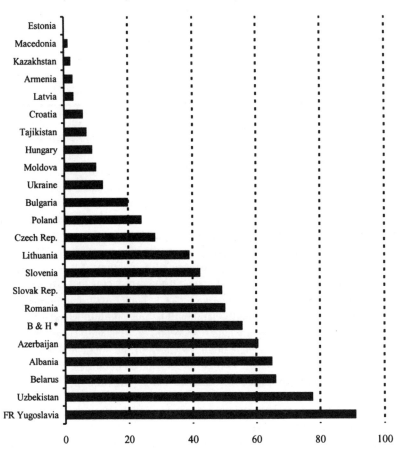

Note :* Bosnia and Herzegovina.

Source : European Bank for Reconstruction and Development.

Figure 6.10   Foreign bank presence and banking sector reform, 2000

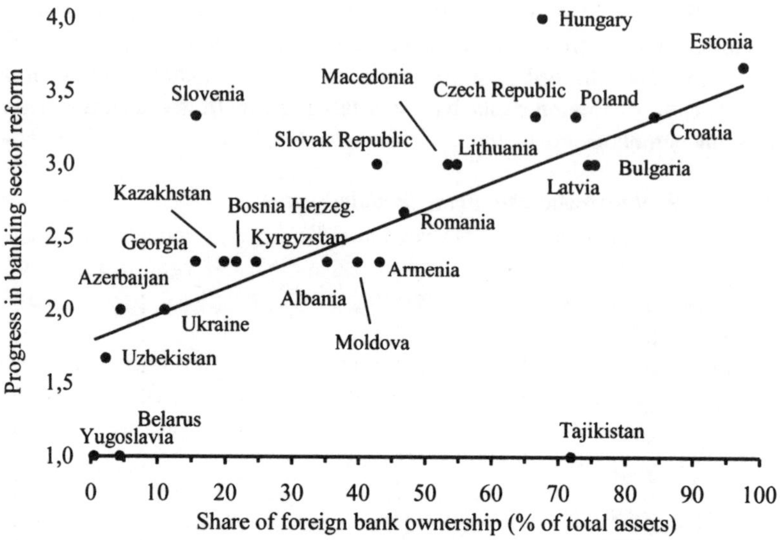

Source : European Bank for Reconstruction and Development.

Capital Markets

While banks have evolved gradually to become the main source of external finance for the real economy, securities markets have grown at a more modest pace. Significant improvements in the sector have been made in the last decade in many areas, including the establishment of formal exchanges, the development of legal frameworks and regulatory institutions, the establishment of internationally compatible accounting standards, and improvements in transparency and corporate governance. However, most capital markets are still in their infancy. Many of the small markets remain illiquid or exist only on paper. Even in the advanced countries, there remains considerable room for improving market depth and liquidity, as well as regulations and institutions.

Stock markets

Some of the stock markets in the region date back to the 19th century. After being closed during the socialist regime, the markets' re-emergence was prompted by the privatization programs in the region. The manner and speed of the introduction of stock exchanges in 20 out of 26 countries during the transition period was in part a reflection of the different privatization methods followed by different countries (Claessens et al., 2001). The Czech and Slovak Republics (Czechoslovakia at the time) in 1992, followed by Bulgaria, Lithuania, FYR of Macedonia, Moldova and Romania launched their stock markets in order to enable the transfer of ownership rights following voucher mass privatization. Croatia, Estonia, Hungary, Latvia, Poland and Slovenia established their stock markets with a small number of stocks offered by direct sale through initial public offerings (IPOs) to those outside the business.

Most CIS countries (Armenia, Azerbaijan, Kazakhstan, Kyrgyzstan, Russia, Ukraine and Uzbekistan) combined the transfer of voucher shares and the listing of companies traded through IPOs. In other CIS countries the stock exchanges are inactive, or only government T-bills are traded, as is the case, for example, in Albania.

As expected, the number of listed companies on the stock exchanges initially increased in countries that used the voucher privatization scheme. After an initial high trading volume, however, many companies were delisted and as the ownership structure became concentrated, the number of shareholders fell. Most stocks became and remained illiquid. Trading volumes remained relatively high in the stock markets of countries that developed their markets through a small number of IPOs.

The strength of the reform process in the non-bank financial markets is important for capital market development. Another important factor, mentioned above, that has shaped the development of capital markets in transition countries has been the privatization process. Figure 6.11 shows that progress in privatization (and often the method chosen) played a major role in the development of capital markets, as measured by the ratio of stock market capitalization to GDP.

Although some progress has been made as regards both institutional reforms and the volume of trading, stock markets in the transition countries remain underdeveloped. The stock market capitalization of the transition economies of Central, Eastern and Southern Europe, as well as the former Soviet Union, increased from about US$1 billion in 1992 to US$108 billion in 2000. The average market capitalization to GDP ratio increased from 2 per cent to nearly 25 per cent during the same period. The region, which accounts for almost 8 per cent of the world's population, accounts for 1 per cent of world market capitalization (EBRD, 2001b).

In terms of market size relative to economic activity, the stock market capitalization to GDP ratio reached 22 per cent in the Czech Republic, 26 per cent in Hungary and 20 per cent in Poland (Figures 6.11 and 6.12). By the end of 2001, capitalization was somewhat lower, in line with the global decline in equity markets, in almost all important markets (aside from Russia) in the region. Four markets in the region had a market capitalization close to or over US$10 billion by the end of 2001: Russia (US$76 billion), Poland (US$26

Policy issues and earlier experiences

billion), Hungary (US$10 billion) and the Czech Republic (US$9 billion).
Capitalization increased by over US$35 billion in Russia over 2001, due to
improvements in corporate governance and firm profitability. Total
capitalization in transition countries therefore increased to US$138 billion.
Croatia, Estonia, Kazakhstan, Lithuania, Romania and Slovenia have stock
markets with a capitalization of more than US$1 billion and the rest are
negligible in size.

Figure 6.11 Stock market capitalization and privatization, 2000

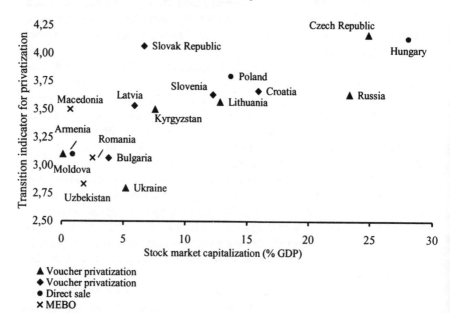

▲ Voucher privatization
◆ Voucher privatization
● Direct sale
✕ MEBO

Note : *MEBO = Management/Employee Buy-Outs, Transition indicator is average
1996
Source : European Bank for Reconstruction and Development.

The stock markets in the region have thus not yet reached a level of
development commensurate with the size of its population and of the economy.
Relative to the size of the economies that they serve, even the largest stock
markets in the region are small. For example, capitalization averages around 30
per cent in Latin America and 52 per cent in East Asia, while in the European
Union and the United States, market capitalization often exceeds the value of
GDP. Compared with a reference group of other emerging markets and
industrialized market economies, the ratios of stock market capitalization to
GDP for all transition economies lie below the estimated benchmark for market

economies at the same level of development (Figure 6.12 and EBRD, 2002).[9] Among these countries, only Estonia has a ratio of market capitalization to GDP that approaches the average for developing market countries at the same level of per capita income.

Figure 6.12 Ratio of stock market capitalization to GDP and per capita income*

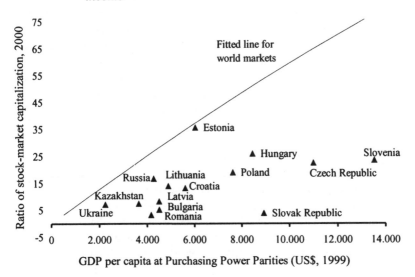

Note: *See text for explanation.

Source : European Bank for Reconstruction and Development.

As a result, many large firms from the region are seeking foreign listings on larger and more liquid markets. These firms tend to list on pan-European and/or US stock exchanges. By the end of 2001, 61 of the region's large companies had issued international equity in the forms of global depository receipts (GDRs) and American depository receipts (ADRs).

Market liquidity on the whole has increased in many of the transition economies, but is still modest in comparison to other emerging markets. Market turnover, defined as the value of trading relative to market capitalization, has increased significantly during the decade. In 2000 it was highest in Hungary at 101 per cent, 61 per cent in Czech Republic, 49 per cent in Poland and 54 per cent in Russia. However, most of the smaller markets are illiquid, in particular those in the CIS. Furthermore, concentration in these markets is substantial, with many regional stock markets dominated by a small number of large firms – typically those in the banking, electric power, natural resource and telecommunications sectors.

The price performance of the stock markets has been mixed. In general, equity markets in Central and Eastern Europe are high-yield, volatile, markets. Over the years 1996–2000, stocks in transition economies have on average yielded a positive total return (measured as capital gains plus dividend income using Standard and Poor's Total Return indices), but these returns have varied widely over time and across countries. The countries that have achieved positive total returns over the period are Hungary, Russia, Poland and Slovenia. Over the same period, the Eastern Europe indices averaged an annualized return of 14.4 per cent and a standard deviation of returns of 43.7 per cent. At the same time, the correlation of returns with those in the developed markets has been low over the period (although is increasing), pointing to potential diversification gains by investing in the region.

Development of fixed income markets
Fixed income markets tend to be more developed than the stock markets, with a number of governments successfully issuing domestic and international bonds over the decade. Gross new issues of domestic bonds increased from US$3 billion in 1991 to US$64 billion in 2000, peaking at US$147 billion in 1998. International issues have also increased from some US$1.5 billion in 1991 to US$10 billion in 2000, with a peak of US$21 billion in 1998. But both domestic and international bond issues have declined significantly since the 1998 Russian crisis. The total domestic bonds outstanding of the four largest markets (Czech Republic, Hungary, Poland and Russia) at September 2001 was just above US$86 billion.

Most of the issuers are central governments, government-related enterprises and local authorities. The number of corporate and bank issuers of debt securities is very limited – with perhaps one exception. In the Czech Republic the issuance of corporate, municipal and bank bonds has developed significantly. Until recently, maturities of bond issues, including those by governments, have rarely extended beyond one year. The most active fixed income markets normally consist of T-bills. However, as macroeconomic stability has improved, the length of maturities has increased in recent years. There has been a sizeable increase of paper with maturities of two to five years. The Hungarian government notably issued ten-year fixed-rate Treasury bonds denominated in euro in 1999 and since 2000 many Central European countries have issued ten-year eurobonds. The Lithuanian government issued a ten-year Treasury bond denominated in domestic currency in 2001.

Pension reform

As in most other European countries (other than Ireland), the growing demographic challenge of an aging population is putting increasing strain on the government budget in many transition countries.[10] Countries have therefore been forced to reform their pay-as-you-go (PAYG) pension systems. Most CEEB countries are implementing the World Bank's three-pillar model of pension provision, with the Czech Republic and Hungary leading the process. This involves the maintenance of a residual PAYG scheme alongside a mandatory private personal retirement account (PRA) and voluntary private schemes for retirement saving. In most of the countries pension reform is still at an early stage.

Progress in pension reform and rapid growth of the insurance markets in transition countries can support the development of domestic institutional investors (and domestic sources of long-term finance) in the coming years, which should feed through into greater liquidity and turnover on the stock exchanges.

6.4 DEALING WITH CAPITAL FLOWS: FUTURE CHALLENGES FOR THE FINANCIAL SECTOR

The level of development of the financial sector in transition countries is such that improving financial stability and reducing the vulnerability of financial systems remain essential policy challenges for all these countries. The increasing integration of the transition countries into the international capital markets further reinforces the importance of removing the remaining structural problems and developing stable and efficient financial markets. The need for financial sector reform is stressed by additional risks introduced by the possibly large and volatile capital flows analyzed in Section 6.2.

The banking sector needs particular attention due to its dominant position in financial intermediation in transition economies. Moreover, as has been shown, the banking sector has been the major intermediary for external capital flows in these countries.[11] The domestic financial sector needs to be strengthened to ensure an efficient use of capital and to deal with the increased competitive pressure from foreign intermediaries. In some advanced transition economies there is already evidence of disintermediation away from the domestic banking system, with international banks increasing their claims on the nonfinancial sectors in these countries, pointing to growing competition between domestic and international banks (EBRD, 2002). The financial system also has to be able to cope with an increasing willingness by both banks and corporations to take on financial risk. Governments should focus on creating or maintaining macroeconomic environment that enhances the sustainability of financial sector development.

The ability of financial institutions to benefit from and withstand the risks associated with international capital flows depends on their capacity to manage financial risk. The major factors underlying differences in the ability of financial systems to withstand the risks associated with capital flows include among others: (i) prudential regulation and supervision; (ii) the risk management and internal governance of financial institutions; (iii) the legal framework; and (iv) accounting standards. Further, weak and unskilled domestic financial institutions with large amounts of unprovisioned non-performing loans, and/or subject to government interference in lending, will be at a disadvantage in competing with sounder foreign institutions. All these factors jointly determine the state of financial sector development.

Prudential Supervision and Regulation

Strengthening financial sector supervision and increasing the autonomy of the supervisory authorities become more important for financial sector stability in the presence of cross-border capital flows. Supervisors should be able to monitor and control the increasing risk taking by financial institution and the ever more complex instruments associated with international capital flows. Recent experience in Asia showed that appropriately imposed prudential rules for financial institutions dramatically reduce the vulnerability of the financial system as a whole. Strengthening supervision and regulation in transition countries requires full harmonization of prudential rules with those of the European Union. Alleviating the risks associated with large capital inflows (such as excessive risk taking by banks) involves applying and enforcing all EU prudential regulations on foreign currency open positions, on bank loan exposures, on collateral valuations, loan classification, etc. Limits on sectoral concentration of credit exposure help mitigate the risk associated with sector-specific shocks.

EU membership requirements have obliged advanced countries of CEEB (including Bulgaria and Romania) to align their regulations with EU directives. However, much remains to be done in other transition countries. Sectoral credit concentration, exceeding the maximum limit to a single borrower, and poor loan classification and provision, magnified by the perverse incentive of banks driven by government interference in lending, still prevail in the banking sector lending in SEE and CIS countries.

Because banks in transition countries are operating as universal banks, particular emphasis should be put on consolidated supervision of the financial sector. The complex cross-ownership of banks and enterprises resulting from voucher privatization in Russia and other CIS countries (in the Czech Republic as well) has created perverse incentives in banks' activities with their financial affiliates. In Russia, banks' engagement in the practice of covering on-balance sheet exposures by taking offsetting positions with their own subsidiaries, has been a common and recurrent issue. Additional emphasis is required on related party lending, especially to shareholders, and strengthening cross-sectoral supervision. In the SEE countries (especially countries that were part of the former Yugoslav Federation), the interconnected financial system poses additional challenges for supervision. Even in Hungary, the case of Postabank illustrates that without appropriate controls, a mismanaged private bank can accumulate hidden losses and increase the threat of a systemic crisis.[12]

Regulation requiring consolidated reporting is missing in a majority of transition countries. Even in the most advanced countries of CEEB, formal reporting on a consolidated basis is either not required or has only recently been adopted. Therefore, there is as yet little experience in preparing consolidated reporting. In a move towards fully consolidated supervision in 2000, Hungary followed the institutional model applied in the United Kingdom in 1997 when supervision agencies for banking and capital markets, pension funds and insurance funds were merged into one regulatory body, the Hungarian Financial Supervisory Authority (HFSA). A similar model was followed in Latvia where the Financial and Capital Market Commission was established in July 2001 and Estonia where a joint Financial Supervisory Authority started operation in January 2002. Hungary, the Slovak Republic and Lithuania introduced regulation requiring bank consolidated reporting in 2001, and the Czech Republic did so in 1999, but more needs to be done for its effective implementation.

Risk Management and Corporate Governance

International capital flows add an additional external dimension to each category of risk associated with domestic financial transactions (market risk, credit risk, liquidity risk and operational risk). Therefore, improving risk management practices and corporate governance of individual financial institutions is particularly important for the survival of these institutions in an environment of free capital flows. Moreover, the prudential supervision and regulation framework must adjust continually to changes in market developments and governance in individual institutions. Ensuring an adequate capitalization of banks is central in limiting banking system risks, including those associated with international capital flows.

Reflecting the concern about the risks associated with international capital flows, the new Basle Capital Accord (intended to be effective by 2005) includes revisions in the capital adequacy framework, requires the development of methodologies for credit, interest and operational risk management and modeling, and promotes sound practices for loan accounting and credit risk disclosure, and for bank transparency and internal control systems.

However, much more needs to be done to improve risk management in transition countries. Even in the most advanced countries, only the largest domestic banks have developed risk management models that adequately address credit risk, liquidity risk and market risk. The CIS and some SEE countries with weak supervisory agencies also suffer from weak skills in the financial sector. Directed and connected lending, prevalent in these countries, aggravate the problem of inadequate capacity and perverse incentives for financial institutions to adequately manage risks (as well as for effective corporate governance).

Corporate governance of individual institutions also plays an important role in risk management. Under the right conditions, foreign ownership can improve corporate governance. In addition, foreign bank ownership supports the diversification of financial systems by introducing new technologies, financial instruments, skills and risk management capabilities. It also tends to strengthen the capital structures of financial institutions and to promote competition for financial products.

Again, even in the most advanced transition countries, there is room for improvement in corporate governance. Improvements in corporate governance practices in these countries require that the roles and responsibilities of management, owners and boards of directors be more clearly defined in financial sector legislation (including appropriate penal actions in case of fraudulent activities).

Further, new instruments available in advanced countries, such as derivatives, and new business areas for banks (e.g., retail lending) often create greater opportunities for taking on risk, without any matching enhancement of institutions' risk management capacity. The monitoring of both risk-taking opportunities and risk management capabilities by the market and by the official supervisory authorities will help enforce discipline on banks and other market participants. In the less-advanced countries of SEE and the CIS, the issues of directed and connected lending (compounded by weaknesses in the legal system and governance) continue to impede effective monitoring by counterparties, shareholders, creditors and supervisors.

Improving transparency and disclosure of financial operations within the banking system is essential for market participants' monitoring and investment decisions. International Accounting Standards (IAS) remain to be adopted in most countries in SEE and the CIS. Even the most advanced countries have only very recently adopted IAS, or are in the process of doing so.[13]

Legal Framework

Financial risks (especially credit risk) are affected by macroeconomic developments and by the legal and regulatory environment (such as bankruptcy laws, collateral recovery, etc.). A strong institutional environment and a stable macroeconomy can contribute significantly to the reduction of financial risks. An important obstacle to enhanced financial development in transition countries is the enforcement of existing laws, rather than the existence of an inadequate formal legal framework.

The EU enlargement process has promoted legal reforms in the financial sector in candidate countries. All accession candidates have accelerated the updating of banking and securities laws to align them with EU laws and directives. However, the enforcement of the legal framework can still be improved significantly.

Figure 6.13 shows that the indicator of effectiveness (substance) of the legal framework is lower than the indicator of extensiveness (form), in all transition countries apart from Poland, which is the only country above the 45 degree line. Remaining problems include slow and inefficient bankruptcy procedures, low collateral recovery, legal restrictions on the disposal of assets (especially assets backed by real estate), and low levels of minority shareholder protection.

In most transition countries, law enforcement suffers from an overburdened judicial process, lack of trained regulatory personnel, and lack of sufficient authority and independence of the supervisory body. Both the development of the legal framework and the effectiveness of law enforcement are major obstacles in many transition countries of SEE and the CIS.

Finally, ensuring financial stability is closely associated with financial market deepening and maturing. The structure of, and ownership diversification in, the financial sector are important sources of strength in the presence of large and possibly volatile cross-border capital flows. Well-developed capital markets can help to fill the funding gap and dampen the destructive impact of a banking crisis on the real economy.

In addition to the remaining challenges for the banking sector (first and foremost strengthening the institutional capacity of regulators), the adequate protection of the rights of creditors and (minority) shareholders is a major challenge to stock market development in transition countries. Corporate governance has become a key issue in all of the transition economies. Abuses of corporate power by managers, owners and controlling shareholders have seriously hurt potential investors' appetite. The lack of sound corporate practices has damaged the region's investment climate. Significant improvements have been made recently and many of the CEEB countries

Figure 6.13 Effectiveness versus extensiveness of legal transition indicators, 2000

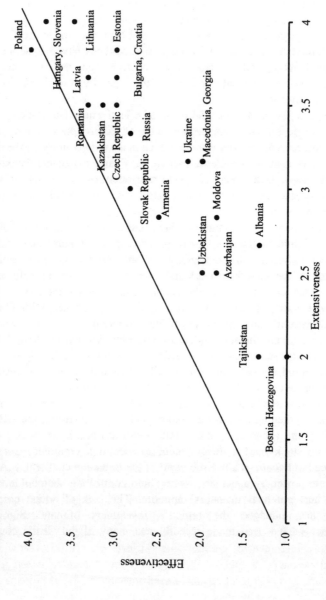

Source: European Bank for Reconstruction and Development.

134

have improved their commercial codes and established financial regulations that protect minority shareholders' rights. However, due to the short history of these improvements, much can still be done to enhance effective corporate governance. Hungary and Poland, the first countries to improve shareholder protection, have also enjoyed the most liquid stock markets in the late 1990s.

6.5 CONCLUSION

More than ten years of transition have brought significant progress in restructuring and developing the financial sector in most (but not all) transition countries. However, progress has been quite uneven across different regions, and even in the most advanced transition countries the banking system (and *a fortiori* the rest of the financial system) has not yet progressed to the point that it can be characterized as a mature, fully functioning market-oriented and efficient banking sector (financial system). In none of those countries is the financial sector transition complete.

Growing two-way capital flows indicate an increasing integration in international capital markets, especially for advanced countries of CEEB. This process increases the pressures for strengthening the institutional infrastructure of the domestic financial sectors. Without significant further progress in this area, the accession countries will be unable to benefit fully from international financial integration and will continue to be exposed to the risks associated with international capital flow reversals.

Major challenges for financial reform remain in each of the accession candidates. First, regardless of the level of banking reform that has been achieved, supervision and regulation have to keep pace with the demands of an ever more complex marketplace. In addition, banks themselves must improve their internal risk management practices and accounting standards and design industry-wide codes of conduct to guard against excessive risk-taking and fraud.

Second, strengthening the legal framework and tightening enforcement of the laws and enforcement of regulatory guidelines are crucial if the level of bank intermediation between domestic and foreign savers and the domestic enterprise sector is to be increased. Specifically, the legal system has to be strengthened in areas such as collateral enforcement and secure transactions, which provide the foundation for all formal financial sector activity. Inadequate enforcement of creditor rights affects the portfolio decisions of banks and investors throughout the region, forcing them to invest a large share of their portfolio in government securities and to avoid projects in the real sector, and especially in small and medium-sized enterprises.

Third, the improvement of corporate governance for both banks and non-bank enterprises remains an important challenge in most transition economies. This is a *sine qua non* for ensuring the soundness of the financial sector – and not only in the accession countries. Good corporate governance in enterprises means transparent and bankable clients for banks.

NOTES

1. CEEB includes: Croatia, Czech Republic, Estonia, Hungary, Latvia, Lithuania, Poland, the Slovak Republic and Slovenia. SEE includes: Albania, Bosnia and Herzegovina, Bulgaria, FYR of Macedonia, FR of Yugoslavia, and Romania. CIS includes: Armenia, Azerbaijan, Belarus, Georgia, Kazakhstan, the Kyrgyz Republic, Moldova, Russia, Tajikistan, Turkmenistan, Ukraine and Uzbekistan.
2. As in Temprano-Arroyo and Feldman (1998), the index can take values between 0 and 100, with 100 representing the maximum degree of liberalization of capital flows under consideration. The index for a given country is constructed by adding up the values obtained in each category of capital flows and dividing the total by the maximum possible score. Flows not subject to controls are assigned a value of 2; flows classified as being subject to partial controls are assigned a value of 1; flows subject to serious controls are given a value of zero. The values for each region are unweighted averages of countries in that region.
3. It is worth mentioning that Russia has followed a different path of capital account liberalization from the rest of the CIS. Capital account liberalization started with FDI under strict rules that were gradually eased. Restrictions on nonresident portfolio investments started to ease in 1994 and after the country achieved current account convertibility in 1996, these restrictions were further relaxed and gradually phased out by early 1998. In August 1998, during the period of financial crisis, Russia reintroduced some capital controls.
4. The EBRD transition indicator for each sector (here for the banking sector), takes values from 1 to 4.3, where 4.3 indicates that the level of reform has reached that of a developed market economy.
5. Measured as short-term debt flows and portfolio flows.
6. Corricelli also argues that these policies contributed to the creation of dichotomies in the system. On the one hand, rather sophisticated financial markets developed, with the participation of banks, foreign investment banks and a few large firms; on the other hand, the bulk of the economy worked on a primitive system based on the widespread use of barter transactions.
7. The differences in fiscal and monetary discipline and the enforcement capacity of governments comprise an explanation for the observed variation in financial and economic development across transition countries (Berglof and Bolton, 2002). The initial conditions at the start of transition determine whether a government will be able to demonstrate fiscal and monetary restraint, and why some countries have or don't have fiscally irresponsible governments. The reasons include the following: (1) differing economic structures and associated differences in the political and short-term economic costs of resisting calls for bailouts; (2) differences in the extent to which large-scale enterprises' coordinated their lobbying efforts for more subsidies and bailouts (Perotti, 1998); (3) differences in governments' ability to raise taxes and other revenues; and (4) differences in countries' geographical proximity and likelihood of accession to the European Union.
8. Figure 6A.2 illustrates the impact of international lending on economic restructuring more generally.
9. The estimated benchmark used in Figure 6.12 for developing and industrialized market economies is calculated by regressing the ratio of stock market capitalization to GDP on per capita income and per capital income squared for a sample of 98 countries. This analysis uses per capita GNP at purchasing power parity exchange rates in 1999, as calculated by the World Bank.

10. Exceptions are the Kyrgyz Republic, Tajikistan, Turkmenistan and Uzbekistan.
11. Even in the CIS countries, most foreign borrowing was channeled into government securities and domestic banks (e.g., Armenia).
12. Postabank was founded in 1988 as a private bank but was partially owned by state institutions. The bank's management, which had close relations with the government, misled the auditors, hiding real losses by convoluted guarantee and investment deals, part of which they kept in secret. The revelation of hidden bank losses by the new management in 1998 prompted a government bailout of 152 billion forint (US$706 million) in December 1998, and a full renationalization of Postabank, the country's third largest bank by assets at the time. The state has bailed out the bank several times in the past two years and acquired a majority in the bank in May 1998 when it raised the bank's capital by 24 billion forint (US$111 million). After the scandal, Hungary's banking supervision legislation was improved, including via the strengthening of the powers of the financial market watchdog, the APTF.
13. For instance, the Slovak Republic expects to do so by the end of 2002.

APPENDIX

Figure 6A.1 Net capital flows to Russia (US$ bn)

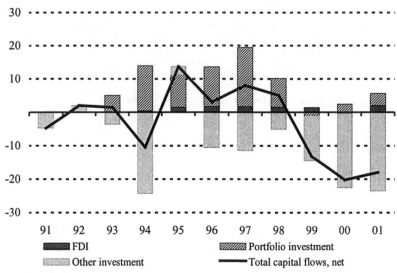

Notes:
a: FDI is foreign direct investment.
b: Figures for 2001 are estimates.

Sources: World Economic Outlook Database and European Bank for Reconstruction and Development.

Figure 6A.2 International bank lending to non-banks versus enterprise restructuring

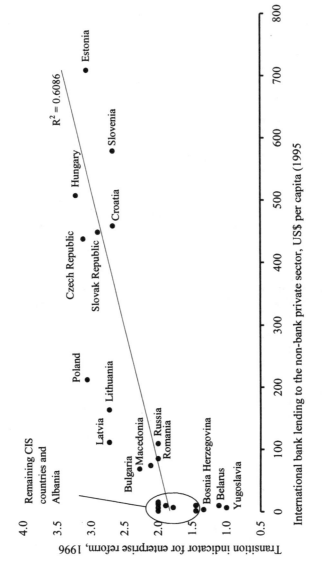

Sources : Bank for International Settlements and European Bank for Reconstruction and Development.

Table 6A.1 Selected indicators of banking sector development, end 2000

	Five largest banks (share)			Domestic credit (% GDP)	Non-performing loans*	Average capital ratio	Net interest margin (%)	Average rate of return on assets (%)
	Assets	Loans	Deposits					
CEEB								
Croatia	66.3	53.9	69.8	45.7	19.7	10.9	3.9	1.4
Czech Rep.	66.1	67.5	74.5	56.0	19.3	4.6	2.1	0.5
Estonia	98.8	99.5	99.5	38.1	1.5	12.6	0.0	1.1
Hungary	53.3	52.9	61.5	35.2	3.1	8.8	3.7	1.3
Latvia	62.3	71.9	66.2	21.7	5.0	8.4	4.0	2.0
Lithuania	88.5	85.0	93.0	16.8	10.8	10.0	3.6	0.4
Poland	48.6	48.4	49.1	36.5	15.9	8.2	4.0	1.1
Slovak Rep.	63.4	63.8	69.1	61.4	26.2	6.4	1.8	0.5
Slovenia	62.5	49.1	53.2	44.6	8.5	8.1	4.2	1.1
SEE								
Albania	89.1	91.2	91.9	31.4	42.6	6.7	2.9	2.1
Bosnia Herzegovina	57.8	–	–	41.9	15.7	16.5	4.0	-0.9
Bulgaria	60.5	–	–	25.6	10.9	0.1	4.1	4.1
FR Yugoslavia	65.4	–	–	61.1	27.8	3.4	–	–
FYR Macedonia	72.4	73.4	81.0	21.2	26.9	23.3	3.2	1.0
Romania	70.1	65.4	–	8.9	3.8	–	7.4	2.3

CIS

Armenia	48.1	52.2	44.3	10.7	6.2	14.6	5.4	2.0
Azerbaijan	–	–	88.3	16.0	–	15.0	3.9	1.9
Belarus	–	–	–	10.9	15.2	–	8.6	0.7
Georgia	53.1	53.3	–	6.9	5.6	33.7	0.1	1.0
Kazakhstan	65.6	69.3	69.6	12.1	2.1	18.5	5.3	1.4
Kyrgyzstan	50.2	61.3	55.8	4.1	16.4	20.5	4.6	–
Moldova	64.5	73.5	71.2	12.8	20.6	30.0	–	8.0
Russia	41.2	46.6	73.0	16.4	15.3	12.1	–	0.9
Tajikistan	76.7	92.3	91.9	26.1	10.8	9.3	2.8	1.8
Turkmenistan	–	–	–	70.0	–	3.0	0.0	0.9
Ukraine	38.3	38.2	–	10.5	32.5	17.5	–	1.0
Uzbekistan	90.5	94.6	–	18.3	0.0	16.4	–	–

Note : * *Includes substandard, doubtful, and non-recoverable loans.*

Source : European Bank for Reconstruction and Development.

PART TWO

Transition Country Experiences

7. Capital account liberalization in Ukraine

Anatolii Shapovalov

7.1 INTRODUCTION

After gaining independence from the Soviet Union in 1991, economic reform in Ukraine has thus far yielded mixed results. As is the case for other transition economies, Ukraine needs to attract large-scale investment in order to reconstruct and modernize its economy. With domestic savings falling substantially short of the funds needed for investment, attracting foreign capital is of crucial importance. Therefore, capital account liberalization forms an important part of economic policy reform.

Ukraine undoubtedly has some specific characteristics that should enable it to attract foreign investment. The country possesses a substantial industrial and technical-scientific potential, abundant natural resources, an experienced and relatively inexpensive labor force and one of the largest domestic markets in the region (of about 50 million people). Furthermore, Ukraine is strategically located, linking Central Europe with Russia and Central Asia.

Despite this potential, Ukraine has so far been a weak competitor on the international market for investment capital. Basic conditions, necessary to create a business environment favorable to international investors, have not yet been met. In addition, crises in Asia and Russia, have had an adverse impact on foreign direct investment (FDI) flows into Ukraine. With international investors being more cautious, the design of a financial system capable of efficiently allocating capital inflows should be a major priority, in order to gain investor confidence. In particular, this will require strengthening the institutional setting of the financial system. The structural improvement of the banking system, financial markets and the legislative environment all represent major challenges for the Ukrainian authorities and substantial progress in these areas is now being made.

The economic outlook for Ukraine is improving. After nine years of economic contraction, a turnaround was recorded in 2000 with real GDP growth of 5.9 per cent. Growth was 9.1 per cent in 2001 and is expected to be 6 per cent in 2002. Recent reforms plus improved economic performance should lead to an improvement in Ukraine's ability to attract foreign investment.

This chapter begins by discussing the financial system in Ukraine. Section 7.3 discusses reforms to date and Section 7.4 highlights experiences with capital flows. Recent initiatives to increase capital inflows are set out in Section 7.5 and Section 7.6 concludes.

7.2 THE FINANCIAL SYSTEM

The Exchange Rate

Various exchange rate regimes have been in place in Ukraine over the past ten years. After introducing the national interim currency, the Ukrainian karbovanetz, in November 1992, a managed float was initially followed. At that time, the National Bank of Ukraine (NBU) set the official exchange rate *vis-à-vis* the US dollar at the fixing rate of the weekly dollar auction. In the absence of an inter-bank foreign exchange market, licensed commercial banks could acquire the foreign exchange needed in their operations through competitive bidding in this auction. In August 1993, a multiple exchange rate regime was reintroduced. In October 1994, however, the exchange rate was again unified. An important step in the further liberalization of the exchange rate was the lifting of the ban on inter-bank foreign exchange transactions in March 1995. In the same month, the NBU started to conduct foreign exchange auctions on a daily, rather than weekly, basis – allowing the official exchange rate to be determined daily. In September 1996, monetary and macroeconomic conditions appeared to be sufficiently stable to introduce the new national currency, the hryvnia. In March 1997, the NBU announced that the exchange rate of the hryvnia would be maintained in a band of 1.70–1.90 *vis-à-vis* the US dollar.

In September 1998, the ruble crisis in Russia led to strong pressures on the hryvnia and the NBU had to widen the currency band to 2.5–3.5 hryvnias to the dollar. After a further devaluation, there was a second widening of the currency band in February 1999. In November 1999 the hryvnia moved out of the then defined band and the NBU let it float. Finally, in February 2000, the introduction of a floating exchange rate regime was officially confirmed.

Over the last two years, the nominal exchange rate to the dollar has been remarkably stable, at some 0.18 and has appreciated somewhat on a real basis (Figures 7.1 and 7.2).

Figure 7.1 Ukraine: nominal exchange rate of the hryvnia
            (monthly averages, against US$)

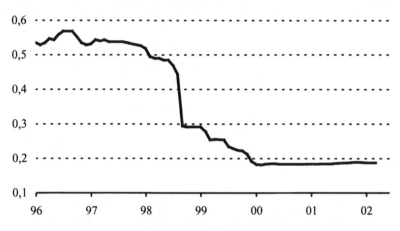

Source : Wiener Institut für Internationale Wirtschaftsvergleiche (WIIW).

Figure 7.2 Ukraine: real effective exchange rate of the hryvnia
            (monthly averages, January 1996 = 100)

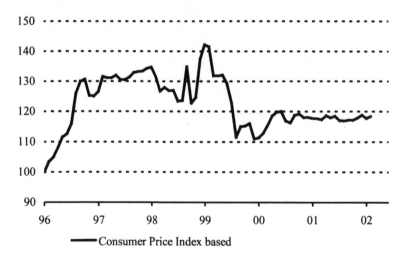

Source : International Monetary Fund.

The Financial System

The banking sector and the capital market in Ukraine are still at an early stage of development. At present there are over 150 commercial banks operating, with the eight largest banks accounting for more than 60 per cent of outstanding loans. Loans to the nonfinancial sector are typically short term (three–six months) and high cost, with the annualized interest rate margin between commercial bank lending and deposit rates reaching more than 20 percentage points. As such, the banks play only a modest role in intermediating savings to enterprises in search of investment capital. In order to put the functioning of the banking sector in perspective, a comparison with other countries is useful. During 1996–99, net annual lending to the economy was around 1–1.5 per cent of GDP, significantly below the 7–9 per cent of GDP seen in countries such as Hungary, Poland and Estonia. Clearly, to become a significant source of enterprise financing, the scale and the efficiency of the banking sector will need to increase drastically.

A segment of the capital market that gained significance during the second half of the 1990s is the Treasury bill (T-bill) market. After being established in March 1995, trading volumes started to increase in 1997, with monthly issues exceeding US$200 million. By that time it had become a dominant source of finance for the government, with overseas investors and domestic commercial banks being major investors. However, relatively high fiscal deficits led to a build-up of government debt, with an increasing percentage of government revenues committed to debt servicing. The contagious effects of the Asia crisis in October 1997 made the situation worse, pushing T-bill yields up to about 50 per cent. As inflation fell to well below 20 per cent that year, real interest rates rose sharply. After the Russian crisis in May 1998, interest rates reached around 80 per cent and foreign investors started to pull back, leading to a restructuring of debt.

After a few years of low liquidity, the situation in the T-bill market is again improving. The market has ceased to be primarily a source of funds to cover the government budget deficit and against this background some positive trends are evident. For example, during the first five months of 2001, the maturity of government securities increased to 148 days, some 12 per cent higher than in the previous year. The strict discipline of the Ministry of Finance of Ukraine in observing the terms for T-bills should help to regain investor confidence and increase market liquidity. The fact that rating agency Moody's upgraded its rating for Ukrainian government bonds in December 2001 is an important indication of an improving situation. The rating of government bonds denominated in hryvnias was upgraded from Caa3 to Caa1 while the outlook for paper denominated in foreign currency, currently rated Caa1, was revised from 'negative' to 'positive'.

The Ukrainian securities market has thus far not succeeded in developing into a source of capital of real importance for the economy. The market consists of several traditional exchanges that primarily function as a market for the initial public offerings of companies that are being privatized. Except for the Ukrainian Stock Exchange in Kiev, secondary markets are illiquid. In addition to the traditional exchanges there is also an electronic trading platform, the Ukrainian First Trading System. This platform attracts most of the trading, accounting for up to 90 per cent of total volume traded. However, the total market capitalization of Ukrainian equity markets is low, at less than 10 per cent of GDP and market turnover, defined as trading volume relative to market capitalization, is only around one-third of the level observed in transition economies such as Russia, Poland and Hungary. In the first half of 2001, investment in corporate securities made up less than 10 per cent of the already modest portfolio investment flows.

7.3 CHRONOLOGY OF REFORMS

Looking back at the first decade of independence, wide-ranging economic policy reforms have been made. Box 7.1 sets out a chronology of the more important steps concerning monetary policy, banking reform and capital and current account liberalization.

In the first years after becoming an independent republic, Ukraine adopted a relatively liberal approach towards foreign investment and the liberalization of capital flows. Soon after 1991, laws were enacted permitting direct foreign investment in most business sectors. Some restrictions were made, such as on financial intermediation, where a license from the NBU is necessary. Regulations require that investments are made in convertible currency or in kind; after paying fees and taxes, foreign investors are free to repatriate dividends and profits. With respect to resident and nonresident accounts, under certain restrictions, domestically held foreign currency deposits are permitted. Regulations concerning this type of account were further liberalized in August 1995.

After the introduction of the interim currency in late 1992, a gradual liberalization of the exchange rate regime took place, as noted above. Although the T-bill market was initially restricted to domestic institutions, individuals as well as nonresidents were premitted to purchase these securities within two years. This gave rise to a substantial increase in portfolio investment flows, which up until that time had been virtually non-existent.

Box 7.1 Ukraine: Chronology of Major Reforms

1991	Aug.	Independence from Soviet Union.
1992	Apr.	Law 'On Banks and Banking' adopted.
	June	Stock exchange trading begins.
	Nov.	Interim currency (karbovanetz) introduced.
1993	Aug.	Multiple exchange rates reintroduced.
1994	Oct.	Exchange rate unified.
1995	Mar.	Treasury bill (T-bill) market initiated.
		Inter-bank foreign exchange transactions liberalized.
	Aug.	Foreign currency accounts for residents and nonresidents liberalized.
1996	Mar.	Law 'On Foreign Investing' adopted.
	Sep.	New currency (hryvnia) introduced.
		Ukraine accepts IMF Article VIII obligations.
1997	Mar.	Formal exchange rate fluctuation bands set.
	Apr.	Full current account convertibility introduced.
	May	Procedure of licensing of credits from nonresidents replaced by registration of such credits.
	June	Export surrender requirement revoked.
	Aug.	First sovereign eurobond.
1998	Jan.	International accounting and reporting standards adopted.
	May	Limits on foreign ownership of banks lifted.
	Sep.	Inter-bank foreign exchange market closed.
		Export surrender requirement reintroduced.
		Exchange rate band widened.
		Start of domestic debt restructuring.
		Restrictions on transferring T-bill proceeds to nonresidents.
1999	Feb.	Exchange rate band further widened.
	Mar.	Inter-bank currency market reopened.
		Restrictions on granting credits in foreign exchange locally eliminated.
	May	Central bank law adopted.
	Aug.	Exchange rate band effectively abandoned.
	Sep.	Restrictions on transferring T-bill proceeds to nonresidents removed.
2000	Feb.	Floating exchange rate regime confirmed.
	Mar.	Commercial debt rescheduled.
	July	Presidential Decree on banking sector issued.

	Dec.	New law 'On Banks and Banking' adopted (enacted in Jan. 2001).
2001	Jan.	Presidential Decree on investment stimulation issued.
	July	External debt rescheduling agreement by Club of Paris.

In 1996, after an initial period of high inflation (which was common to all transition economies), increasing currency stability made it possible to introduce the new national currency, the hryvnia, in September 1996. At the same time, Ukraine accepted the obligations under IMF Article VIII. On accepting Article VIII, Ukraine committed itself to abstaining from policies that introduce limitations to payments and transfers connected to current international transactions and to promoting a multilateral payment system free of limitations.

In addition, for the first time since independence, the right was given to nonresidents, through hryvnia loro accounts opened with the authorized banks, to buy foreign currency in the Ukrainian foreign exchange market provided that it was confirmed that these funds were obtained by nonresident legal entities through export–import transactions. Also, individual nonresidents have been allowed to open accounts with banking institutions in both national and foreign currencies on the same terms as residents.

Given the stable rate of the hryvnia *vis-à-vis* the dollar, the exchange rate regime was in March 1997 changed from a managed float to a pegged rate within bands. In August 1997, the first sovereign Ukrainian eurobond was issued. To increase both capital and competition in the banking sector, restrictions concerning foreign bank ownership were abolished in May 1998. From 1 January 1998, the Ukrainian banking system adopted international accounting standards (based on the accrual concept).

In October 1997 and August 1998, consecutive financial crises in Asia and Russia sent shocks through the global financial system. As was the case with other transition economies, Ukraine could not escape the consequences. Foreign investors withdrew from the T-bill market and the central bank spent considerable reserves in an attempt to defend the exchange rate, before devaluations became necessary.

In order to limit the pressures resulting from the capital outflows, the National Bank of Ukraine had to reintroduce a number of essential capital controls. Ukrainian commercial banks were prohibited from granting credits to residents of Ukraine in foreign currency for subsequent sale in the inter-bank currency market. In addition, commercial banks were only permitted to grant credits to residents in foreign currency and hryvnias against so-called 'critical imports', i.e., for purchasing goods from the list defined by respective decisions of the government of Ukraine. At the same time, the

NBU also set a system of limits in other sectors of the money and credit market. It is clear that these measures held back, to some extent, the development of the national banking system. Moreover, Ukrainian entrepreneurs were restricted in their international operations and their access to global capital markets. This slowed the modernization of the economy more generally.

Fortunately, after an earlier than expected recovery from the Russian crisis, in March 1999 the National Bank of Ukraine was able to implement policies to gradually withdraw almost all the limits and bans set in 1997–98. This included the effective floating of the hryvnia. Debt restructuring (both domestically and by the club of Paris) has also helped stabilize the situation following the earlier crisis.

7.4 FOREIGN INVESTMENT

Foreign Direct Investment

Over the last decade, foreign investment has not been the source of funding hoped for to allow the much-needed structural reform of Ukraine's economy to occur. As at June 2001, cumulative FDI since 1991 amounted to only US$4.3 billion. This represents around 10–12 per cent of GDP. For other transition economies in Central and Eastern Europe, the percentage was considerably higher. As early as in 1997, cumulative investment as a percentage of GDP in Hungary and the Czech Republic had reached levels of 36 and 28 per cent, respectively. On a per capita basis over the 1998–2000 period, net FDI inflows for Ukraine totaled US$68 per person, whereas for Hungary, the Czech Republic and Poland, the respective amounts were US$1,964, US$2,102 and US$751. Over this 12-year period, the last three countries received approximately two-thirds of the total amount invested in all transition economies. Their success in attracting foreign investment can be attributed to the rapid implementation of economic reforms in these countries, the creation of a sufficiently favorable investment climate and a stable political environment. Against this background, foreign investment in Ukraine appears exceptionally moderate (see Figure 7.3). The limited changes in the structure of Ukrainian exports are one consequence of the low level of investment inflows. For example, raw materials continue to be the dominant export category.

In Ukraine, the number of enterprises having received foreign investment has increased from 2,123 in 1994 to 7,680 in the first half of 2001. There has also been some increase in the level of total investment per enterprise.

Whereas in 1994 foreign capital invested averaged US$225,000 per enterprise, in the first half of 2001 the amount had risen to over US$550,000.

Figure 7.3   Ukraine: net foreign direct and portfolio investment
             (% GDP)

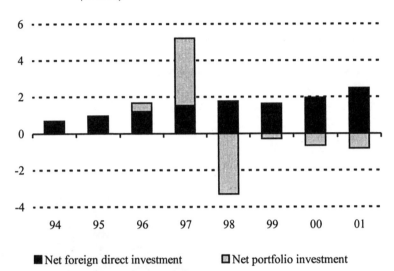

■ Net foreign direct investment   □ Net portfolio investment

Source: International Monetary Fund.

The main investors in Ukraine are the major industrialized countries who account for up to 90 per cent of total FDI. The share of Baltic and Commonwealth of Independent States (CIS) countries in Ukrainian FDI is 10 per cent. At a country level, the United States of America, the Netherlands, Germany, Great Britain and Russia are the biggest individual investors in Ukraine. As at mid-2001, these countries accounted for around 50 per cent of total investment, and their share of total investment has remained relatively stable in recent years. At present, the major part of foreign capital, some 19 per cent, is directed to the food industry and agricultural sector, that is, to the areas where quick recoupment is possible. Wholesale trade and intermediary services (13 per cent) occupy second place. Machine building and financial services jointly rank third with some 8 per cent each.

Focussing on the financial sector, the total stock of foreign investment in the banking system was US$216.2 million in October 2001. This represents 13.8 per cent of the total registered authorized funds of Ukrainian commercial banks. Foreign investment in this sector has been actively encouraged and the NBU abolished the limit on nonresidents' participation in the Ukrainian banking system as early as 1994.

In total there are currently 29 commercial banks, out of a total of around 150 banks, with foreign capital participation, including:

- seven with 100 per cent participation;
- 12 with 50 per cent or more; and
- ten with less than 50 per cent foreign capital.

Figure 7.4 illustrates the development of foreign participation in the banking sector. Foreign-owned banks are here defined as those banks where foreign investment is at least 50 per cent of total capital.

Figure 7.4 Ukraine: participation of foreign-owned banks
(percentage of total number of banks)

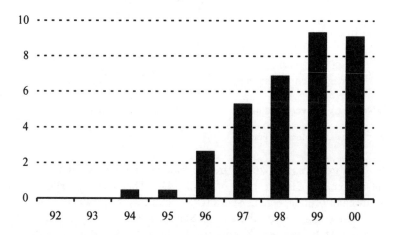

Source: European Bank for Reconstruction and Development.

As noted above, per capita FDI flows in Ukraine have so far been low compared with other transition economies. The appropriate conditions to attract capital from abroad have yet to be created. The following factors impede the wide-scale attraction of foreign investment by Ukraine:

- an unfavorable legal environment (legislation is too intricate: about 70 normative acts and regulations cover investment, plus there are frequent changes of legislation);
- imperfection and lack of development of the national investment infrastructure and management;
- the national taxation system;

- a lack of effective insurance for foreign investments;
- a lack of coordination between state authorities;
- an insufficient number of free economic zones; and
- an unreadiness by managers of many Ukrainian enterprises to accept foreign investment.

Furthermore, foreign investment in Ukraine is hindered by the lack of an efficient network of investment banks, consultancy firms and information sources. An imperfect accounting system prevents foreign investors from obtaining objective information about the reputation of a business partner. The procedure for settling disputes arising between domestic and foreign investors also needs to be improved. Domestic enterprises need experience and funds to develop high-quality investment projects that meet international standards. Finally, there is no full statistical monitoring of the demand and supply of foreign investments, and nor is their use monitored.

Portfolio Investment

Unlike foreign direct investment, portfolio investment by nonresidents is currently not regarded as unambiguously positive in Ukraine. This is because of their short-term nature and the high levels of interest required. Our experience following the Russian crisis in 1998 is that these funds can be rapidly withdrawn from the economy, posing problems for exchange rate stability. Because of these characteristics, long-term investment at a more moderate interest rate is considered more effective.

As of July 2001, portfolio investments in Ukraine totaled US$2.5 billion with US$241 million in corporate securities and US$2.2 billion in debt securities such as bonds and bills. This is a reduction of US$267 million on the level at the beginning of the year, despite the rapid economic growth experienced. This confirms the limited importance of such portfolio investments to date.

Portfolio investment in Ukraine is hindered by the lack of an effective domestic stock market. To be effective, a stock market has to meet the following requirements. It must:

- secure the rights of investors;
- ensure the transparency of securities transactions;
- create conditions for easy and reliable transfer of ownership for the securities' holder and establish a user-friendly clearing mechanism for securities transactions; and
- provide the possibility of gaining income from securities investments.

Improvements in these areas will increase the attractiveness of investment in Ukraine.

7.5 RECENT INITIATIVES TO INCREASE FOREIGN INVESTMENT

In recent years, a wide-ranging program to increase foreign investment inflows has been put forward. Initiatives focus across a number of sectors.

Banking

Because of the importance of a sound banking system in gaining investors' confidence, the National Bank of Ukraine, the Cabinet of Ministers and Verkhovna Rada (the parliament) have together initiated a number of measures to strengthen the banking environment.

The Laws 'On Banks and Banking' and 'On the National Bank of Ukraine', adopted in 1999 and 2000, have brought about many improvements with respect to banking legislation. One feature is that the transparency concerning regulations with respect to both the establishment of new banks and the liquidation of insolvent banks, has increased significantly. In addition, the mandate of the NBU to act in these cases was substantially enlarged.

An additional objective of the Law 'On Banks and Banking' is to improve the normative and legal framework for banking regulation. This will eventually bring banking supervision into accordance with international standards, ensuring the implementation of the Core Principles worked out by Basle Committee on Banking Supervision and the Directives of the European Union in this area. Furthermore, differences between residents and nonresidents with respect to the amount of authorized capital required for establishing banks have been abolished. Previously, the minimum authorized capital required was the equivalent of around US$5 million for banks having less than 50 per cent of their authorized capital belonging to nonresident parties as of the date of incorporation, whereas it was around US$10 million for banks with over 50 per cent foreign participation. Now there is no difference in requirements for residents and nonresidents concerning the size of authorized capital of newly established banks.

A further important initiative is the Complex Program on the Development of the Banking System. This program is currently being considered for adoption by the Administration of the President of Ukraine and aims to contribute to raising the credibility of the Ukrainian banking system. It envisages not only bank capitalization measures, expansion of credit resources, provision of creditors' fund safety and the strengthening of banking supervision, but also the removal of the remaining restrictions for banks with foreign participation. The recent restructuring of two state banks into open corporations (fully owned by the government) will also help to strengthen the banking system as it implies increasing authorized capital and improvements in the quality of the credit portfolio.

Financial Markets

In order to provide for the gradual development of foreign exchange forward markets (e.g., futures, options and other derivatives), the NBU has taken initiatives to prepare amendments to the Rules on Carrying out Transactions in the Inter-bank Foreign Exchange Market. These rules currently aim to provide protection to exporters, importers as well as to banks. The introduction of financial instruments such as forward transactions between foreign currencies (i.e., with no hryvnia participation) will provide an additional means of hedging currency risks.

The Investment Climate

The adoption in 1999 by the President of Ukraine of a Decree simplifying the receipt by residents of foreign currency credits from foreign creditors, represented a further step to liberalize capital inflows. A procedure requiring an official license from the central bank for such credits was replaced by a simple procedure requiring only registration. The transfer from a permission to a registration system has eliminated lengthy administrative procedures and should help in attracting funds from abroad. For the first half of 2001, the National Bank of Ukraine registered foreign credits attracted by Ukrainian economic entities of over US$1 billion. By comparison, some US$825 million was recorded for the same period of the previous year.

In order to regulate capital transactions related to investments of foreign exchange funds abroad by residents, the National Bank set out in 1999 a new procedure for issuing, amending and revoking individuals' licenses to invest abroad, according to which the number of documents required was considerably diminished. One of the consequences of the change is that for the first time since independence, Ukrainian individuals are entitled to invest abroad. As of 1 July 2001, total foreign investments of Ukrainian residents amounted to US$154.2 million. This is an increase of some 50 per cent over the first half of 2000.

Capital Flight

An issue related to increasing foreign investment is the return of capital that earlier left Ukraine. The OECD estimates that the total amount of capital that has fled the country since independence is at least US$10 to US$20 billion. There are strong arguments to assume that financial stabilization, economic amnesty and a favorable investment climate will help to bring back a significant part of this capital. Since any repatriated sum of exported capital will contribute to the restructuring of the national economy, proposals for an economic amnesty for 'shadow capital', which would mean taxing repatriated capital by a uniform 10 per cent, are being considered.

7.6 CONCLUDING REMARKS

Today, the situation in international capital and credit markets is characterized by tough competition for foreign investment. According to IMF data, the share of the world flow of foreign direct investment that the least-developed countries attract has been continuously decreasing in recent years. In contrast, capital investments in the CIS and Central and Eastern European countries have been gradually increasing. Ukraine, which tarried at the starting line of economic reforms, so far has not succeeded in using this trend to its advantage.

For Ukraine, the attraction of foreign investment is particularly important. Without investment from the West, Ukraine will be unable to modernize its economy. However, with demand for foreign investments exceeding supply, international investors are reluctant to invest in economies lacking a favorable investment environment. Fortunately, due in part to favorable developments in Ukraine's major export markets, the economic situation in Ukraine has improved over the last few years. After two years of robust economic growth in 2000 and 2001, economic growth of over 6 per cent is again expected in 2002.

Given the importance of attracting foreign direct investment, the NBU sees the creation of the necessary conditions for free movement of capital as a key priority. Prospects for membership of the World Trade Organization and possible integration into the EU add further emphasis to this point. Consequently, the NBU is initiating further work regarding capital liberalization. In furthering liberalization, emphasis should be placed on attracting FDI inflows to Ukraine, as well as foreign creditors. This includes developing a more active privatization process including the participation of nonresidents. In addition, the liberalization of foreign economic activities of residents and of operations in the stock and inter-bank currency markets are important. Nevertheless, although much remains to be done, Ukraine has made significant progress in economic reform in recent years and is beginning to experience the rewards of that progress.

8. Capital account liberalization experiences in Armenia

Vache Gabrielyan and Armine Khachatryan

8.1 INTRODUCTION AND BACKGROUND

The literature on the use and liberalization of capital controls and regulations cannot be considered either exhaustive or definitive. It is quite difficult to assess the effects of capital controls, which may bring a number of benefits as well as costs. At the same time, it is very important to correctly evaluate the timeliness and sequencing of capital liberalization and its relationship to prudential policies in the financial sector. It is also essential to consider the ability of a country to withstand external shocks with and without capital controls. In this regard, the case of Armenia is of particular interest. This section continues by providing the background to the capital liberalization experience of Armenia. The following section discusses the period of more rapid reforms from 1994 onward while Section 8.3 sets out financial market and prudential issues. Section 8.4 concludes. Box 8.1 below provides a summary of the key liberalization moves.

Armenia is a small country with a not very sophisticated financial sector that is dominated by banks. As a newly independent country, Armenia embarked on liberalization early on, while the financial system was being established. In terms of sequencing, liberalization in all sectors of the economy took place more or less simultaneously, and to a certain extent, under the direct influence of external factors. As in many former Soviet republics, Armenia had to face the consequences of the swift Russian price liberalization in January 1992. This was a unique time – politically the Soviet Union had been replaced by the Commonwealth of Independent States (CIS), but economically all countries, including the Baltic states, remained in the ruble zone. In addition, a common market remained – with a common currency and without significant customs duties and tariffs – although this was rapidly decaying.

Following on from the Gorbachev era was a period of very high inflation. Because of political differences between Russia's parliament, government and central bank, price liberalization in 1992 was not matched by a monetary policy tightening. Hyperinflation across the CIS was the result, and the Central Bank of Russia was printing different types of rubles for Russia and the rest of the republics. Huge quantities of 'old rubles' were chasing a decreasing supply of goods in those republics that did not manage to introduce their own currencies. The resulting hyperinflation was therefore most severe in those republics that for some reason or another delayed introducing a new currency. Armenia was one of these countries – being among the last of the CIS countries to introduce a new currency. The Armenian dram (AMD) was introduced in November 1993. Inflation peaked in 1993 at 10,996 per cent (and averaged 1,922 per cent over the year as a whole), much higher than the CIS average.

Banks and bank-like institutions had started to attract deposits and lend extensively by the end of the Soviet era (although a proper supervision framework was lacking). Central bank functions were still undertaken by Gosbank, implying that the amount of money issued in each republic was centrally determined. Following the collapse of this planning system, and as a result of accelerating inflation and the increasing supply of imported goods, the flow of deposits to the banking system declined. Bank-like institutions rapidly found themselves bankrupt – they often invested in rather unprofitable businesses, were run by unscrupulous management, and faced difficulties in debt recovery, especially given the high rates of inflation.[1] The situation was exacerbated by the dire political and economic circumstances. Nagorno-Karabakh (and Armenia by proxy) were involved in a territorial dispute with neighboring Azerbaijan. Economically, the conflict included an economic blockade of Armenia by Azerbaijan. Among other consequences, this led to frequent and long-lasting electricity outages every day during 1992–94. The resulting adverse impact on the economy was substantial – GDP declined by more than 50 per cent.

The introduction of the national currency made it possible to consider the conduct of monetary and other stabilization policies, along with foreign exchange regulation and control. In the initial period following the introduction of the currency (1993–95), it was necessary to establish certain rules. This was the period when the main laws concerning the regulation of the financial system were adopted. The Law on Foreign Exchange Regulation and Control and the Law on the Central Bank of Armenia are perhaps the most relevant for this chapter. Given the hyperinflation and the substantial decline in economic activity, there was a need to set up rules that would support the strengthening of the dram. This was the part of the stabilization package that the government and the Central Bank of Armenia (CBA) implemented to stabilize the economy. During this stage of development, a surrender requirement for export proceeds and other current account restrictions were introduced.[2] In addition, banks faced differentiated forex position requirements, depending on their capital size.[3]

However, after the inflation rate declined below 100 per cent and the exchange rate depreciation stabilized in 1995, the CBA undertook measures to reduce foreign exchange control in order to allow market forces to determine prices in the forex market. With all instruments at its disposal, the CBA tried to encourage an increase in liquidity and turnover on the foreign exchange market. These steps included both institutional measures (e.g., setting the official exchange rate on a daily basis, licensing and regulating banks and transactions) and financial measures (intervening in the market). The CBA started to follow market trends and announce daily exchange rates based on the operations that had taken place in the foreign exchange market during the previous day. As in other financial market segments (more precisely, in markets where the CBA undertook operations in the national currency), the CBA started to act as if it was the market maker of last resort – i.e., buying and selling at the lowest and highest market rate. For example, if market participants were not able to obtain foreign exchange from the market, the CBA would sell at the highest market rate. When necessary, the opposite would also occur, with the CBA buying at the lowest market rate.

8.2 REFORMS TAKE OFF

The general economic situation started to improve in 1994. First of all, the conflict between Azerbaijan and Nagorno-Karabakh came to a halt as a tripartite agreement between Azerbaijan, Nagorno-Karabakh and Armenia established a truce. Though still far from a permanent peace and the elimination of the blockade, it improved the investment climate in the country.[4] Around the same time, the banking sector started to concentrate as many banks collapsed and others faced tougher regulation (see Box 8.1).[5] During this second stage of reform (1995–97) it was important to stimulate the inflow of foreign capital into the country, as domestic savings, given the background of the problematic banking sector and fresh memories of hyperinflation, would not be sufficient to attain sustainable growth. To this end, the Central Bank of Armenia sought to stimulate capital and current account transactions through the gradual easing and eventual elimination of restrictions in these areas. During the first half of 1995 surrender requirements were first decreased (from 50 to 30 per cent) and were then eliminated. In mid-1995, nonresidents were permitted to open accounts in Armenian banks without restriction.

Box 8.1 Armenia: Chronology of Major Reforms

1993 Oct.   Requirement to surrender 50 per cent of export proceeds.
1993 Nov.   Introduction of the dram (AMD) at a conversion rate of
            one dram to 200 (pre-1993) Soviet rubles.
1994 Mar.   The dram becomes the sole legal tender.
1994 Dec.   Banks with a general foreign exchange license required
            to offer a minimum set of international transaction
            services.
1995 Jan.   Surrender requirement for export proceeds reduced to 30
            per cent.
            Reduction in number of categories for export licenses
            and tariffs.
1995 Apr.   Surrender requirement for export proceeds abolished.
1995 July   Inter-bank foreign exchange transactions permitted.
            Nonresidents allowed to open accounts at Armenian
            banks without restrictions.
1995 Dec.   The official exchange rate determined on a daily basis
            instead of tri-weekly.
1996 Jan.   Regulation No. 8 regulating foreign exchange accounts
            held by residents abroad and in Armenia issued,
            eliminating all restrictions on current account operations.
1997 May   Armenia accepts IMF Article VIII obligations.
1998 Mar.   Banks' overall open forex position limited to 40 per cent
            of their total capital, while the position for certain other
            currencies (as defined by the CBA) limited to 10 per cent
            of capital.
1999 Jan.   Tariff schedule revised.
            The limit on the overall foreign exchange position of
            banks lowered to 30 per cent of capital.
1999 Sep.   The CBA eliminates the option for banks to hold 50 per
            cent of required reserves against foreign exchange
            deposits in either foreign or domestic currency.
2000 Jan.   The limit on the overall foreign exchange position of
            banks lowered to 25 per cent of capital and the open
            position in non-convertible currencies lowered to 5 per
            cent.

During 1996 all restrictions on current account transactions were abolished. In addition, the CBA made an announcement regarding Armenian exchange rate policy and regulation. The main theme of the announcement was to declare that the Armenian authorities (and particularly the CBA) would adhere to a floating exchange rate regime and that restrictions on capital account transactions were abolished. The declaration stated that the CBA would intervene in the foreign exchange market only on a temporary basis and in order to smooth out sharp fluctuations. Moreover, should the need arise for the reintroduction of capital controls, these will be announced to the market one month ahead of their implementation. Simultaneously, the CBA supported an increase in the number of participants in the foreign exchange market by licensing foreign exchange bureau, brokerages and dealers. This step was also important and significant in encouraging the flow of foreign exchange into the economy. As evidence of the growth of the market's liquidity, the participation of the central bank in the foreign exchange market declined remarkably (see Figure 8.1). By mid-1996 Armenia was ready to accept Article VIII of the Articles of Agreement of the International Monetary Fund (IMF), although the country formally accepted the Article one year later.[6]

Figure 8.1 Armenia: forex turnover and central bank interventions (US$ m)

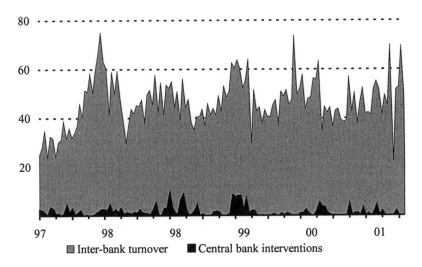

Source: Central Bank of Armenia.

As Figure 8.2 shows, exchange rate developments have been more in line with general economic developments in the country, rather than determined by central bank interventions. The one exception is perhaps a period during 1999 when, in ten days, the government spent the whole portion of a World Bank structural adjustment credit and the central bank had to quickly reduce the supply of base money. For a short period of time, the only instrument available was the sale of foreign exchange, and this contributed to an appreciation of the AMD.

Figure 8.2 Armenia: exchange rate developments of the dram
                (against US$, monthly average)

Source : Central Bank of Armenia.

8.3 FINANCIAL MARKET DEVELOPMENTS AND REFINEMENT OF PRUDENTIAL REGULATIONS

What were the consequences of reforms? The evidence is mixed. Or, alternatively, one's conclusion depends upon the prior position held. To judge by investment flows, it is premature to speak of a glowing success. But, if the objective was to ensure the country's ability to withstand external shocks, the record is much better. This section assesses the factors behind the Armenian performance.

Even with fully liberalized foreign exchange regulations and the fairly stable macroeconomic situation, investment in Armenia remains one of the lowest amongst CIS and Eastern European countries (see Figure 8.3). One of the reasons for this relatively poor performance was the sequencing and coordination of reforms. In particular, rapid liberalization in the area of foreign exchange control was not accompanied by steps aimed at developing the domestic financial system, including non-bank financial institutions. The only institutions acting as intermediaries between those wishing to save and those wishing to borrow were banks. This limitation continues to exist, and hinders the process of attracting long-term foreign capital.

Figure 8.3 Foreign direct investment* (% GDP)

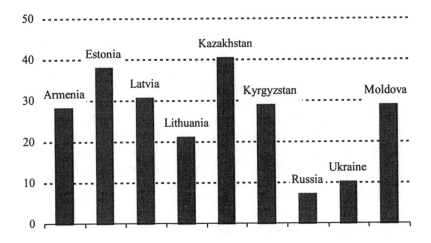

Note : * Cumulative FDI for 1995–2000, GDP as at 2000.

Source : International Monetary Fund.

In Armenia, the capital market is extremely limited. There are several reasons for this. First, it is a reflection of the level of economic development. Many countries with similar per capita income levels lack both the strong enforcement of property rights and the public pressure to do so. Most of the joint-stock companies in Armenia were created through voucher privatization, whereby the management came to own the majority of the companies. As a result, in the vast majority of cases, there is no desire to raise capital through a public share issue, as this would threaten the dominant ownership. Hence, although the capital market has all of the infrastructure needed (the regulation and 'rules of the game' are meticulously copied from 1930s' American law), it lacks substance. The total turnover in the Armenian Stock Exchange amounted to some US$9 million in 2001 (mostly not the result of active trading, but the transfer of ownership from one large shareholder to another at prices which sometimes differed from both the bid and asking prices on the particular day). The only remaining security are Treasury bills (T-bills) and bonds, which are actively traded, mostly in the inter-bank market (with a weekly turnover of around US$1–2 million). The current state of the market, in conjunction with the strict requirements of the CBA for banks, makes the entry of new institutions to the financial sector rather difficult. It is worth noting that the development of capital markets would have substantially eased the CBA exchange rate policy, as it would have been possible to influence exchange rate expectations without explicit interventions in the foreign exchange market. In addition, the lack of financial derivatives removes this potential source of information about financial market perceptions.

A further important factor in influencing investment flows was the lack of institutional credibility regarding government economic policy, alongside the high political and country risks. Political instability during 1996–97 had a substantial impact on the flow of direct investment into Armenia.[7] Regional issues also played a role here. Crises in other parts of the world (Asia, Brazil etc.) raised doubts concerning economic stability in Russia and in Former Soviet Union (FSU) countries more generally.[8] The crisis in Russia was the final link in that chain of events. Armenia suffered a number of effects due to the Russian crisis – a real exchange rate appreciation, a slowdown in the flow of transfers and factor income remittances from Armenian guest workers abroad, a decline in demand for Armenian exports, etc. (Figure 8.4 provides a decomposition of the current account dynamics over the period.) Nevertheless, the losses in financial markets were minimized by the prudent policies implemented by the authorities.

Figure 8.4 Armenia: current account balance (US$ m)

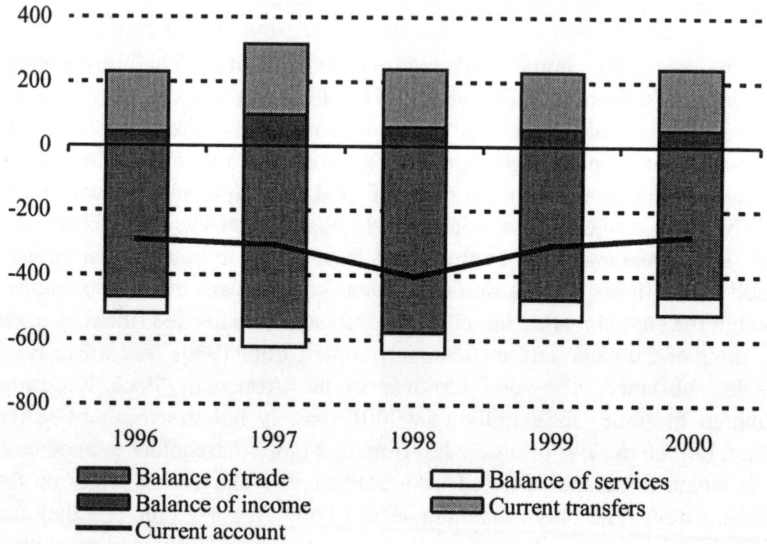

Balance of trade   Balance of services
Balance of income   Current transfers
Current account

Source: Central Bank of Armenia.

As mentioned above, the main financial instruments in Armenia are forms of government debt. The first issue of T-bills was in 1995. At that point the process was quite unorganized, making it difficult to use the issue in debt management and monetary policy implementation processes. In early 1996, in an attempt the support the issue of the newly introduced T-bills, the CBA entered into foreign exchange forward contracts with nonresident institutional investors, essentially eliminating their foreign exchange exposure risk. As a result, the share of nonresident holdings of T-bills reached 60 per cent. Although the overall stock of holdings was not large, it nevertheless created the perception that the CBA was encouraging the inflow of 'hot money'. During late 1997, the CBA announced that it would cease entering into these forward contracts as they hindered the foreign reserve position and could undermine confidence in CBA policies.

Instead, the CBA suggested that nonresidents sign competitive contracts with commercial banks if they still wished to hold Armenian T-bills. This approach was firmly implemented during 1998. During that year the CBA also tried to strengthen its independence by refraining from direct lending to the government and improving short-run fiscal and monetary policy coordination.

Given those developments, and in line with the increase of interest rates in Russia, some portfolio investors withdrew from Armenia and transferred their funds to Russian markets. As a result, even during the short period of internal political instability that occurred in early 1998 and in the aftermath of the Russian crisis, Armenia did not lose substantial foreign exchange reserves and even managed to develop the T-bill market.[9] Figure 8.5 shows the sharp decrease of foreign participation in the Armenian T-bill market in 1998.

Since 1998 the CBA has entered a new phase in the development of the financial market. After relative macroeconomic and financial stability was achieved, the CBA took steps to ensure that it was ready and able to sustain that stability by all means at its disposal. With the advice of international financial institutions, the authorities decided to improve prudential management. To reduce the exposure of banks to foreign exchange risk, the CBA lowered the limit on overall foreign exchange position of banks from 40 to 30 per cent in early 1999 and to 25 per cent from early 2000. The option for banks to hold 50 per cent of their required reserves against liabilities in foreign exchange in either foreign or domestic currency was abolished in 1999. As a result, banks were required to hold 100 per cent of the required reserves in domestic currency. These changes acted to stabilize the foreign exchange market. Around 30–40 per cent of forex turnover takes place in the inter-bank market and banks are the major players in this market (bank–client transactions amount for another 40–50 per cent of the trade volume in a market with US$1–2 million turnover daily. Because a depreciation would

Figure 8.5 Armenia: ownership of Treasury bills (AMD bn)

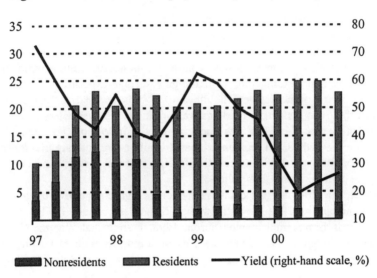

Source : Central Bank of Armenia.

result in an automatic increase in the volume of required AMD reserves that banks would have to hold against foreign exchange liabilities, the changes encouraged banks to stop engaging in such speculation.

An additional important factor that allowed Armenia to refrain from administrative capital controls was the CBA's prudent policy in managing foreign exchange reserves. Starting from mid-1996, the CBA aimed to build up sufficient levels of gross international reserves to maintain about three and a half months of import coverage (Figure 8.6). As is the case for any country following a program with the IMF, the central bank was under constant monitoring, including regarding the level of net international reserves. In these circumstances, the authorities signaled to the public that they were not ready to defend the exchange rate at any price. The main arguments were poor export performance, low fiscal discipline and an insufficient level of international reserves. These factors also created a credible environment for the floating exchange rate regime. Since then, the CBA has increased the stock of international reserves, allowing the exchange rate to fluctuate if needed. The volume of CBA interventions in the inter-bank forex market also vividly illustrates this tendency.

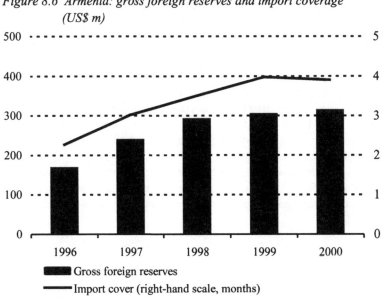

Figure 8.6 Armenia: gross foreign reserves and import coverage (US$ m)

Source : Central Bank of Armenia.

8.4 CONCLUSIONS

The Armenian experience of capital account liberalization shares some features with other cases depicted in literature. Perhaps it is premature to fully assess the consequences of such a rapid liberalization, and whether it hindered or supported private capital inflows and, subsequently, economic growth. But the process has proved to be sufficiently resilient to perform reasonably well in periods of distress in world financial markets. There are several factors that shaped Armenian efforts towards capital account liberalization:

- Armenia has quite a small financial market that is not well developed. It has only a limited choice of instruments and almost no integration with highly speculative international markets. The received wisdom is that hard pegs make sense for a country with a high inflation history and which is closely integrated to other economies through both capital and current account transactions (Fischer, 2001). Although it has experienced hyperinflation, Armenia lacks not only integration with world markets, but also substantial international reserves. As a consequence, there seemed no alternative to a floating foreign exchange rate regime and sound macroeconomic policies. This argument was serious enough for authorities to resist the temptation of fixing the currency. After the floating regime was adopted, dealing with capital controls was much easier.

- As in similar cases – Kenya, Argentina, Peru – rapid capital account liberalization was part of a general reform package aimed at attracting foreign capital financing and achieving sustained growth (Ariyoshi et al., 2000 and Mishra et al., 2001). In Armenia, even the philosophy of privatization was changed and the emphasis has shifted from vouchers to foreign institutional investors.
- As in Argentina, attempts were made to strengthen the supervisory and regulatory framework at the same time as policies were directed to achieving and maintaining macroeconomic stability (Ariyoshi et al., 2000).

NOTES

1. These included not only 'proto-banks', but also the first investment funds. They were created through attracting privatization vouchers and cash, and eventually repeated the fate of Russian and Albanian 'Ponzi' schemes.
2. Given the Soviet heritage of tight regulation of the economy, the monopoly on foreign trade, fixed (and multiple) exchange rates, and the continuing Russian practice of forex surrender, this was not seen as something extraordinary, but rather, as an obvious and necessary step. In fact, surrender requirements were actually introduced some two months before the national currency was in circulation. On 1 October 1993 it was decided that 50 per cent of export revenues were required to be surrendered, applying retroactively from 1 August 1993.
3. Despite the CBA's efforts, this particular prudential standard cannot be very strictly enforced even today (banks can use various transactions to circumvent the prudential requirement of limiting their forex position to 25 per cent of their capital).
4. In 1994 the Law on Foreign Investments was passed, completely liberalizing foreign direct investment (FDI) inflows (except for the purchase of land, although leases for several decades were permitted). The law also contained grandfathering clauses for the protection of foreign investors – granting a five-year immunity from any newly passed laws (except for tax rates) if these laws restricted an investor's business.
5. During the years of Perestroika, when private property was still permitted, the first non-state banks were created as cooperatives. However, they were considerably different from standard banks and were rather small private enterprises. These cooperatives were often controlled by only one or two people and lacked any meaningful capital. (Capital could be as low as 20,000 rubles or some old buildings and almost no cash.) There were also no real prudential regulations. As a result, concentration (whether through collapses, the revoking of licenses or mergers) was inevitable.
6. The delay was due to bureaucratic procedures (e.g., arrival of IMF missions, consultations, etc.) both on the side of the Armenian government and the IMF.
7. The numbers, though, from 1998 onward are quite high. This is mainly the result of a policy change in the second phase of privatization – i.e., attracting large institutional investors, rather than giving large enterprises to insiders. In addition, institutional investors were

sought which possessed name recognition, resources, distribution networks, etc. on a worldwide basis.

8. A recent IMF study (Mauro et al., 2000) found that as compared to the 1870–1913 period, financial markets have become more volatile, and globalization and contagion have become essential features of the system.

9. This was achieved at some cost, of course. In 1998, T-bills slightly increased the budget deficit, rather than contributing to its financing. However, this was essential for the development of the government debt market and the maintenance of stability in the market. Armenia can now boast one of the longest government bond instruments in the CIS.

9. Capital flows and capital account liberalization in Croatia

Boris Vujčić

9.1 INTRODUCTION

Capital flows can play a useful role in creating welfare. Typically, emerging economies seek foreign savings to solve the intertemporal savings–investment problem. At the same time, countries with a current account surplus seek opportunities to invest savings. To the extent that capital flows from surplus to deficit countries are well intermediated and, therefore, put to a productive use, they create welfare. Capital flows can, however, also be dangerous, as has been witnessed in many currency and banking crises. They can make countries more vulnerable to exogenous shocks. In particular, if serious macroeconomic imbalances exist in a recipient country and if the financial sector is weak in terms of risk management, prudential regulation and supervision, large capital flows can easily lead to a serious banking and currency crisis. A number of recent crises, such as those in Korea, Mexico, Sweden or Turkey (described, for example, in Ishii et al., 2002), have demonstrated the potential risks associated with capital flows.

In some instances, it appears to have been sufficient for a country to belong to a particular regional or investment grade group of countries to experience problems with capital flows, even if its economic fundamentals were sound. This phenomenon has been labeled 'contagion' and has been thoroughly analyzed in recent years. In many cases, the findings are interpreted in line with one's prior beliefs. One group of economists claims that financial markets will hit a country even if it conducts sound economic policies because of the notorious herd behavior of investors. (An interesting recent paper that tries to identify the costs of information gathering and contagion effects is Calvo and Mendoza, 2000.) Many proponents of this view come from countries that have been hit by crises in one way or another. Other economists claim that affected countries were hit precisely because their fundamentals were weak. Such a thesis is often heard in the market. A combination of these two views seems to be the most reasonable conclusion and is increasingly accepted. Emerging markets are often hit by a reversal of capital flows or a worsening in borrowing conditions, even if their policies are sound. Those hit hardest, however, are countries that have weaker fundamentals.

It seems that markets have recently begun to distinguish better between different countries. Although, given the costs of information gathering, it is very unlikely that herd behavior will ever be completely eliminated, the recent investor reactions to problems in Argentina and Turkey during 2001 were encouraging.

Because of the dangers associated with a high degree of capital volatility, a number of countries have at times resorted to various forms of capital controls. The effectiveness of such controls has also been the subject of debate. The most widely known controls, of the Chilean type, are praised by some (for example, Valdes-Prieto and Soto, 1998) and discounted by others (for example, Edwards, 2000). The consensus conclusion from the debate on capital controls seems to be that capital account liberalization should be carefully and gradually implemented. As is now accepted by the vast majority of economists, liberalization of short-term flows in emerging economies should not be undertaken before major economic reforms have been accomplished (for example, Wyplosz, 2001).

In this chapter, we briefly describe monetary policy in Croatia, before analyzing the development of the banking and financial system. We then describe capital flows into Croatia since the end of the war in 1995 and the role of capital controls and capital account liberalization. We conclude by asking what the future holds.

9.2 MONETARY POLICY

Croatia became independent in 1991. At that time an open war was being fought in the country. The war or semi-war situation lasted until 1995. The first few years of transition were, therefore, characterized not only by transition, but more significantly by a war-related slump and a high degree of macroeconomic instability. In the three years prior to the October 1993 stabilization program, GDP fell by some 40 per cent on a cumulated basis and inflation reached an annualized rate of 1200 per cent.[1] The stabilization program succeeded almost immediately in stabilizing prices (see Table 9.1) and the exchange rate, enabling the process of recovery to begin in 1994. Average GDP growth from 1994 until 2001 was 4.4 per cent per year, second only to Poland among the peer group of Central and Eastern European (CEE) countries.

Table 9.1 Croatia: inflation (%)

	Headline CPI*	Core-CPI
1993	1,149.3	
1994	-3.0	-3.7
1995	3.7	3.1
1996	3.4	2.8
1997	3.8	2.5
1998	5.4	5.7
1999	4.4	4.2
2000	7.4	4.6
2001	2.8	1.7

Note: * CPI = Consumer price index.
Source : Central Bureau of Statistics, Croatia.

The post-stabilization nature of monetary policy in Croatia can best be described as a quasi-currency board. Since the stabilization program was launched in October 1993, domestic money has been almost entirely created through foreign exchange interventions. Some 99 per cent of central bank assets are foreign assets, i.e., foreign currencies. As can be seen from Figure 9.1, international reserves of the central bank were always higher than the dollar value of the money supply and are currently almost twice as large. That puts the central bank in a comfortable position regarding control of the exchange rate and inflation.

Monetary policy was a kind of 'quasi'-currency board in that the exchange rate was never fixed, nor did the central bank ever pre-commit to defending any kind of exchange rate band. That was a deliberate choice in order to retain two-way risks in the market. The aim was to reduce the risk of excessive short-term capital inflows that can be associated with a one-way bet in which the exchange rate is perceived as moving in only one direction. In other words, a managed float was used by the central bank as an implicit capital control (although Figure 9.2 indicates that the float was tightly managed). An additional reason for avoiding a fixed exchange rate regime is the fact that exchange rate flexibility, even when limited, allows the exchange rate to reflect movements in economic fundamentals.

The main reason for this type of monetary policy lies in the high level of currency substitution in Croatia and its long history of macroeconomic instability. Croatia's financial market history since the mid-1960s was more

Figure 9.1 Croatia: international reserves and money supply (US$ bn)

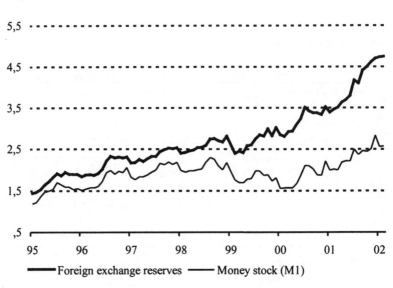

Source : Croatian National Bank.

Figure 9.2 Croatia: nominal exchange rate of the kuna
(against the euro)

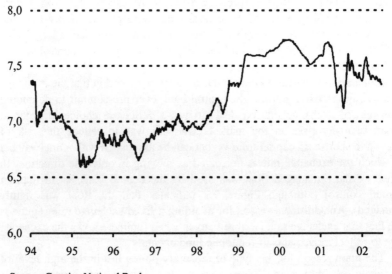

Source : Croatian National Bank.

that of a Latin American than of a communist economy. Periods of inflation were followed by hyperinflation, stabilization, and again inflation, particularly during the 1980s and early 1990s. Dual exchange rates existed and the exchange rate was notoriously unstable. Such a financial history, coupled with a much more liberal policy than in countries behind the 'iron curtain' – people were allowed to travel and work abroad as well as to have foreign exchange accounts open with domestic banks – has led to widespread currency substitution.

At the beginning of the 1990s, during the war, foreign currency deposits fled the domestic banking system. They were either hoarded at home or taken abroad. These withdrawals were due to war-related uncertainty, macroeconomic instability and banking sector weaknesses. After the rehabilitation of large state-owned banks and the end of the war in 1995, the level of currency substitution, as measured by the share of foreign currency deposits in broad money, began to increase again (Figure 9.3). This was due to the flow of foreign currency deposits back into the domestic banking system. By the end of 2001, foreign currency deposits represented almost three-quarters of M4. That makes Croatia the most euroized country among its peer group of CEE countries.

Figure 9.3 Croatia: composition of broad money (kuna bn)

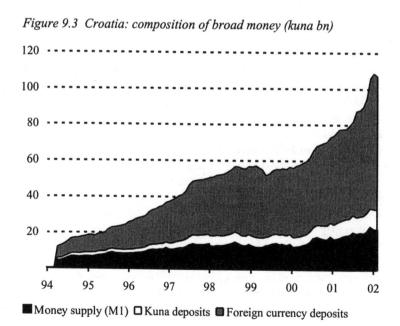

■Money supply (M1) ☐Kuna deposits ■Foreign currency deposits

Source: Croatian National Bank.

In such circumstances, a currency board-like monetary policy is an optimal strategy for a central bank. Incentives for conducting a prudent monetary policy in a country with such a history are very high, since the stability-oriented policy is rewarded not only by foreign direct investment, but also by the return inflow of the substantial capital kept in foreign currencies at home or abroad. On the other hand, any 'misbehavior' is met by an immediate reaction from both foreign investors and the domestic population, which has a built-in instinct to flee from a weak currency. The fear of a weak currency dates back to the former Yugoslavia's hyperinflationary episodes and occasional partial expropriations of foreign currency savings, with the last episode being the freezing of foreign currency savings by the Croatian government after independence. In such an unusual situation, capital flows can to a large extent be the consequence of residents (mostly households) moving foreign exchange deposits in and out of the domestic banking system.

9.3 THE BANKING SYSTEM

The development of the Croatian banking system to a large extent resembles the typical transition story. Although Croatia began the transition process with a two-tier banking system and many market-based practices, many banks were burdened with non-performing loans inherited from the pre-transition period when banks were, perversely, owned by their main clients (large enterprises). In the first few years of transition a number of new small and medium-sized banks emerged. These new, smaller banks initially did well, primarily due to the very high interest rate spreads created by a few large state-owned banks (see Figure 9.4). In 1996–97 the Croatian banking sector comprised some 60 banks and over 30 saving banks. At that time the banking market was clearly overbanked and foreign participation was low. Foreign banks shunned Croatia until the war ended (see Table 9.2). Once macroeconomic stability had been achieved, major efforts were undertaken in 1995 and 1996 to rehabilitate four troubled state-owned banks that represented nearly 40 per cent of the banking industry. These banks had borrowed heavily on the inter-bank market, pushing interest rates to levels as high as 30 per cent on overnight loans, in spite of the very stable macroeconomic environment, low inflation of 3–4 per cent and a stable exchange rate. The state separated out the bad loans, replaced management and recapitalized these banks. Soon afterwards the money market normalized and interest rates fell rapidly, creating favorable conditions for further monetary policy and payment system reforms.

Figure 9.4 Croatia: spread between deposit and lending rates (%)

Source: Croatian National Bank.

Table 9.2 Croatia: banking sector by ownership (share of total)

	1996	1997	1998	1999	2000	2001*
Number of banks	58	60	60	53	43	42
State-owned banks (share)	78	42	43	46	6	6
Private domestic banks (share)	21	54	50	15	10	10
Foreign-owned banks (share)	1	4	7	40	84	84

Note: * 2001 data is for March.
Source: Croatian National Bank.

The rapid decline in interest rates, however, exposed weaker small and medium-sized banks to market conditions to which many were unable to adapt. Those that got into trouble were banks that were undercapitalized, poorly managed, or both. Most of these banks were very aggressive prior to their failure, pushing deposit interest rates up and aggressively collecting deposits from both domestic residents and from Croatians living abroad. On top of the flow of deposits returning following the end of the war, macroeconomic stabilization and bank rehabilitation, these aggressive tactics contributed to a further increase in capital inflows between 1995 and 1997 (shown under the currency and deposits item in the capital account in Table 9.3).

Table 9.3 Croatia: financing of the current account deficit (US$ m)

	1995	1996	1997	1998	1999	2000
Current account	-1,442	-1,091	-2,325	-1,531	-1,390	-433
Capital account	1,096	1,995	2,652	1,469	2,143	927
Direct investment	109	486	347	835	1,445	1,086
Portfolio investment	5	628	577	15	574	722
Other investment	1,425	1,398	2,134	752	478	-320
Currency & deposits	694	784	424	192	85	-1,053
Reserve assets	-443	-533	-428	-152	-378	-582
Net errors	346	-904	-326	62	-752	-494

Source: Croatian National Bank.

Following the failure in 1998 of the fifth and sixth largest banks in the market, the process of banking sector consolidation began. In 1998–99 the process was characterized by what has been labeled a 'mini-banking crisis', during which 11 small and medium-sized banks went bankrupt. These failures exposed unsound practices in the banking industry, which were later found in a number of other banks. Wrongdoings ranged from poor credit risk assessment to large credits and exposure to insiders and connected persons. There were even a number of allegedly criminal activities for which some bank management has been prosecuted. Since 2000 consolidation in the banking industry took a different course as the number of banks decreased due to mergers and acquisitions. Overall, the number of banks declined from 60 in 1997, to 42 four years later. At the consolidated banking group basis there are even fewer banks – some 35 at the end of 2001.

The ownership structure has changed rapidly during this consolidation process. State ownership was previously predominant, but comprised only 6.1 per cent of total assets at the end of 2000, and only three banks remain majority state owned. In 1999, before the sale of three large rehabilitated banks to foreign strategic partners, the share of state owned banks was some 40 per cent. An even more dramatic change has taken place if we consider the split between domestic and foreign ownership. By 2000, although only 20 banks out of 44 were foreign owned, 84 per cent of the banking system, measured by assets, was already in the hands of foreign-owned banks (Table

9.2). The speed of change is well reflected in the fact that only 7 per cent of the banking system was foreign owned in 1998. In only two years the banking sector was almost completely sold to foreign banks.

The entry of foreign banks has helped the process of consolidation in the overbanked market by speeding up the process of mergers and acquisitions. Foreign bank entry has improved corporate management, enabled positive technology spillovers and allowed domestic banks cheaper access to sources of financing. That has quickly resulted in strong competition and increased efficiency in the banking sector, which is in turn reflected in a continued decline in the interest rate spread (Figure 9.4). In spite of the rapidly declining spread in the banking market, the profitability of the banking sector increased following the exit of weak banks from the banking market in 1998–99. That is a simple, though clear, demonstration of the increased efficiency of the banking sector.

9.4 CAPITAL FLOWS

Three distinct periods of capital flows can be identified. The first was a period of net capital outflows during the war, when the current account was in surplus, and lasted until 1995. Croatia became independent at the end of 1991, while the first current account was compiled in 1993, still during a semi-war situation. In the 1993–94 period, there was a capital account deficit recorded. Capital fled Croatia, or at least the banking system. As explained above, several of the largest banks had serious problems at that time. The macroeconomic situation prior to 1994 was completely unstable with the inflation rate reaching 1150 per cent per annum prior to the launch of the stabilization program (see Table 9.1).

The situation changed from 1995 onwards. The war ended in 1995 and the inflation rate was only 3.7 per cent, the exchange rate was stable and the rehabilitation process had started in four large state-owned problem banks. GDP growth was 6.8 per cent and the current account moved into deficit. This second phase, from 1995–98, was characterized by substantial capital inflows. Those inflows financed large current account deficits and at the same time enabled a rapid build-up of foreign currency reserves. It should be noted that in 1991, when it became an independent state, Croatia had zero foreign currency reserves as Belgrade had kept all the reserves of the former Yugoslavia. The 2000 reserve level of almost a quarter of GDP or five months of imports was therefore established from scratch.

There were two main sources of capital inflows in the second phase. One was the flow of foreign currency savings back to the domestic banking system. That, on average, amounted to some 4.5 per cent of GDP each year between 1995 and 1997. Both the outflow of these deposits during the war, and their reflow, were to a large extent a consequence of the high level of dollarization (actually 'deutschmarkization') of the economy. The other major source of capital inflows was new debt creation.

From the maturity side, loan inflows never presented a problem as the vast majority consisted of long-term borrowing. Although the central bank introduced in 1998 some capital restrictions on short-term inflows (explained below), the term structure of foreign debt never became a serious problem (Figure 9.5). Short-term debt was kept low and the debt repayment schedule for Croatia looks smooth. Total foreign debt, however, has grown rapidly since 1996–97 when the London and Paris club debts were included in the statistics. Total foreign debt reached 57 per cent of GDP in 2000 – a level at which policy makers must become careful not to create future servicing problems.

Figure 9.5 Croatia: term structure of foreign debt (% GDP)

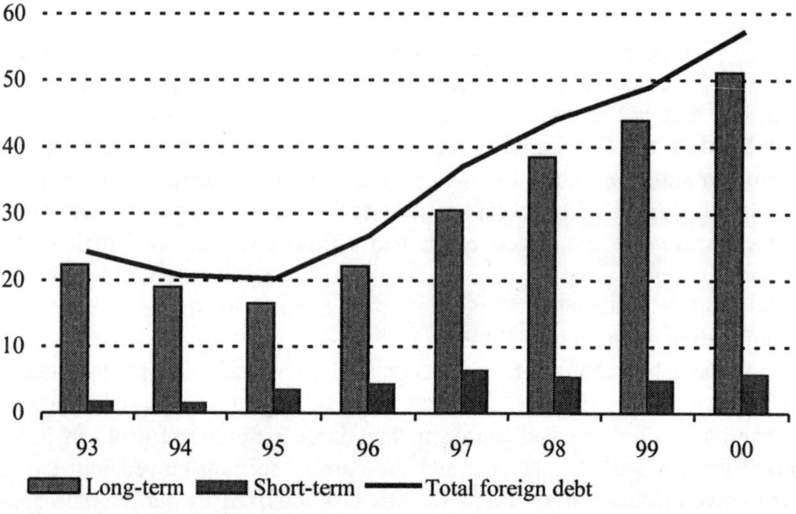

Long-term   Short-term   Total foreign debt

Source: Croatian National Bank.

The third phase in capital inflows is from 1998 onwards, when foreign direct investments (FDIs) became the main source of capital inflows. Although beginning relatively late, Croatia has rapidly joined the second group of CEE countries in terms of FDI inflows per capita (Figure 9.6). FDI inflows were mainly characterized by brownfields, i.e. (large) privatization projects, rather than greenfield investments. Much of the FDI inflows were state asset sales which were used to finance budget deficits (see Figure 9.7). That, however, is a dangerous strategy for the future. If fiscal adjustment does not occur, but state-owned assets have been sold, the government might find itself in a difficult financing situation. This is why there is currently an emphasis on fiscal adjustment. The consolidated government budget deficit was 6.8 per cent of GDP in 2000, 5.3 per cent in 2001, and is budgetted to be 4.25 per cent in 2002. If the budget deficit is not reduced, the risk of a sudden stop in FDI inflows might contribute to exchange rate instability. If, however, other forms of FDI inflows can substitute for state privatization projects, this risk will be reduced.

Figure 9.6 Foreign direct investment per capita
(US$ m, cumulative 1990

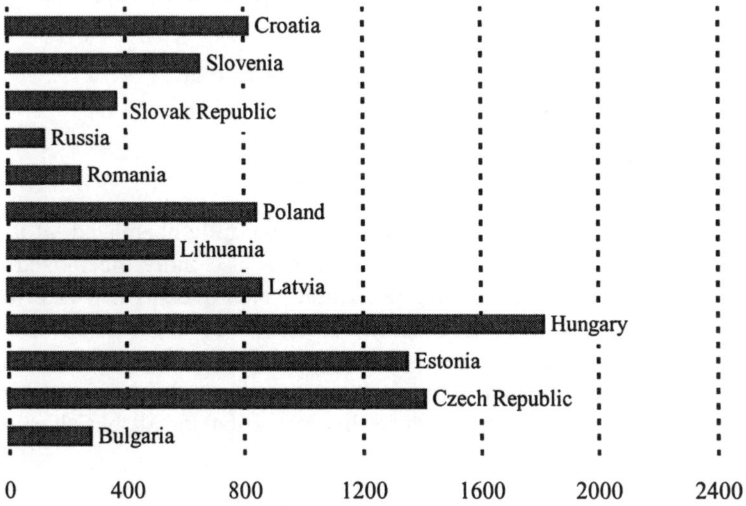

Source: Croatian National Bank.

9.5 CURRENT CAPITAL CONTROLS

In 1995 Croatia adopted Article VIII of the International Monetary Fund (IMF) Articles of Agreement, thereby fully liberalizing current account transactions. A number of restrictions remaining on capital movements have gradually been relaxed (see Box 9.1).

*Figure 9.7   Croatia: foreign direct investment and budget capital
revenue   (% GDP)*

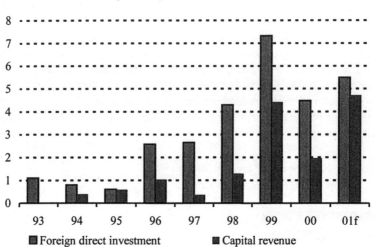

Note: f = forecast.

Source: Croatian National Bank.

Foreign direct investments by nonresidents are fully liberalized, as is the repatriation of profits. Credit operations are also fully liberalized for residents, while nonresidents face restrictions. Nonresidents can take loans from residents only through a company established or acquired through foreign direct investment (i.e., a company established through FDI in Croatia can grant a loan to its parent company in another country). There is currently a new law proposed that will reduce this restriction for all but short-term loans.

Non-residential accounts are subject to money-laundering reporting requirements (i.e., for all transactions in excess of 105,000 kunas, or around €15,000). Also, nonresidents cannot withdraw more than 15,000 kunas (around €2,000) per month from their accounts nor deposit more than US$20,000 without central bank approval. These limits will be substantially relaxed under the proposed new law, which is expected to become effective in 2003. Individual residents can hold (and freely use) money in their foreign currency accounts, but can only transfer money abroad for current account transactions.

Legal entities (companies) face a surrender requirement for foreign currency within 150 days (with a possibility of a 60 day extension). The surrender requirement will be completely removed under the proposed new regulation. Legal entities can hold accounts abroad for the purpose of doing business (usually investment activities or construction business) or for hedging purposes, while individual persons cannot hold accounts abroad.

Box 9.1 Croatia: Chronology of Major Reforms

1991 July   Securities trading begins on the Zagreb Stock Exchange.

1992 Jan.   Yugoslav dinar replaced by the provisional currency, the Croatian dinar (HRD), at a ratio of 1:1. The dinar is the sole legal tender and is pegged to the German mark.

    Apr.   Managed floating exchange rate regime, based on the domestic–foreign inflation differential over the past month and the expected differential in the current month.

    June   Exchange rate allowed to fluctuate on a daily basis.

    Dec.   The Republic of Croatia accepts IMF Article XIV obligations.

1993 Oct.   Under a new foreign exchange law:
- the exchange rate is floated;
- payments for current transactions abroad are liberalized; and
- the obligation of compulsory surrender of foreign exchange arising from goods and services export is cancelled.

1994 May   The kuna is introduced, replacing the Croatian dinar at a ratio of HRD 1,000.00 to HRK 1.00.

1995 May   The Republic of Croatia accepts the IMF Article VIII obligations.

2001 Apr.   Amendments to the foreign exchange law liberalize foreign exchange operations and allow:
- foreign exchange loans to domestic legal entities for all payments abroad and for deposit into foreign exchange accounts;
- domestic legal entities to purchase foreign exchange and deposit it in foreign exchange accounts without having to state any payment purpose; and
- foreign currency trades without having to state any payment purpose.

Regarding portfolio investments, restrictions exist for both residents and nonresidents. Portfolio investments abroad are not allowed except for financial institutions (investment funds, pension funds, banks, etc.) which are able to invest abroad subject to prudential regulations. Substantial liberalization is now proposed by the new law, whereby investment abroad will only be subject to restrictions regarding the asset rating of the investment. Nonresidents will be allowed to freely invest in Croatia, except for in short-term instruments.

Nonresidents can invest in real estate, subject to reciprocity and to approval by the Ministry for Foreign Affairs. In reality, real estate investment for nonresidents is quite liberal. Under the proposed new law, residents will be allowed to invest in real estate abroad subject to reciprocity and to approval by the Ministry of Finance.

New regulations (and in particular a new law on foreign exchange) will be adopted this year. The changes will mark a further substantial liberalization, in accordance with the Stabilization and Association Agreement (SAA) signed last year with the European Union. When the SAA Treaty comes into force, Croatia will further liberalize most of the remaining restrictions on capital movements, except for those concerning short-term capital flows. Restrictions on short-term capital inflows will remain in place for at least four years after the ratification of the SAA Treaty.

In reviewing recent experiences, two episodes deserve a closer look. One is the introduction of Chilean-type capital controls in 1998. The other is the liberalization of the foreign exchange market in 2001 and its consequences.

Croatia has received relatively little short-term foreign capital. However, in late 1997 and at the beginning of 1998, at the peak of the boom phase when economic activity, credit expansion and the current account deficit were high, short-term capital inflows emerged. At that time interest rates were still relatively high and only one large investment bank had over US$200 million of kuna-denominated assets (which was a significant amount given the narrow and shallow Croatian market). Domestic banks were increasingly borrowing abroad short term and converting those inflows into kunas in order to finance the lending boom.

In order to curtail those surging short-term inflows, a set of Chilean-type capital controls were introduced at the beginning of April 1998:

- for all financial credits which were accepted for conversion into domestic currency, banks were required to deposit with the central bank (in domestic currency) 30 per cent of the amount for short-term credits (up to one year) and 5 per cent for longer-term credits;
- when issuing guarantees on the credits for conversion into kunas, banks were required to deposit (in domestic currency) 10 per cent of the amount of guarantee; and
- 15 per cent of the foreign exchange deposits of foreign banks were to be deposited (again in domestic currency) in a separate account with the central bank.

These capital controls worked well initially and the inflow of short-term capital declined significantly. By autumn of 1998, however, the international financial crisis had significantly reduced the problem. Foreign investors suddenly lost their appetite for emerging markets and it became quite difficult for both domestic banks and the corporate sector to raise any kind of capital abroad. Due to the changed circumstances, all capital controls for financial credits or deposits with a maturity exceeding one year were removed by the Croatian National Bank (CNB) in October 1998.

It is therefore possible to conclude that capital controls of the type introduced in Croatia worked well initially, but that their lifetime (particularly the effective one, prior to the 1998 crisis) was too short to allow for any firmer conclusion. The presumption in most of the literature on capital controls is that such controls often work well initially, but can lose effectiveness over time as economic agents find ways to avoid them. The Croatian experience confirms the first part of that hypothesis, but the controls were not in place for sufficiently long to test the second part.

The second interesting episode concerns an important liberalization move. In summer 2001 the corporate sector was allowed to fully participate in the foreign exchange market for the first time. Prior to that, companies were only allowed to buy foreign currency if that was justified by their import needs. In other words, they could buy foreign exchange only in order to pay for imports or to make loan payments which became due, but not in order to hold foreign currency in their accounts regardless of foreign trade or financing needs. That restriction was removed in late spring 2001, allowing corporates free access to the foreign exchange market. Prior to that, the surrender requirement, obliging companies to repatriate foreign currency receipts was lengthened from 90 days to 150 days, with the possibility of a further 60-day extension. The effect of the substantial extension of the surrender requirement was negligible and the proposed new law now incorporates the complete removal of the surrender requirement. This should take place in 2003.

The obvious benefits of the liberalized participation of the corporate sector in the foreign exchange market are twofold. First, companies are allowed to freely decide on the currency composition of their portfolio holdings. That enables them to better manage risk. Second, liberalization deepens and broadens the relatively shallow and narrow foreign exchange market.

The downside is that this liberalization caused an unusual depreciation in the foreign exchange market. As can be seen in Figure 9.2, in August 2000 the exchange rate rapidly depreciated by 8 per cent. Given the remarkable stability of the nominal exchange rate in Croatia from late 1993, when the exchange rate fluctuated in a relatively narrow (*ex post*) band of ±6.5 per cent, such an abrupt depreciation created nervousness in the market and triggered speculation. Figure 9.8 illustrates the source of the depreciation pressure in the market. After the April decision to liberalize capital controls, companies did not react immediately because they expected the usual seasonal summer appreciation of the kuna.[2]

Figure 9.8 Croatia: foreign exchange deposits of the corporate sector (€ m)

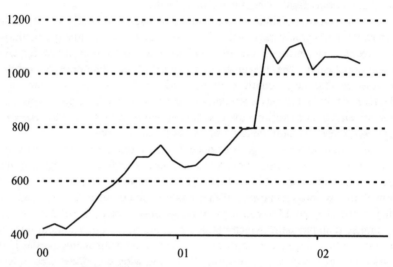

Source : Croatian National Bank.

In August, however, when foreign currency was cheap and kuna liquidity abundant, expectations changed and were further fueled by some rumors about a possible kuna depreciation. A few large companies decided to buy significant sums of foreign currency. Figure 9.8 shows how abruptly the corporate sector increased their foreign currency deposits within a single month. In a small market in which the average daily turnover is approximately €30 million, news that a couple of companies are buying €200 million or more immediately drives up the price of foreign currency. Of course, that was not a very smart move by the companies, as they effectively bid up the price at which they themselves in the end purchased. Obviously, at that time the overall situation was not clear to many companies, partly because they were unaccustomed to free participation in the foreign exchange market. In addition, some banks tried to take advantage of the situation and fueled the corporate sector demand by rumoring that companies should buy foreign exchange as soon as possible as the domestic currency was likely to depreciate further.

In order to stop the nervousness, the central bank had to intervene heavily. Thanks to a comfortably high level of foreign exchange reserves (Figure 9.1) it was possible to calm the situation purely through market intervention. However, the central bank was constrained in doing so because of the very tight floor on the foreign exchange reserves set by the IMF within the stand-by arrangement. Ironically, the floor had been substantially raised less than one month before the depreciation pressures started. In order to stop the speculation and also observe the floor, the central bank resorted to an unorthodox measure. To sterilize local currency liquidity, the CNB asked banks to hold 20 per cent of their reserve requirement on foreign currency deposits in local currency.[3] This was later increased to 25 per cent. By increasing the demand for local currency, this measure propped up the exchange rate, and broke the speculative pressures.[4]

Another important point to make is that the holding of local currency reserves on foreign exchange deposits is particularly useful as an automatic stabilizer in a highly euroized economy. This is due to the very high foreign exchange deposit base. When the domestic currency depreciates, banks are required to deposit more of the domestic currency as a reserve requirement. In contrast, when the currency appreciates, more domestic currency is freed from the reserve requirement. That helps to reduce currency fluctuations, which is particularly important in a situation when exchange rate movements are the most important monetary policy transmission channel. These effects would, of course, be weaker in countries with lower levels of euroization.

9.6   WHAT DOES THE FUTURE HOLD FOR CROATIA?

Until now, capital flows in Croatia have been significant but well managed. Their structure is quite favorable, although atypical due to the high level of euroization. Overall, the flows have not caused any serious macroeconomic problems or imbalances which might imperil the future of the country.

The future will clearly bring further and more rapid integration into international financial markets. That process will be boosted by EU convergence, which has so far been missing from the Croatian transition story. Further integration is likely to attract more of both FDI inflows ('good cholesterol') and short-term capital inflows ('bad cholesterol'). Increased capital flows in principle reflect the fact that the country has been doing well and, in that sense, should be positively regarded. However, they are a mixed blessing to the extent that it might become more difficult to control them, and consequently also the exchange rate and/or interest rates. That increases risks in the foreign exchange market and consequently, overall economic risks.

With an increasing degree of integration into the international capital market, and the accompanying increase in risks, it might be desirable to shorten the period before the adoption of the euro. An early adoption of the euro would eliminate the problem of exchange rate control and diminish the interest rate control problem. It would also bring down interest rates and diminish the risks associated with sudden reversals in capital flows. Exchange rate risk would, of course, remain but on a macroeconomic level – in the balance of payments. That would, then, require more flexibility in other economic variables, as discussed in the optimum currency area literature.

If the early adoption of the euro remains impossible in the near future, Croatia will have to be careful in liberalizing the remaining capital flow restrictions. Under the new foreign exchange law proposed, the most important remaining restriction will be on short-term capital inflows. Capital controls, or the possibility of introducing them as a monetary policy tool in an open and heavily euroized country, should be retained for some time to come.

It is true that due to a much healthier banking system and better regulation and supervision, most of the worries usually associated with the capital flows are now less present in Croatia than was the case before the 1998–99 mini-banking crisis. In 1998, prior to the introduction of Chilean-type capital controls, a significant amount of capital inflows were converted into kunas and poorly intermediated by a number of unsound banks. In that sense, a typical danger that a surge in short-term capital inflows (which often shows up as an expansion in short-maturity bank deposits) will be poorly managed is now substantially lessened.[5]

However, a successful EU candidate country will become an increasingly attractive target of significant capital inflows, which can cause a rapid appreciation of the real exchange rate or, alternatively, an increase in inflation. Even if the sharp real appreciation from a sudden large capital inflow is subsequently reversed, it might still have a strong effect on exports due to a hysteresis effect. In addition, as long as these inflows are of a short-term nature, they also present a danger of a sudden reversal and can easily trigger a currency confidence crisis in a highly euroized environment. The possible adverse impact of capital flows on monetary policy is reinforced by the fact that, due to the high level of euroization, the country is unable to develop a set of full-blown indirect monetary policy instruments.

Of course, capital controls are not a long-term solution, particularly because they tend to lose their effectiveness as economic agents find ways to avoid them.[6] Nevertheless, although not a panacea, capital controls could be a useful additional instrument for restricting short-term capital flows, therefore lowering the pressure on the exchange rate or on prices and the probability of a sudden reversal in capital flows.[7] If not misused, capital controls can, at times, have a useful role to play in a small, open and heavily euroized country in which capital flows can be particularly volatile and in which indirect monetary policy instruments are insufficiently developed. Therefore, their complete removal can best wait until the accession process is completed.

NOTES

1. One should, however, be careful in interpreting official GDP data at that time due to methodological problems, as well as difficulties with statistical coverage during the period when approximately one-third of the territory was effectively occupied (for more on this issue, see Vujčić and Lang, 2001).
2. Which always happens due to the importance of the tourism sector in the economy coupled with underdevelopment of the foreign exchange market.
3. Previously, the reserve requirement on foreign currency deposits was held solely in foreign currency, while reserve requirements on local currency deposits were held in local currency.
4. A negative aspect of such a requirement is that it creates a mismatch in banks' balance sheets, but that has not proved to be an important issue. Banks are not allowed to have net foreign currency positions in excess of 20 per cent of their liable capital.
5. Nevertheless, there are examples of banks that have relatively rapidly accumulated a substantial level of bad debts even after bank recapitalization and full or partial privatization have been accomplished.
6. That is, however, primarily a problem with restrictions on outflows.
7. Although it may be difficult to design capital controls to target specifically short-term inflows. In addition, it is difficult to design policies that influence only outflows or only inflows. In Yugoslavia and Chile at the beginning of the 1990s, for example, the liberalization of outflows – which might theoretically help counteract heavy capital inflows – in fact induced heavier inflows due to the credibility effect *vis-à-vis* foreign investors. It is also difficult to distinguish with certainty whether certain flows are short or long term. For a more detailed discussion, see IMF (1995).

10. The liberalization of the capital account in Hungary: experiences and lessons

Roger Nord[1]

10.1 INTRODUCTION

The political transition in Central and Eastern Europe in 1989–90 was accompanied by far-reaching economic reforms towards a market economy. Three central European countries, Hungary, Poland and the Czechoslovak Federation (which separated into the Czech Republic and the Slovak Republic in 1993), embarked on the process of economic liberalization at a particularly high speed. The main pillars of the transformation were the privatization of most of the economy, price deregulation, trade and financial sector liberalization and the introduction of marked-based instruments of macroeconomic management. By 1995 the share of the private sector in the economy ranged from 75 per cent in Poland to 80 per cent in Hungary and the Czech Republic (EBRD, 2001a).

Despite the similarities, there were significant differences in approach to the transition process, which stemmed as much from differing initial conditions as from specific political constraints and preferences. Hungary and Poland had introduced some market-oriented reforms of the economy well before the political transition in 1989. Czechoslovakia, on the other hand, continued to rely heavily on central planning until the very end of the 1980s. Moreover, both Hungary and Poland entered the 1990s with a significant stock of external, foreign exchange-denominated debt, representing an important constraint on economic policy.

This chapter will focus on the process of capital account liberalization in Hungary. In many ways, the opening of the capital accounts in Central Europe was an important step in reintegrating the countries with Western Europe and the rest of world. Trade liberalization – including the rapid re-orientation of trade from the former ruble zone to the European Union (EU) –

and attracting much-needed foreign capital for investment depended crucially on the freeing of capital flows. But in still-fragile economies, with significant macroeconomic imbalances, capital account liberalization also posed risks, both of sudden capital outflows should there be a large shock to domestic or foreign confidence, as well as of surges of capital inflows putting strain on the policy framework. Hungary attempted to address these risks by following a gradual liberalization strategy that achieved a fully free capital account – after more than a decade of transition – in June 2001. Its success in managing this process may provide useful lessons for other countries embarking on this road.

10.2 THE HISTORY OF CAPITAL ACCOUNT LIBERALIZATION IN HUNGARY

The liberalization of the capital account in Hungary took place around three key events: (i) the political transition in 1989, (ii) the accession to the Organisation of Economic Co-operation and Development (OECD) in 1996 and (iii) the adoption of a new, wide-band exchange rate regime in 2001 (for a full chronology of the liberalization, see Box 10.1).

Following the political transition in 1989, the first democratically elected government in 1990 adopted a medium-term program aimed at establishing a modern market economy. Many new laws were put in place aimed at opening up the economy to competition, both domestically and from abroad.[2] Trade liberalization was an early priority, marked by the introduction of a unified trade system on 1 January 1991 and the regional trade agreements with the EU (the Europe Agreement of 1991).[3] While the emphasis was on the current account, especially merchandise trade, Hungary chose to abolish most restrictions related to inward foreign direct investment (FDI) and thereby attract foreign capital.

The 1990–95 period was marked by substantial progress in current account liberalization, which was completed when Hungary adopted the obligations of Article VIII of the IMF's Articles of Agreement, effective from 1 January 1996. Capital account restrictions were relaxed only gradually, primarily by a more liberal implementation of existing approval processes rather than by changing the underlying laws.

The second broad phase of capital account liberalization occurred in the context of Hungary's membership application to the OECD. Complete freedom of capital account transactions was not a condition of membership and Hungary lodged reservations regarding the liberalization of a large number of operations (other than foreign direct investment) when it joined in May 1996. Nevertheless, membership in the OECD was preceded by significant further changes in the Foreign Exchange Act, including permitting nonresidents to purchase most Hungarian securities with maturities longer than one year and eliminating the requirement to seek prior approval for the sale of significant equity stakes in Hungarian banks.

Between 1996 and 2001, controls on capital account transactions were further loosened, both on the inflow and the outflow sides. The final push occurred in June 2001, when Hungary eliminated nearly all remaining capital controls. On the outflow side, key steps were the lifting of the obligation to repatriate all foreign exchange; abolishing restrictions on opening bank accounts abroad; and eliminating prior approval and notification requirements on outward FDI. On the inflow side, all restrictions on both residents and nonresidents concerning short-term portfolio investments were lifted. This meant the elimination of the two principal controls on capital inflows that remained in effect: the prohibition on the purchase by nonresidents of domestic securities with an original maturity of less than one year, and the barring of any borrowing by nonresidents in Hungarian forint in the domestic market.

Figure 10.1, based on the methodology developed in Tamarisa (1999), illustrates the gradual liberalization of Hungary's capital account during the 1990s. However, it is based on a binary choice for each type of transaction, awarding either one (a control exists) or zero (no control exists) and hence does not capture gradual changes in the intensity of controls or their implementation, as is likely to have occurred in the first half of the 1990s.

The gradual liberalization of the capital account was probably motivated as much by political considerations as by economic rationale. The political transition led to increased freedom to travel abroad and a radical re-orientation of foreign trade. Together with a rapid expansion of the private sector, it required a liberalization of external payments, including for some capital transactions. The importance of political commitments such as membership in the OECD and the overriding objective of joining the EU also played an important role. Meanwhile, economic rationale also supported encouraging the inflow of foreign capital to supplement domestic savings and provide additional resources for investment and growth. The decision to maintain controls on short-term capital, however, is likely to have had a different objective: not to discourage capital inflows, but to support Hungary's choice of a tightly managed exchange rate regime.

In evaluating these choices, it is useful to ask two separate questions. First, did the maintenance of capital controls throughout the first decade of transition harm the Hungarian economy by depriving it of needed foreign capital? Second, if it did not, did the short-term controls, in particular, in fact help Hungary, for instance by staving off undesirable, speculative capital flows? The remainder of this chapter will seek to answer those two rather different questions.

Box 10.1   Hungary: Chronology of Major Reforms

1991 Jan.	Joint ventures no longer subject to licensing and may be established in duty-free zones. Foreign participation up to 100 per cent permitted without prior approval.
1995 Apr.	Resident enterprises allowed to open foreign exchange accounts for international trade transactions.
1996 Jan.	Hungary accepts IMF Article VIII obligations.
	Foreigners allowed to buy most Hungarian securities with maturities longer than one year without prior approval.
	Outward equity investment is permitted provided that the equity share exceeds 10 per cent.
1996 Mar.	Foreign investors permitted to purchase stakes exceeding 10 per cent of the equity of a domestic bank.
1996 July	Residents permitted to invest (through resident brokerage firms) in foreign government debt securities with a maturity exceeding one year, and in securities with a maturity exceeding one year issued by OECD-based enterprises with the highest credit rating.
	The acquisition by nonresidents of domestic securities is permitted provided the instrument has an original maturity of one year or more.
	Share purchase in the parent enterprise by resident employees of subsidiaries of foreign enterprises liberalized.
1997 Jan.	Investment by residents in securities with a maturity exceeding one year issued by non-resident enterprises with investment grade rating further liberalized.
	Futures and options transactions in two foreign currencies by domestic banks liberalized.
	Foreign participation in banks fully liberalized.
	Short-term lending to nonresidents by banks limited to 50 per cent of total foreign exchange liabilities (previously 50 per cent of foreign exchange liabilities from nonresidents).
1998 Jan.	Legal framework for the establishment of branches of non resident companies introduced.
	Investment by residents in foreign real estate liberalized.

	Investment by residents in securities with a maturity exceeding one year issued by nonresident enterprises permitted irrespective of their credit rating.
	Investment by nonresidents in the futures index of the Budapest Stock Exchange and foreign currency-denominated outright forward, options and futures transactions of nonresidents with resident financial institutions permitted.
	Financial credits from nonresidents to residents with a maturity exceeding one year permitted without prior approval.
	Granting of non-restricted sureties, guaranties and financial back-up facilities by residents to nonresidents liberalized.
	Operation by residents of deposit accounts with nonresident financial institutions liberalized.
1999 Jan.	Commercial bank liabilities to nonresidents with a maturity of less than one year subject to reserve requirements (initially zero). Obligatory reserves held against liabilities to nonresidents remunerated at the same rate as reserves held against liabilities to residents.
2000 Jan.	Offshore investment by residents in collective investment securities issued by nonresident investment funds liberalized.
	Lending by residents to nonresidents of OECD countries with a maturity exceeding one year fully liberalized.
	Operation by residents of deposit accounts with nonresident financial institutions further liberalized.
2001 Jan.	Remaining foreign exchange restrictions eliminated.

10.3 DID THE EXISTENCE OF CAPITAL CONTROLS HURT HUNGARY?

Economic theory generally regards capital account liberalization as beneficial. Welfare economics would see unambiguous benefits in the flow of capital to those uses where its marginal product is highest, regardless of international borders. Capital mobility also allows for portfolio diversification, risk sharing and the inter-temporal smoothing of consumption. And, finally, there are arguments that the cost of enforcing capital controls is high, and possibly rising because of the increasing sophistication of international financial markets.

Figure 10.1   Hungary: capital controls, 1991–2001
(fully restricted = 1, fully liberalized = 0)

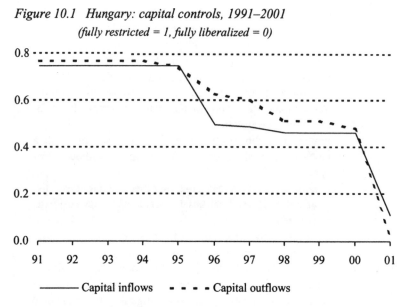

Source : Author's calculations.

But theory also suggests that there are exceptions, where 'second-best' solutions aimed at compensating for other, pre-existing distortions, may dominate.[4] Information asymmetries may lead to adverse selection, moral hazard and herding behavior in international financial markets, causing sub-optimal results in the cross-border allocation of capital. Domestic distortions can have a similarly detrimental effect, for example the presence of government subsidies to certain sectors or guarantees to the banking system.

In Hungary's case, starting from a position with significant restrictions on both current and capital transactions, the direction of change was always clear: towards increased liberalization. But the pace, and the sequence of reform was a gradual one. In the absence of a full counterfactual, it is impossible to say what would have happened had Hungary opened up its capital account at a more rapid pace. But there are certainly indications that its more cautious approach did not discourage foreign investors. Realizing the need to attract foreign investment – both as providers of capital and of know-how – Hungary's first focus was on opening up to foreign direct investment. This was true not only for Hungary: in Poland and the Czech Republic as well, the first decade of transition was marked by very large inflows of FDI (Figure 10.2). In the first half of the 1990s, Hungary pursued this strategy most aggressively of all, culminating in 1995 when FDI inflows reached some 10 per cent of GDP.

Figure 10.2 Net foreign direct investment (% GDP)

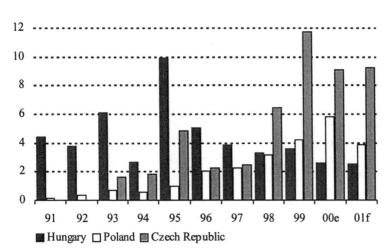

Note: e = estimate, f = forecast.
Source: European Bank for Reconstruction and Development.

The second phase consisted in attracting other long-term capital, notably portfolio capital. Table 10.1 shows how from 1998, Hungary benefitted from substantial net portfolio inflows as non-resident investors felt increasingly comfortable holding Hungarian public debt. The appetite for Hungarian debt was undoubtedly related to the success of the stabilization program implemented in 1994–95, which was reflected in a steady improvement in Hungary's sovereign ratings, which improved from BB+/Ba1 (non-investment grade) in the early 1990s to investment grade by the mid- and late 1990s (Table 10.2).[5] The spreads on Hungary's foreign borrowing fell correspondingly, from over 250 basis points in early 1995 to barely above 50 basis points by mid-1997 (Figure 10.3).

As theory would predict, the controls did succeed in driving a wedge between domestic and foreign interest rates. Certainly in the first half of the 1990s, real interest rates remained significantly above those in Germany, for example – and also above those in the Czech Republic, which may be a more valid comparison (Figure 10.4). But, as addressed in more detail below, in the second half of the 1990s, Hungary would have appeared to fare significantly better.

Overall, Hungary succeeded in attracting a large volume of foreign capital during the 1990s. By the end of the decade, the stock of foreign direct investment had reached 42 per cent of GDP.[6] Relative to the size of the economy, these inflows exceeded those to other Central European countries,

Table 10.1 Hungary: net capital flows (€ m)

	1990	1995	1996	1997	1998	1999	2000	2001
Investment:								
Direct	244	3,474	1,815	1,922	1,815	1,873	1,783	2,715
Abroad		-33	2	-389	-428	-239	-603	-368
Inward	244	3,474	1,815	1,922	1,815	1,873	1,783	2,715
Portfolio			-320	-919	1,786	1,851	-429	1,735
Equity			274	867	453	1,141	301	88
Bonds and notes			-544	-1,708	1,229	770	126	1,186
Money market			-63	-86	-21	-16	4	320
Derivatives			13	-815	124	-45	69	142
Other			-2,231	-13	-590	956	1,656	-3,341
GDP in euro[a]	26.0	34.5	36.1	40.5	41.9	45.1	50.3	50.4
Memorandum:								
Total inflows (%GDP)[b]	0.9	10.0	-2.0	1.5	6.2	9.9	4.8	1.5

Notes:
a: Preliminary estimate for 2001, billions of euro.
b: Between 1990 and 1995, only the proportion of FDI to GDP is available.
Source: National Bank of Hungary.

Table 10.2 Hungary: portfolio investment risk*

	1995	1996	1997	1998	1999	2000	2001
A. Foreign currency bonds							
Standard's & Poor's	BB+	BB+	BBB-	BBB	BBB	A	A
Moody's	Ba1	Baa3	Baa3	Baa2	Baa1	A3	A3
FitchIBCA		BBB-	BBB	BBB	BBB+	A	A
B. Local currency bonds							
Standard's & Poor's		A	A	A	A	A+	A+
Moody's				A1	A1	A1	A1
FitchIBCA		BBB+	A	A	A	A+	A+

Note:* End-year ratings on long-term sovereign bonds.
Source: National Bank of Hungary.

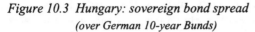

Figure 10.3 Hungary: sovereign bond spread
(over German 10-year Bunds)

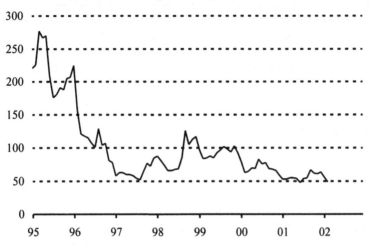

Source : National Bank of Hungary.

Figure 10.4 Real long-term interest rates (%)

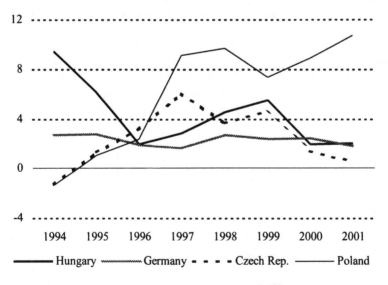

Sources : Darvas and Szapáry (2000) and additional calculations by Darvas.

including those with fewer controls such as the Czech Republic. The existence of capital controls, particularly on the short end, would not appear to have discouraged foreign investment. In fact, they may have enhanced Hungary's attractiveness for foreign investors by providing macroeconomic stability – together with other factors, such as market-oriented reforms of the legal and regulatory framework in the first half of the 1990s. And by the late 1990s, the conviction that Hungary would be among the first to join the EU in its next round of enlargement encouraged significant portfolio inflows as foreign investors began placing 'convergence plays', which put downward pressure on interest rates even before the capital account was completely opened in mid-2001.

10.4 DID THE SHORT-TERM CONTROLS HELP?

If the existence of capital controls does not appear to have hurt, a more interesting question in some ways is whether the maintenance of controls on short-term capital in fact helped. Particularly in the wake of the emerging market crises of the second half of the 1990s, there has been a wave of research into the value of using capital controls as a defense against the vagaries of fickle short-term capital flows, building in some ways on the existing literature on dealing with surges in capital inflows, and the well-known Chilean unremunerated reserve requirement as one instrument to curb short-term inflows.[7]

A short detour would be useful at this point, to place the Hungarian capital controls in context. A key moment in the early transition experience in Hungary was the economic crisis of 1993–94, which had its roots in the output collapse in the early 1990s and the breakdown of the traditional CMEA trade flows.[8] A dramatic widening of the current account deficit to 11 per cent of GDP in 1993, driven by a large government deficit and soft budget constraints in the public enterprise sector, occurred at a point where Hungary's gross external debt was already a substantial 57 per cent of GDP – high for a transition economy. The immediate objective of the stabilization program launched in early 1995 was to reduce the external deficit to a manageable size and avert a major external crisis through the pursuit of sound macroeconomic policies. But the program also aimed at reigniting the stalled economic reform process by accelerating structural reforms, including privatization, further liberalizing trade (and certain parts of the capital account) and pushing ahead with the consolidation and clean-up of the financial sector. An important element of the macroeconomic package was the introduction of a crawling band exchange rate regime.[9] The exchange rate served as a nominal anchor, but its built-in depreciation was meant to ensure the competitiveness of Hungarian exports. Cottarelli et al. (1998) point to the heterodox aspect of monetary policy: despite the narrow exchange rate band, Hungary succeeded in maintaining some measure of monetary policy independence as sterilized intervention partially shielded domestic interest rates from external pressures.

Despite severe pressures on the balance of payments, the government did not intensify capital controls during the crisis, possibly out of a concern to avoid frightening foreign investors.[10] But the continued existence of short-term capital controls, together with the decisive macro- and microeconomic policy programs, did support its strategy. While long-term capital became increasingly abundant – and posed growing monetary policy problems later in the 1990s – the maintenance of short-term controls gave the National Bank of Hungary (NBH) some room for maneuver and protection from volatile capital movements. To do so, the NBH used two main controls: nonresidents could not purchase government debt with an original maturity below one year, nor could domestic financial institutions lend in forint, i.e., in domestic currency, to nonresidents. The first of these restrictions may not have been very binding, particularly as secondary markets for longer-term government securities became more liquid and nonresidents were permitted to purchase these securities, even if the remaining maturity was less than one year.[11] The second restriction, however, was much more binding, as it limited the extent to which nonresidents could short-sell the currency.

The protection provided by the controls became particularly evident in 1998, during the Russian crisis.[12] Nonresident investors liquidated a significant share of their holdings of Hungarian bonds, leading to a drop in the NBH's gross foreign reserves of about US$1 billion, and the exchange rate fell from the upper to the lower edge of the band (i.e., by 4.5 per cent). The intervention by the NBH was accompanied by an increase in its policy interest rates, resulting in a corresponding rise in short-term market rates (and putting a severe squeeze on resident brokerages, which were heavily leveraged and hence very exposed to an exchange rate depreciation). But the balance of payments risk for Hungary from financial contagion was limited to the unwinding of long positions held by nonresidents, which were amply covered by official reserves. The capital controls effectively limited the NBH's downside risk by precluding nonresident investors from taking bets by borrowing forint and going short.[13]

While the existing controls would have appeared to have helped Hungary weather some of the storm caused by cross-border financial contagion, few if any conclusions are warranted regarding the use of short-term controls in a crisis situation. Imposing controls *de novo*, rather than maintaining existing controls for a slightly longer period of time, is likely to be regarded quite differently by investors, foreign as well as domestic. Also, in a crisis situation, a country typically faces strong capital outflows, which are inherently more difficult to curb except by resorting to extremely blunt measures.[14]

10.4 THE END OF INTERMEDIATE EXCHANGE RATE REGIMES?

Much has been written about the difficulty of maintaining soft pegs and other intermediate exchange rate regimes in a world of globalized capital flows, which seems to be pushing countries inexorably towards 'corner solutions'.[15] Is this the reason why Hungary finally abandoned its controls?

Full liberalization of the capital account took place only in June 2001, in the context of the widening of the exchange rate band and the introduction of inflation targeting. Two main factors motivated the Hungarian authorities: first, the need to allow domestic economic agents to engage in derivative transactions consistent with the higher exchange rate risk. But second, and no less important, was the desire to mark another clear step in the direction of harmonizing its legislation and policy framework with that of the EU.

Abandoning capital controls would hence seem to have been the result primarily of domestic rather than external considerations, in line with text-book advice on an optimal exit policy.[16] It is also consistent with the suggestion by Berger et al. (2001), who question whether the trend towards capital account liberalization in recent years is less the result of exogenous forces and rather the consequence of conscious domestic policy choices. Maybe capital account liberalization is not so much imposed by the globalization of international capital markets pushing countries towards corner solutions, as the rational choice resulting from a separately motivated decision to move away from intermediate exchange rate regimes? This argument is attractive in the case of Hungary, where the credibility of the 1995 stabilization program depended heavily on the success of the crawling-peg regime in delivering disinflation while maintaining export competitiveness. As the role of the crawling peg declined – because Hungary's credibility had been established and/or was increasingly determined by other factors – its benefits began to be outweighed by its costs, and the capital controls lost much of their *raison d'être*.[17]

10.6 CONCLUSIONS

Hungary's successful transition to a market economy has placed it on the cusp of EU accession. Looking back, the productive use of foreign capital – in a context of sound domestic macroeconomic policies and far-reaching structural reforms – has been a key element in this success. The early opening to inward foreign direct investment provided two scarce resources: capital and know-how. The liberalization of other types of capital flows has been more gradual, but this did not discourage foreign investors and Hungary remained a prime recipient of capital inflows for most of the decade of the 1990s. It would therefore be difficult to argue that capital controls have harmed the Hungarian economy, and in fact they may have added to Hungary's attractiveness to foreign investors by ensuring a stable macroeconomic environment.

The main reason for maintaining short-term capital controls after the economy had stabilized following the 1993–94 crisis was the choice of exchange rate regime. The narrow crawling band, serving a heterodox dual purpose of providing a nominal anchor for disinflation and maintaining export competitiveness was successful, certainly in the initial years of operation. The experience of the Russian crisis, when the limited exposure of Hungary to short-term capital outflows helped minimize economic disruption, is illustrative of the effectiveness of the controls – at least regarding the activities of nonresident investors. But at the same time, the role of the controls should not be exaggerated: they were always considered temporary and were more akin to 'sand in the wheels' rather than to draconian prohibitions.

Abandoning the remaining controls, including the short-term controls on capital inflows, in mid-2001 was primarily motivated by the change in the exchange rate regime, itself the result of a shift in domestic policy priorities in favor of bringing inflation down to EU levels. Political economy considerations, placing the decision in the context of ever-closer EU accession, also played a role. Pressure from international capital markets, on the other hand, was not a primary motivation.

Hungary would appear to be a good illustration of gradual capital account liberalization. However, it should not be forgotten that this represented only one element in Hungary's economic policy package. The credibility of Hungary's approach hinged critically on supportive macroeconomic and structural policies, which transformed it steadily into a market economy. Few if any conclusions are warranted regarding the use of short-term controls in a crisis situation. Imposing controls *de novo*, rather than maintaining existing controls for a slightly longer period of time, is likely to be regarded quite differently by investors, foreign as well as domestic. But for countries embarking on the road towards free capital flows, Hungary's experience may bear some interesting lessons.

NOTES

1. The views expressed in this chapter are my own and should not be attributed to the International Monetary Fund. I am grateful for comments from Helge Berger, Robert Feldman and György Szapáry; to Natalia Tamarisa for help and advice on the capital account liberalization indices; and to Etelka Lux-Kovács for excellent research assistance. Any remaining errors are my own.
2. It should be noted that, in contrast to some other countries in Central and Eastern Europe, Hungary embarked on a selective liberalization of its economy well before the political transition in 1989, although the emphasis here should be placed on the word 'selective'. For a description of Hungary's early transition experience, see Boote and Somogyi (1991).
3. For a full description, see Cottarelli et al. (1998).
4. For a comprehensive overview of the literature on capital controls, see Dooley (1996).
5. For an overview of developments in financial linkages between the EU and a range of Mediterranean and transition economies, see Feldman and Temprano-Arroyo (1998).
6. See NBH (2000). Note that the statistics on FDI do not include reinvested earnings by foreign-owned enterprises; if they did, the stock of FDI would likely be even higher.
7. See, for example, Ariyoshi et al. (2000) for an overview of country experience with the use of capital controls to limit short-term capital inflows.
8. See Cottarelli et al. (1998) for comprehensive description of the crisis and the subsequent recovery program.
9. Following an up-front devaluation by 9 per cent in March 1995, the National Bank of Hungary introduced a pre-announced crawling exchange band of 2.25 per cent on either side of the central parity. The rate of devaluation of the central parity started at a relative high 1.9 per cent per month, but was gradually reduced during the lifetime of the regime. By the time it was abandoned in May 2001, the monthly rate of crawl amounted to only 0.2 per cent per month.
10. See Oblath (1998) for an analysis of the monetary policy response during the crisis period.
11. Moreover, prudential controls on banks' open positions and close scrutiny by the NBH (combined with occasional moral suasion) ensured that nonresidents could not easily circumvent the control, for example by entering into repurchase agreements with domestic banks.
12. See Darvas and Szapáry (2000) for a description of the impact of the Russian crisis on Hungary and other Central European economies.
13. Of course, the controls could not similarly limit the ability of residents to speculate, and in the event, many brokerages went bankrupt. But this represented a risk for the financial sector (with most brokerages owned by banks) rather than for Hungary's external accounts – and foreign ownership of the majority of the financial sector ensured that these losses did not have systemic consequences.
14. Ghosh et al. (2002) discuss policy responses during selected capital account crises; the evidence that capital controls, where used such as in Malaysia and Russia, were helpful is mixed, at best.
15. See, for example, Fischer (2001).
16. See Eichengreen and Masson (1998).
17. In the initial years of the crawling-peg regime, capital inflows were used to build up foreign exchange reserves and pre-pay some external debt obligations. However, in the late 1990s, the sterilization costs resulting from large and sustained capital inflows became increasingly burdensome for the NBH.

11. Capital account liberalization and financial market reform in the Republic of Moldova

Veronica Bacalu[1]

11.1 INTRODUCTION

The Republic of Moldova gained independence in August 1991, following the collapse of the Soviet Union. The years since then can be characterized as a period of transition from a centrally planned economy to a market-oriented one, with a variety of associated problems, challenges and experiences. Although all newly independent states that were previously part of the Soviet Union have aspects of their transition paths in common, the differences between them provide an interesting opportunity for analysis. Capital liberalization in transition countries is a field that offers an opportunity to draw comparisons between the different approaches taken. Overall, capital liberalization policies in the Republic of Moldova can be characterized as being only a part of the overall package of reforms undertaken in policies relating to trade, investment and the foreign exchange regime.

After the collapse of the Soviet Union, Moldova experienced a severe shock due to trade distortions, accompanied by a short conflict in a part of its territory that ceased to be controlled by the Moldavian authorities. The inherited structure of the economy was not favorable. Some 50 per cent of GDP was produced in agriculture and related industries, while industrial production was concentrated mainly in the breakaway part of the territory. Reforms aimed at restoring growth, attracting foreign investment, trade development and financial sector consolidation were given top priority. As a small open economy, with an external sector accounting for up to 70 per cent of GDP, Moldova needed to address the issue of liberalization in an orderly and consistent way.

The chapter continues with a summary of capital liberalization to date, while Section 11.3 describes the key remaining capital controls. Banking sector reform is discussed in Section 11.4 and Section 11.5 concludes with the lessons learned.

11.2 A SUMMARY OF CAPITAL ACCOUNT LIBERALIZATION MOVES SO FAR

The Republic of Moldova, like other transition economies and particularly former Soviet Union countries (with some exceptions), is an example of a country that has rapidly implemented reforms aimed at developing a market economy. However difficult the path of reforms, they were initially rapid and successful at the beginning, but are now controversial and sluggish. Despite the difficulties, the liberalization policies were carefully sequenced and contributed to financial stability.

The introduction of the national currency in late 1993 marked the beginning of the implementation of independent macroeconomic, financial, monetary and foreign exchange policies. Moldova faced the challenges of increasing the foreign reserves of the National Bank of Moldova (NBM), choosing an exchange rate regime, establishing a foreign exchange market, building up a banking system and liberalizing foreign trade.

Current account liberalization was rapid, being finalized with the acceptance of Article VIII obligations, Sections 2, 3 and 4, of the IMF Articles of Agreement in June 1995. Since then the national currency has been convertible for current and some capital account transactions. It is worth noting that currency convertibility was maintained even during the Russian crisis. During and after the crisis no restrictions were adopted, although many countries in the region (some of which were Moldova's main trading partners) introduced foreign exchange restrictions and have maintained them since then. The lessons learned during the Russian crisis with respect to external shocks and capital mobility will be discussed in Section 11.5.

Current account liberalization took place against a background of central bank reform. The ability to conduct an independent monetary policy, the introduction of indirect monetary instruments, the liberalization of interest and exchange rates, the strengthening of the banking system and the establishment of a normally functioning Treasury bill (T-bill) market are successes in the reform process. The measures and steps described in Box 11.1, below, contributed to a number of positive outcomes:

- liberal foreign exchange regulations contributed to the creation of a normally functioning foreign exchange market. The exchange rate is determined by demand and supply; its fluctuations reflect both seasonal tendencies and the external position. Foreign exchange regulations are also quite simple, allowing banks, which are major participants in the foreign exchange market, to improve the quality of their services; and

---

Box 11.1 Moldova: Chronology of Major Reforms

1991	June	Law on the National Bank of Moldova.
		Law on banks and banks' activities.
1995	July	Law on the National Bank of Moldova.
		Law on financial institutions.
	Nov.	Regulation on business transactions, including credit extension, with connected or related parties of commercial banks.
	Dec.	Regulation on large credits.
1996	Aug.	Regulation on the licensing of banks.
	Sep.	Regulation on the credit extension to bank employees.
	Oct.	Regulation on the issuing of a certificate on the competence of bank auditors.
	Nov.	Regulation on the opening of branch offices by the banks.
		Regulation on holding significant interest in a bank.
1997	Mar.	Regulation on the requirements of bank administrators.
	Aug.	Regulation on the procedures for the preparation and submission of audit reports.
		Regulation on bank liquidity.
	Nov.	Regulation on open foreign exchange positions.
	Dec.	Regulation on risk-based capital adequacy.
1998	Apr.	Regulation on equity investments by banks in legal entities.
	May	Regulation on past due credits.
	June	Regulation on credit classification and allowance for loan losses.
1999	Sep.	Regulation on managing interest rate risk.
	Dec.	Regulation on bank investment in real estate.
2000	June	Regulation on mergers and acquisitions of banks in the Republic of Moldova.
2001	Dec.	Regulation on publishing information on financial activity by commercial banks of the Republic of Moldova.
	Oct.	Regulation on risk-based capital adequacy.

- while implementing its monetary policy, the NBM was able to build up
  and maintain gross international reserves at a level sufficient to maintain
  exchange rate stability and to keep the import cover ratio between 2.5
  and 3.5 months (unlike many other countries in the region). The
  exception was the period of regional crisis in 1998: the exchange rate
  depreciated by 40.3 per cent and reserves fell to 1.4 months of import
  cover. The foreign reserves–liquidity ratio also varied, from 1.3 in 1998
  to 0.6 in 1999. The low point was reached due to the low level of foreign
  exchange reserves at the beginning of 1999, as well as the high level of
  external debt service payments based on the then prevailing schedule.
  The liquidity ratio returned to a comfortable level of 1.2 in early 2001.

11.3 A BRIEF SUMMARY OF CURRENT CAPITAL ACCOUNT CONTROLS

Along with the rapid and orderly current account liberalization, a range of
capital account transactions were also liberalized. Controls on capital inflows
were never imposed. This was dictated by the high priority placed on
attracting foreign investments of any type. For statistical purposes, loans and
guarantees granted by nonresidents to residents are to be registered with the
NBM. Apart from this registration requirement, payments to nonresidents of
principal, interest and commissions are permitted without restriction. By
keeping a register of private debt, the NBM is able to project the outflows
related to private debt servicing, which allows for a more efficient
implementation of monetary policy.

Nonresidents can freely purchase T-bills and repatriate their invested and
earned funds without taxation (up until 2005 according to current legislation).
This regulation is quite effective. Foreign participation in the T-bill market
accounted for some 42 per cent of the total stock in 1997, contributing to the
development of this market, raising foreign investment and improving the
balance of payments (Figure 11.1). Although the real exchange rate
appreciated by 5–6 per cent annually, there was no crowding out of exports
and they continued to increase. Nevertheless, the current account deficit was
high. More recently, the attitude of foreign investors towards the local T-bill
market has become more cautious. In the second half of 1997 and during the
Russian crisis in 1998, nonresident participation disappeared. Regarding the
banking system, the participation of nonresidents is free of any limitations,
except for those of a prudential and supervisory nature. The banking sector
continues to be one of the most attractive areas for investment in Moldova
(Figure 11.2). Moldova assumed very liberal obligations in various sectors
after joining the World Trade Organization (WTO) in mid-2001.

Figure 11.1 Moldova: amount of Treasury bills sold (US$ m)

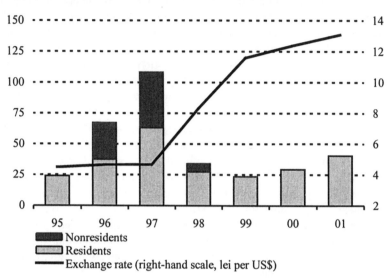

Source: National Bank of Moldova.

Figure 11.2 Moldova: banking capital structure
(share of total)

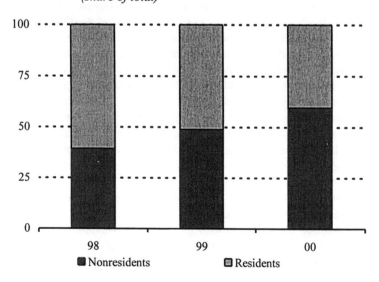

Source: National Bank of Moldova.

Policies related to the liberalization of outflows were cautious and a gradual approach was adopted. At the initial stage, immediately after current account liberalization, overall economic conditions remained very fragile. Growth was problematic, the balance of payments deficit was growing and the fiscal deficit was high. There was considerable uncertainty regarding whether complete capital account liberalization would bring any visible results. The experience of the Kyrgyz Republic, which undertook an early liberalization of both the current and capital accounts, illustrated these uncertainties.

Capital outflows are subject to authorization by the NBM. The extension of loans or guarantees with respect to nonresidents, as well as investments and equity purchases abroad, are permitted only upon authorization by the NBM. Banks are exempt from this rule for the purpose of investing their foreign exchange assets in financial instruments which are guaranteed by governments of G7 countries. The purpose of these restrictions was initially to preserve the limited financial resources in the country. Subsequently, after gaining some experience and preliminary statistical information, the major reason for retaining controls became one of a fiscal character, i.e., avoiding tax evasion and corruption.

An analysis of the authorizations issued by the NBM suggests some clear conclusions:

• requests to authorize a transaction are quite rare. Hence, the number of issued authorizations is small and the amount of legally permitted outflows is low. This fact raises the issue of the efficiency of controls;
• requests are usually based on one of the following purposes: trade facilitation investments, export promotion, assurance of raw material imports for further local production, etc. In these cases, bank guarantees are also commonly issued; and
• the maintenance of controls may be justified by the desire to retain an additional instrument to limit tax evasion, and not necessarily to regulate the outflow of foreign exchange. This latter role is efficiently performed by a freely floating exchange rate.

The abolition of the remaining controls may take place after sustainable growth, based on irreversible structural reforms, has been achieved for several consecutive years. This growth and the accompanying reforms would contribute to a strengthening of financial sector stability, deepening in financial markets, increasing foreign direct investments and the integration of Moldova into European financial markets.

11.4 INFORMATION ON THE DOMESTIC BANKING AND FINANCIAL SYSTEM

A sound banking system is crucial for the financial stability of a country. At the beginning of the transition period, the following key banking sector reforms were implemented:

- a two-tier banking system was created;
- the establishment of private banks was allowed;
- former specialized banks became universal banks; and
- the legal framework and supervisory structure for the banking sector were introduced.

The former specialized banks, originating from the old monobank system, inherited the burden of bad loans extended to large state-owned enterprises. New private banks appeared, which were quite small. In order to build a viable and sound banking system, the priority was given to bank capitalization and the implementation of modern banking supervision. The minimum capital requirement has been raised seven times since independence.[2]

A unique strategy was adopted with respect to the mode of privatization of former state banks. As the result of a decision by parliament, the share of the state in five state banks was estimated and during a relatively short period of time this share was repaid to the state. Thus all banks, but one (the former savings bank) became private joint-stock companies. The share of the government in the savings bank is maintained at 56 per cent.

Simultaneously, a certain portion of the bad loans extended to large loss-making state-owned enterprises was recovered under existing government guarantees. Because of that, it is difficult to estimate the fiscal cost of bank recapitalization in Moldova. Nevertheless, the quite unique 'velvet' bank privatization process contributed to the rapid reforms in the banking sector, including minimizing the influence of the state in the banking sector, strengthening prudential regulations and building up a strong supervisory capacity at the central bank. Box 11.1 shows a list of the major regulations adopted in the field of banking legislation, and especially supervision. Bank licensing and supervision are among the major functions of the National Bank of Moldova. The development of the banking system is an example of one of the most efficient sectoral reforms in Moldova. Although overall macroeconomic conditions in the country were problematic, the banking sector led the reform process. The consequent introduction of Basle standards of prudential regulations, combined with the implementation of international accounting and auditing standards, contributed to efficient supervision.

Supervision is handicapped if proper accounting and financial reporting mechanisms are lacking.

As Figure 11.3 shows, the size of the banking sector is relatively modest in terms of absolute volume, as well as in relation to GDP. But, due to openness, sound practices and competitiveness, the banking sector has grown more rapidly than the economy as a whole over recent years (Figure 11.4). Banking assets amounted to 26.6 per cent of GDP in mid-2001. Domestic credit stood at 12.4 per cent of GDP, compared to 12 per cent in Russia and 25 per cent in Hungary. The concentration of the banking sector is high: the five largest credit institutions have a combined market share of 68.6 per cent.

Figure 11.3 Moldova: bank assets (%)

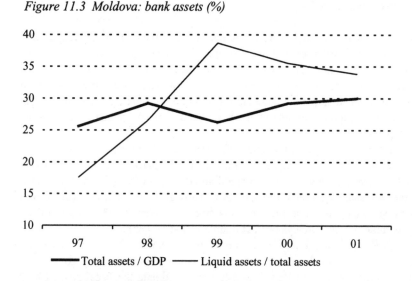

Source: National Bank of Moldova.

The number of banks has varied around 20. The consolidation strategy encourages banks to increase their capital or to merge. There is no analysis of the optimal number of banking institutions for a country like Moldova. The NBM holds the view that the market will determine the optimal number and promotes competition and equal treatment of all banks. Since independence, nine banks have been liquidated. The relatively high number of bank failures illustrates the following:

- bankruptcy legislation is effectively enforced;
- banking supervision is efficient;

- bad management practices were the main reason behind these failures; and
- the failures did not lead to problems for the banking system as a whole.

Figure 11.4 Moldova: banking sector and GDP (% growth)

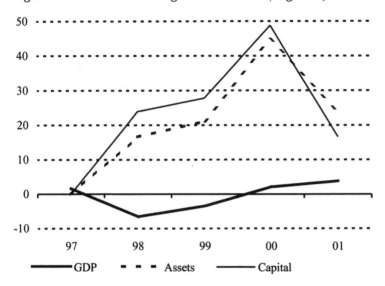

Source : National Bank of Moldova.

Interest rate spreads are also a major determinant of banking sector profitability (Figure 11.5). An analysis shows that spreads were quite high, providing sufficient compensation for the banks to exercise their financial intermediary function. As inflation stabilizes below 10 per cent, the margin between deposit and lending rates will decrease, but this process will take some time and will also require a considerable improvement in the legal environment with respect to creditor rights regarding collateral, the enforcement of court decisions, and so forth. The evolution of the quality of banks' loan portfolios demonstrates the growing capacity of banks to efficiently manage the risks associated with their credit activities (Figure 11.6). The very low level of non-performing loans at present is also the result of lessons learned during and after the Russian crisis when their share temporarily rose to 9 per cent.

Figure 11.5 Moldova: inflation and interest rates (%)

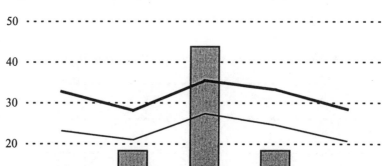

Source : National Bank of Moldova.

The banking sector continues to provide an attractive investment opportunity in Moldova. The share of foreign capital is quite high and is increasing (Figure 11.7). Unfortunately there are no major international banks in Moldova. The main reasons for this are the small size of the economy, the limited local consumption capacity and the stop–go pattern of the reform process in recent times. Based on WTO accession obligations, the Moldavian banking sector is free of cross-border restrictions, constituting an evident advantage in comparison with the countries in the region. The capital adequacy ratio stands at a relatively high level of 48.2 per cent, mainly as the result of capital injections.

The volume of cross-border liabilities of resident banks is 1.1 per cent of GDP. They are related mainly to trade facilitation activities and could increase as Moldova integrates into international financial markets and as foreign trade develops. The absence of restrictions on inflows should also facilitate this process. Although the banking sector is the pioneer of reforms in Moldova, its development is limited by the overall performance of the economy. However, the banking sector today is able to absorb any reasonable degree of growth and to contribute to the financial stability and sustainability of the economy.

Figure 11.6 Moldova: banks' loan portfolios
        (Share of total, year end)

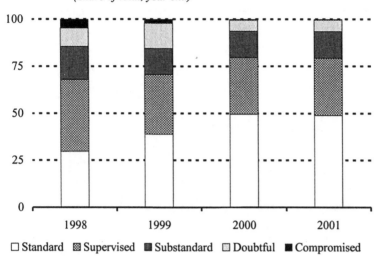

□ Standard   ▨ Supervised   ■ Substandard   ▨ Doubtful   ■ Compromised

Source : National Bank of Moldova.

11.5 THE CONSEQUENCES OF LIBERALIZATION MOVES TO DATE AND THE LESSONS LEARNED

Following the description of liberalization moves so far and of the controls currently in place, an analysis of the consequences of the implemented policies can be made, particularly with regard to the impact of these policies on the overall economic performance of the country. While implementing a package of consecutive liberalization steps, a country wishes to maximize the expected benefits and minimize the risks associated with capital mobility. Each country experience is in this respect unique, due to differences in the structure of economies, the speed of reforms, external conditions, etc. Nevertheless, the conclusions about the design, effectiveness, timing and sequencing of steps of liberalization are to a large extent similar for all transition economies. This section elaborates on the influence of current and capital account liberalization to date on financial stability and macro-economic development in Moldova.

Figure 11.7 Moldova: foreign direct investment (US$ m)

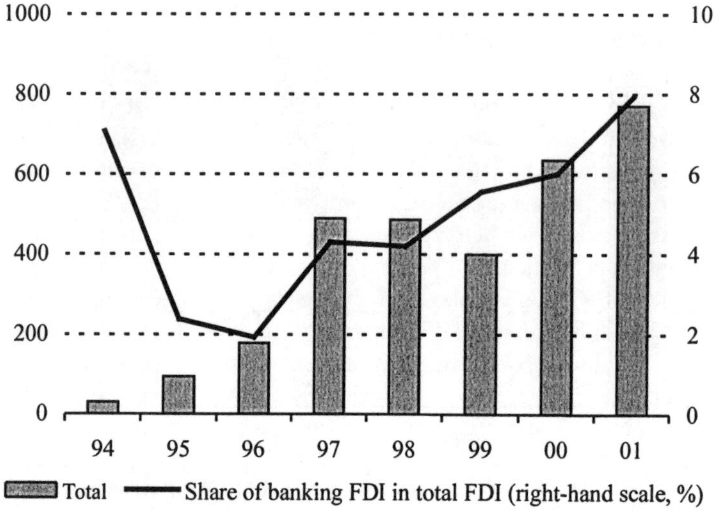

Source : National Bank of Moldova.

Rapid, consecutive liberalization was the optimal strategy, taking into account the openness of the economy. Moldova benefitted from that strategy for a number of reasons:

- the NBM maintained sufficiently high and stable foreign exchange reserves, except for the period of the Russian crisis;
- while conducting its foreign exchange interventions, the NBM was able to ensure the smooth functioning of the foreign exchange market;
- simple, transparent foreign exchange regulations resulted in the growing trust of economic entities and the population in the foreign exchange policies promoted by the NBM, thus contributing to the credibility of the national currency;
- the credibility of the banking system rose;
- non-repatriation of export earnings and capital flight decreased considerably and took place mainly for tax-evasion purposes; and
- strong prudential regulations, proper supervision based on modern accounting practices and a strong central bank ensured that banking crises were avoided.

It is difficult to identify any significant negative consequences resulting from the liberalization policy to date. That said, the benefits from the liberalization strategy would have been considerably higher if overall macroeconomic policies and structural reforms had been pursued in the same non-controversial and go-ahead manner. Structural reforms and privatization currently lag behind. The reform of the energy sector, crucial for the Moldavian economy, has been extremely slow. The direction of foreign trade continued to be oriented towards countries of the former Soviet Union. Thus, the risks associated with trading partner credibility have persisted. Foreign direct investments were low, the balance of payments deficit continued to be high and it took some time for economic growth to be achieved.

The Russian crisis was a real stress test for the economy and for the financial system in particular. The first pressures were experienced in the second half of 1997, when echoes of the Asian crisis encouraged foreign investors to withdraw from the T-bill market. Their withdrawal was smooth, due to the flexible exchange rate regime and excessive pressures on the foreign exchange market were balanced by NBM interventions. As a consequence, towards the beginning of the Russian crisis, nonresident holdings of T-bills were minimal. Nevertheless, the Russian crisis had a dramatic impact on the Moldavian economy and highlighted all of the country's economic shortcomings. Exports were directed mainly to Russia and Ukraine and the crisis coincided with the seasonal peak in exports. The resulting shortage of foreign exchange put pressure on the exchange rate. Depositors rushed to the banks to withdraw deposits and convert their savings into foreign currency. Their behavior precipitated further panic. Companies also tried to convert their earnings into hard currency.

At the beginning of the crisis, the NBM attempted to smooth out the sharp fall of the exchange rate, but after some time it gave up defending the national currency and allowed it to float freely without intervention. In four months, the exchange rate depreciated by 40.3 per cent before stabilizing at a new, lower, level. The foreign exchange reserves of the NBM dropped by a third, aggravated by the necessity to service a put option for a private placement by the Ministry of Finance in December 1998. During these months, special attention was paid to the supervision of banks. Open foreign exchange positions were reported daily, their financial situation weekly, and some special reports and controls were organized at the request of the NBM. Additional liquidity was pumped into banks which helped them to cope with withdrawals and supported the ongoing functioning of the payments system. The situation stabilized after four months. There were no bank failures in Moldova following the regional crisis. Banks did not lose money in Russia because they had not been allowed to invest in local currency Russian government securities (GKOs). In the end, the most obvious consequence for the banking system was a rise in the dollarization ratio of deposits from 19 to 50 per cent.

The overall consequences of the regional crisis for the national economy were very serious: inflation rose to 43.8 per cent in post-crisis 1999 and foreign trade decreased by a third. GDP fell by 3.4 per cent and living standards dropped dramatically. In Moldova the quality of banking supervision was quite high and the central bank was able to promote independent and correct policies on a timely basis, helping to avoid bankruptcies. The twin-crises experience of some countries, where a balance of payments crisis is followed by a banking crisis, was therefore avoided. The rapid stabilization also demonstrates that regulations with respect to current and capital account operations are efficient. Due to the credibility of the banking system, there was no major capital flight during the crisis.

On the basis of Moldavian experiences with capital liberalization and the lessons learned during the regional crisis, the section concludes with some general points that are more likely to be common across transition countries. Capital account liberalization is part of the overall process of economic and structural reform that occurs after the establishment of current account convertibility. In particular, capital account liberalization should be accompanied by financial sector reform. In many countries, liberalization was accompanied by tight macroeconomic policies in the context of programs supported by the International Monetary Fund. In general, the elimination of controls led to an increase of capital inflows, an accumulation of foreign exchange reserves and some worsening of the current account position.

Controls are inefficient in the medium and long terms, because of the many techniques and schemes invented to legally avoid any restriction. Controls are also inefficient in countries where law enforcement is weak and where nobody is afraid to violate regulations because of the absence of punishment. Costs associated with a low degree of law enforcement are very high for a society because of expanding corruption. Most former Soviet Union countries retain some capital controls, not only to avoid the risks usually associated with capital mobility, but also to combat tax evasion. Experience shows that capital controls are no substitute for proper policies (monetary, fiscal, investment, privatization), or for sound, prudential regulation of the financial sector.

Further reforms are needed to deepen financial markets and to ensure sustainable growth. These objectives can be supported by the promotion of codes and good practice guidelines that countries can use during the capital account liberalization process.

NOTES

1. The views expressed in this chapter are those of the author and should not be viewed as representing those of the International Monetary Fund or the National Bank of Moldova.

2. Capital requirements were increased to 1 million lei in December 1994, to 4 million in December 1995, to 8 million in December 1997, to 12 million in June 1999, to 16 million in December 1999, to 24 million in June 2000 and to 32 million in December 2000.

12. Capital account liberalization in Poland

Ewa Sadowska-Cieslak[1]

12.1 A SUMMARY OF CAPITAL ACCOUNT LIBERALIZATION TO DATE

Capital account liberalization in Poland occurred in three stages and reflected the pace of the market reforms initiated in January 1990 and the economic and regulatory environment. The first basic moves were a part of the initial transformation process in January 1990 and lasted until the application for membership of the Organisation for Economic Co-operation and Development (OECD) in November 1994. The second stage encompassed the OECD accession negotiation period (November 1994–November 1996) and the third, post-accession phase, which was completed in October 2002. This section describes the reform process and the following section documents the remaining controls.[2] Section 12.3 provides an overview of the Polish banking sector, while Section 12.4 concludes with the lessons learned.

Launching the Transformation Process (1990–94)

Liberalization of the Polish economy began with the introduction of internal convertibility for the Polish currency. The abolition on 1 January 1990 of permits for the purchase and sale of foreign currency by exporters and importers and the introduction of a uniform exchange rate for all kinds of transactions was a milestone in the reform process. The uniform exchange rate was applied to all transactions with the exception of those undertaken by private non-banking foreign exchange offices, which were not permitted to purchase foreign currency from the banking system. The revised foreign exchange law removed this restriction in 1995. Most capital movement operations as well as some operations on current account remained restricted.

The authorities initially concentrated on setting up the regulations and institutions necessary for a market economy. The biggest challenge was hyperinflation. The disinflation process resulted in CPI inflation falling from above 585 per cent in 1990 to around 32 per cent in 1994 (the year in which the Polish government applied for OECD membership). Real interest rates for depositors were negative in 1994, aside from those on long-term deposits. The real interest rate for borrowing was around 10 per cent. Much of this difference was attributed to high costs of intermediation, reserve requirements, along with the levels of bad debts in the banking system and the associated reluctance of banks to extend new credits. In 1993, the Act on Financial Restructuring of Enterprises and Banks helped to clean up banks' balance sheets, leading to increased lending and a lengthening of loan maturities.[3]

After fixing the zloty exchange rate against the US dollar in January 1990, the zloty was devalued by 11.5 per cent in May 1991 (due to the high inflation rate) and was fixed against a basket of five currencies weighted by their share in Polish foreign trade.

In November 1991 the authorities switched to a more flexible crawling-peg against the basket. The pre-announced monthly rate of crawl was gradually reduced, in line with falling inflation, although devaluations occurred in February 1992 (12 per cent) and August 1993 (8 per cent).[4]

On the monetary side, a rapid accumulation of foreign exchange reserves, originating from the trade surplus and capital inflows, was registered in 1994. The inflow of foreign direct investment (FDI) amounted to US$1.8 billion (compared to US$1.7 billion a year earlier). Portfolio investment, particularly in government securities, also picked up. The authorities' response was to conduct sterilization operations.

In the early 1990s the Warsaw Stock Exchange (WSE), which opened in April 1991, was small and illiquid. Large institutional investors were lacking, although the regulations met international standards. New issues by domestic companies were limited and foreign companies were prohibited from issuing shares or being listed on the WSE. Since September 1994, however, foreign investors were permitted to buy shares on the same terms as domestic investors, provided the company concerned was not in a sector in which there were licensing requirements for FDI. Before placing an order, foreign investors had to open a securities account with one of the brokerage houses and deposit 30 per cent of the transaction, with the remaining 70 per cent due three days after the transaction. Personal and corporate income from capital gains were tax free until the end of 1994 and foreign investors were free to repatriate these gains without a foreign exchange license.[5]

The money market comprised an inter-bank market and markets for both Treasury bills and bonds. The market in corporate bonds was in its infancy and was constrained by the tax system, outdated regulations and high inflation. At that time only one international company issued three-year bonds. Foreign investors were initially permitted to purchase only bonds with a maturity longer than one year. The restriction was removed in 1993. However, profits on all securities could be repatriated without the need for a special foreign exchange permit.

The largest transactions between residents and nonresidents were for current account operations. Direct investment flows and portfolio investment in Treasury bonds also occurred, although to a more limited extent.

OECD Accession (November 1994 to November 1996)

In November 1994 the Polish government applied for OECD membership and the process of capital movement liberalization and other reforms speeded up (see Box 12.1). The OECD accession negotiations took two years and required considerable regulatory and institutional changes.

The new foreign exchange law passed by the parliament in late December 1994 replaced the very restrictive law of February 1989. Although an improvement with respect to the 1989 version, the new law remained restrictive by OECD standards. Restrictions in some areas were maintained, but the law authorized the Minister of Finance to liberalize further by means of ordinance when the economic situation permitted. This method avoided the need for a lengthy parliamentary procedure when making changes. The Minister of Finance made changes by ordinance during OECD membership negotiations and also subsequently, until a new law was passed in December 1998. Although this method of liberalization is not recognized as reliable by international investors, it was chosen for practical reasons: OECD membership negotiations were advancing rapidly and the process of putting changes through parliament would have delayed accession. No liberalization moves introduced by ordinance were rescinded and all changes were confirmed in the foreign exchange law passed by the parliament in late December 1998.

The liberalization of capital movements has been sequenced and adjusted to the macroeconomic and regulatory status of the country. It depended very much on monetary policy developments. For the monetary authority, inflation remained the number one problem. Although the disinflation process continued, an increasingly important inflationary factor in 1994–95 was the rapid accumulation of foreign exchange reserves resulting from a large trade surplus (taking into account unrecorded trade) and, increasingly, from capital inflows. The monetary authorities reacted to the expansion of reserves by sterilizing inflows, complemented by a firming in the exchange rate and a series of interest rate cuts. Between summer 1994 and early 1996, the annualized rate of crawl of the nominal exchange rate was reduced from 21 to

Box 12.1 Poland: Chronology of Major Reforms

1989 June   Free elections.
      Sept.   First democratic government.
1990 Jan.   Stability Pact for Poland introduced.
              Single exchange rate introduced.
              Zloty exchange rate fixed against US dollar.
1991 Apr.   Warsaw Stock Exchange (WSE) established.
      May   Zloty devaluation against dollar (14.4 per cent) and
              exchange rate fixed against basket of five currencies.
      Oct.   Crawling-peg exchange rate mechanism (1.8 per cent
              devaluation monthly) within a ±2 per cent band and NBP
              quotation system (±0.5 per cent) introduced.
1992 Feb.   Zloty devaluation against the basket (by 12 per cent).
      June   Treasury bonds introduced.
1993 Aug.   Devaluation of 8 per cent and reduction in crawling-peg
              adjustment to 1.6 per cent per month.
1994 Feb.   First quotation of subscription rights on the WSE.
      Sept.   Crawling-peg adjustment reduced to 1.5 per cent per
              month.
      Nov.   Crawling-peg adjustment reduced to 1.4 per cent per
              month.
1995 Feb.   Crawling-peg adjustment reduced to 1.2 per cent per
              month.
      Mar.   Widening of the zloty quotation band to ±2.0 per cent.
      May   Exchange rate band widened to 6–7.0 per cent.
      June   Poland accepts IMF Article VIII obligations.
      Dec.   Zloty revaluation of 6.0 per cent.
1996 Jan.   Crawling-peg adjustment reduced to 1.0 per cent per
              month.
      July   National Investment Fund certificates (mass pri-
              vatization) listed in single-price auction.
      Nov.   OECD accession.
1997 Aug.   Laws on public trading in securities; investment funds;
              and banking passed.
1998 Jan.   Futures index introduced on WSE.
      Feb.   Crawling-peg adjustment reduced to 0.8 per cent per month.
              Widening of the exchange rate band to ±10.0 per cent.
      July   Crawling-peg adjustment reduced to 0.65 per cent per
              month.
              NBP stops foreign exchange market direct interventions.

	Sep.	Crawling-peg adjustment reduced to 0.5 per cent per month.
		Trading in US dollar futures introduced.
	Oct.	Monetary Policy Council public announcement on floating zloty in the 1999-2003 period.
		Widening of the exchange rate band to ±12.5 per cent.
1999	Jan.	Change of exchange rate basket to 2 currencies (euro 55 per cent, dollar 45 per cent).
	Mar.	Crawling peg adjustment reduced to 0.3 per cent per month.
		Widening of the exchange rate band to ±15 per cent.
	June	Central bank exchange rate fixing mechanism abolished.
2000	Apr.	Zloty floated.
		Amendment to the Law on Public Trading in Securities allows operations in securities on foreign capital markets.
2001	Sept.	Foreign Exchange Law liberalizing capital movements with the OECD member countries passed.
2002	Oct.	New Foreign Exchange Law expected to come in force.

12.5 per cent, nominal interest rates were reduced by between 5 and 7 percentage points and the real effective exchange rate (producer price based) appreciated by 12 per cent. Foreign investors' involvement in purchasing domestic Treasury bills increased significantly in 1995 to US$1.5 billion. In addition to these exchange and interest rate policy actions, regulatory measures were taken or considered to counteract the forces underlying reserve accumulation. Import tariffs and the import surcharge were cut several times. In December 1995 the surrender requirement for export proceeds was abolished, reducing the conversion costs borne by enterprises. The monetary authority pushed for a restriction in the purchase of Treasury bills by nonresidents, but the government did not follow their advice.[6]

The banking sector remained state dominated at the end of 1995 but the health and performance of most banks had improved. The burden of non-performing loans fell sharply and profitability increased. Some troubled banks were taken over, while others with low or negative solvency ratios were liquidated. However, banks were technologically outdated and staff lacked the necessary skills.

In June 1995 the Polish government, acting together with the President of the National Bank, accepted the obligations of Article VIII of the International Monetary Fund (IMF) Articles of Agreement. After accepting Article VIII, the liberalization process speeded up: capital movements directly related to international trade finance, such as commercial credits and foreign direct investment inflows and most outflows were liberalized (according to the OECD/IMF benchmark definition). Some exceptions have been maintained, such as foreign investment in real estate, broadcasting companies, air and shipping transport, certain telecommunication services, gambling and betting due to other than foreign exchange policy reasons. Accordingly, the law on foreign direct investment was shortened and adjusted to the market economy requirements. In January 1996, outward direct investment operations of up to ecu 1 million were liberalized for businesses as were outward real estate investments of up to ecu 50,000 per person. Long-term portfolio investment on recognized OECD markets was also allowed.

New forms of portfolio inflows appeared, such as the issue of eurobonds in mid-1995, the issue of debt instruments by Polish companies on the American market and the issue of municipal bonds on international capital markets. These new securities increased the inflow of foreign exchange and widened the sources of finance available to Polish companies.

On accession to the OECD in November 1996, the Polish government attached a long list of restricted capital operations to the OECD Code of Liberalization of Capital Movements and the OECD Code of Liberalization of Current Invisible Operations. In accepting these initial restrictions and acknowledging the justifications for maintaining them, the OECD Council gave the Polish government the obligation of gradually removing all capital account reservations of a foreign exchange nature by the end of 1999.

The general philosophy behind the liberalization was an unconditional liberalization of long-term flows (first inflows and then outflows), as these were considered stable and indispensable for the process of restructuring the national economy. Most reservations did not apply to authorized foreign exchange banks. Moreover, restrictions were generally limited and applied either to particular categories of economic entities or to specific kinds of securities. According to the OECD accession agreement only two of the nine restrictions on money market operations were full, the other operations were allowed for authorized banks. Among four restrictions concerning operations in collective investment securities, only two were full. The last full restriction applied to purchase of foreign currency with Polish zloty abroad by residents. All other restrictions, which seemed to be extensive by number, were limited either to non-banking sector entities, to short-term sensitive flows or to special kind of operations. Nevertheless, fully restricted operations could be conducted following authorization by the National Bank of Poland (NBP).

After OECD Accession

In February 1997, two months after OECD accession (and in fulfillment of the accession obligations), the authorities liberalized all transfers of foreign exchange related to previously liberalized transactions. Other liberalization moves taken at the same time included allowing both residential investment of up to ecu 1 million in securities listed on OECD markets and residential investment in collective investment securities and trust funds. Restrictions were also eased on the granting of long-term financial credits by residents in favor of nonresidents (and which are related to international transactions in which a resident participates) and on granting sureties and guarantees by residents.

The approach was cautious: liberalization of some operations was divided into steps by gradually increasing the ceiling for permitted transactions. For example, the issue of foreign securities on the domestic capital market was initially limited to ecu 200 million per year. The ceiling was later raised to ecu 300 million per year before the restriction was finally removed. The same cautious approach was taken with a number of other capital account operations. Developments were monitored and when flows did not disrupt monetary policy, transaction limits were gradually raised and then removed.

The authorities, keeping in mind their accession obligations, began drafting a new (liberal) foreign exchange law in late 1997. Unfortunately, progress was disrupted in August 1998 as a result of the financial crisis in Russia and the ongoing impact of the Asian crisis. These had a rapid impact on the Polish economy via the exchange rate and raw material and fuel prices. In addition, Polish exports were adversely affected – both by the reduction in exports to Russia and by the indirect impact on other countries. The current account deficit increased and the financial position of enterprises deteriorated throughout 1998.

However, high real interest rates, the sound fundamentals of the Polish economy and good short-term economic prospects encouraged short-term capital inflows via authorized banks and the London zloty market. The authorities tried to discourage the inflows by widening the exchange rate band and shifting some of the exchange rate risk to investors. The rate of crawl of the central parity in the fluctuation band was progressively reduced from 1 per cent a month in February 1998 to 0.5 per cent in September 1998 and in October the exchange rate band was widened to ±12.5 per cent. Exchange rate variability increased monetary policy autonomy effectiveness in conditions of relatively free capital mobility. This modification of the exchange rate policy increased the exchange rate risk for short-term overseas portfolio investments and contributed to the gradual reduction in short-term portfolio inflows visible in the first half of 1998. The next step towards greater exchange rate flexibility was a widening in the fluctuation band to ±15 per cent, along with a further reduction in the rate of monthly crawl.

Serious imbalances in the economy continued in 1999. With macroeconomic policies insufficiently restrictive, the sharp supply shocks on the world fuel market and on the domestic food market led to an increase in the inflation rate. For the first time since the beginning of the transformation process, the 1999 end-year inflation rate (9.8 per cent) was higher than the rate a year earlier (8.6 per cent). Inefficiencies in the fuel and foodstuff markets contributed to the increase in inflation.

Monetary policy was tightened from September to November 1999 in response to the increase in inflation. High real interest rates stimulated short-term capital inflows which were mainly invested in Treasury debt securities. Portfolio inflows in 1999 amounted to US$1.4 billion (equivalent to 20 per cent of direct investment inflows). Together with the proceeds from privatization, these capital inflows led to a zloty appreciation (see Figure 12.1). The current account deficit increased dramatically and stood at 7.6 per cent of GDP by the end of 1999 (up from 4.3 per cent in 1998).

Figure 12.1 Poland: nominal effective exchange rate of the Zloty
(1995 = 100, increase = appreciation)

Source: National Bank of Poland.

In spite of these developments, the new foreign exchange law came into force in January 1999. The new law codified all liberalization moves introduced by ordinance of the Minister of Finance. However, given the economic circumstances at that time, it did not include additional liberalization measures and was therefore less liberal than had earlier been anticipated. Nevertheless, the law authorized the minister of finance to introduce further liberalization action by implementing regulations for operations falling within the scope of the law. This could be done with respect to all (or selected) entities as well as for all (or specific) transactions by regulation, provided that any such regulations did not threaten the implementation of monetary policy or the stability of the financial system.

Taking into account the worsening situation on the monetary side, the government did not consider it appropriate to pursue further liberalization of short-term capital flows and at the end of 1999 decided to re-lodge the existing restrictions on short-term capital flows in the OECD codes of liberalization. The primary reason given by the authorities for deferring liberalization of the short-term capital account operations was that lifting these controls could result in added external pressures on the Polish economy, which was already showing signs of significant macroeconomic vulnerability. Excessive short-term inflows could have increased the vulnerability of the financial system in the event of any reversal in investor sentiment. The OECD Council accepted these arguments and Poland retained the right to maintain the restrictions on short-term flows, deposit accounts and operations in negotiable instruments.

Reforms continued with the floating of the zloty exchange rate from 12 April 2000. In September 2000 the National Bank took steps to reduce excess liquidity in the banking system in order to increase the effectiveness of interest rates as the basic instrument of monetary policy. Reflecting earlier policy decisions, the macroeconomic situation improved in 2000 and 2001. Both inflation and the current account deficit declined. By the end of 2001, the inflation rate was 3.6 per cent while the current account deficit had fallen to 3.9 per cent of GDP. The declining trend in inflation allowed interest rates to be lowered six times during 2001.

Given the improving macroeconomic situation, further liberalization measures have been undertaken by amendment of the foreign exchange law in October 2002. The law meets the requirements of forthcoming European Union membership as well as ensuring full compliance with Poland's OECD commitments. All capital movements with OECD member countries were unconditionally liberalized although some restrictions on short-term movements with other countries remain.

12.2 A BRIEF SUMMARY OF CURRENT CAPITAL ACCOUNT CONTROLS

Capital controls remain in place for a number of transactions considered sensitive from a monetary policy perspective. The foreign exchange law currently in force maintains full or limited restrictions on sensitive short-term and deposit operations. Fully restricted money market operations include the sale or public issue of foreign securities on the domestic money market. Other money market operations are liberalized for authorized resident banks, but remain restricted for other market players. Restrictions remain on operations in negotiable instruments and non-securitized claims (although some transactions are permitted for authorized resident banks). The issue of foreign mortgage debt securities on the Polish capital market is prohibited. Short-term financial credits and loans are liberalized for authorized banks only. Financial back-up facilities granted by residents in favor of nonresidents in transactions where no resident participates in the underlying international transaction are only permitted for authorized resident banks.

There are also partial restrictions on residents' use of foreign currency accounts held at nonresident institutions. However, the purchase abroad by residents of foreign currency with domestic currency is only restricted for purchases not linked to an underlying transaction. With the exception of funds held in accounts for authorized transactions, residents are required to transfer any foreign exchange or zloty to Poland.

Some direct investment operations are restricted for industrial policy reasons. These include FDI in real estate, broadcasting companies, air and shipping transport, certain telecommunication services and gambling.

Nevertheless, the foreign exchange law gives the investors the right to request from the National Bank a permit for conducting fully restricted operations. A decision has to be issued within one month and decisions can be appealed to the Upper Administrative Court. These provisions ensure that administrative procedures are not arbitrarily used to block capital flows. Data from the Foreign Exchange Authorization Division of the NBP show that some 2,300 decisions for conducting non-liberalized operations were issued by the end of the year 2000. Of these, 72 per cent were positive and 1 per cent were negative. The remainder are due to factors such as the withdrawal of the application or a revised decision.

12.3 THE DOMESTIC BANKING AND FINANCIAL SYSTEM

The Polish financial sector has developed significantly since early 1990s in terms of size, level of intermediation, quality of services, ownership structure, concentration, technology and the variety of products offered. This section briefly summarizes recent developments and the current situation in key market segments.

Banking Sector

Following the regulatory and economic reforms implemented in the last decade, a strong banking sector has emerged. The Polish financial sector is bank driven and banks are the key agents of financial intermediation. The banking sector consists of 70 commercial banks and numerous tiny cooperative banks (accounting for 4.4 per cent of banking sector assets and oriented towards small, mostly rural businesses). The total assets of the banking system amounted to 62.3 per cent of GDP in December 2000. Banking concentration has increased considerably as a result of the consolidations, mergers, takeovers and liquidations. The net assets of the five (ten or 15) largest banks make up 50.1 per cent (72.2 per cent or 81.3 per cent) of the total net assets of the banking sector.[7] However, by international standards the banks remain small. On average, banks perform well in terms of profitability and their return on equity reached 14 per cent in September 2001.

The ownership structure of the banking system changed significantly during the transition period. Only one bank remains fully state owned, two others are directly controlled by the state and four are indirectly state controlled. The other banks are majority private-owned banks. Of the 70 banks, 46 are foreign controlled.[8] The value of foreign capital invested in the Polish banking sector amounted to about US$1.3 billion in September 2001. The capital base and net assets of the foreign-controlled banks amounted to 79.2 per cent and 68.8 per cent of the banking system's total capital base and net assets, respectively. Foreign investors have modernized the banks taken over, trained personnel and introduced a new banking culture.

The biggest investors originate from Germany and their share in the total invested capital amounts to 24 per cent. Foreign investors in Polish banks are mostly large banks which are highly rated on international financial markets. Most banks are listed on the Warsaw Stock Exchange and contribute almost 30 per cent to the market capitalization of the WSE.

The majority of banks are universal commercial banks, although there are also a number which specialize in lending for car purchases or for mortgages. Some banks are also related to particular industries (e.g., sugar) or to regional and local governments.[9]

Capital Markets

The principal institutions of Poland's capital markets are the WSE, which organizes both a cash and derivatives market for securities, and the National Depository for Securities, which settles transactions concluded on the regulated market and stores securities in the form of computer records. The

WSE commenced activity in its present form in April 1991, with electronic paperless trading and regulations based on the best international standards. It operates on the basis of the Law on Public Trading in Securities of August 1997 and under the supervision of the Polish Securities and Exchange Commission. Treasury bonds are traded on both the inter-bank market and the WSE, enabling individual investors to participate in trading. The regulated off-exchange market is organized by CeTO (a group of persons, equipment and technical aids organized in order to compile, present and make available information concerning offers to buy and sell with regard to securities and transactions which had been accomplished. It was established in the form of a stock exchange. The shareholders of CeTO can only be brokerage companies). CeTO comprises a small number of securities, mainly the shares of small companies and municipal bonds.

Capital markets play a limited role in the financing of the corporate sector in Poland and the capitalization of the WSE stood at 13.7 per cent of GDP at the end of 2000. In spite of the privatization and restructuring process, less than 30 per cent of total capitalization is freely trading. The so-called strategic investors in privatized companies own about 44 per cent of shares. The State Treasury owns some 15 per cent and a further 11 per cent is owned by investors holding 5 per cent or more of a company's shares.

A total of 130 companies are listed on the WSE and their market capitalization is PLN 100.2 billion (some €27 billion). Regarding turnover, Polish individuals account for around 50 per cent. Among institutional investors, residents carried out 22 per cent of total turnover and nonresident investors 28 per cent. The WSE faces strong competition from foreign exchanges. A total of 13 Polish companies are listed on stock exchanges in London, Frankfurt and New York. Although there is weak domestic demand for shares, the demand from pension funds is expected to increase.

Money Market

The Polish money market is relatively well developed.[10] There is an active and liquid market in Treasury bills, although the volume of issues is declining as the authorities move towards a greater use of long-term capital market instruments to meet the public sector borrowing requirement. An inter-bank deposit market for deposits has been developing since 1993. Around 70 per cent of the deposits are for a maturity of less than two months. There is also a fragmented and illiquid market for commercial paper. Resident banks hold over 30 per cent of the paper, while nonresidents account for only 5 per cent. Domestic insurance groups also hold commercial paper in their portfolios. There is a small market in certificates of deposit, although because the inter-bank deposit market is cheaper, and certificates of deposits sold to non-banks are subject to reserve requirements, this market has not developed significantly.

Foreign exchange swaps provide a basic market for short-term nonresident investment. Polish banks are actively involved in this market, although there are also some London-based participants. Most contracts (some 84 per cent) are US dollar–zloty contracts.

Long-term Debt Markets

Treasury bonds dominate long-term debt markets, although there are also bonds issued by commercial entities, local governments, the National Bank and mortgage banks. The Ministry of Finance started to issue Treasury bonds in 1991. Since 1994, both fixed and floating rate bonds have been issued and these are listed on the WSE. Wholesale issues are available to resident and nonresident investors. Around 22 per cent of Treasury bonds were held by nonresidents, 36 per cent by domestic banks and 42 per cent by the domestic non-banking sector. The value of these bonds amounted to 13.7 per cent of GDP by the end of 2000.

In contrast, issues of local government and commercial bonds remain small by value and have limited liquidity. Domestic mortgage banks have also begun issuing bonds since 2000. Nonresident mortgage banks are prohibited from entering the market.

Foreign Exchange Market

Domestic banks and London-based institutions dominate the foreign exchange market. Five domestic banks account for 62 per cent of market turnover. The share of nonresidents in the resident bank turnover amounted to over half of it. Over 70 per cent of transactions are carried out in US dollars and the average monthly gross turnover amounted to the equivalent of US$3.4 billion by the end of 2000.[11]

Derivatives, Swaps and Options

Derivatives, swaps and options markets are also developing, although the options market, in particular, remains small. The most well-developed derivatives market is for futures on the main WSE index (the WIG20) where liquidity is high and turnover is growing rapidly.

12.4 THE RESULTS OF LIBERALIZATION TO DATE AND THE LESSONS LEARNED

Capital account liberalization was implemented gradually and in a very cautious manner, helping the Polish economy to avoid currency and financial crises during the transition period. The liberalization process was linked to progress in creating the legal framework for a market economy and setting up adequate institutions. Liberalization also took account of macroeconomic developments.

The change in the exchange rate mechanism from fixed to fully floating gradually created favorable conditions for the full liberalization of capital movements. Nevertheless, it took more than ten years before the exchange rate was fully floated (1 January 1990 to 12 April 2000). During that process, changes in the exchange rate mechanism were linked to progress in reducing inflation and maintaining a reasonable current account deficit.

The framework for monetary policy has changed from a focus on monetary aggregates to fully-fledged inflation targetting. The reason behind this switch is that inflation targetting is viewed as the most effective and credible way of reducing inflation and of ensuring that the central bank is accountable. In contrast, a continued focus on monetary aggregates would have proved difficult given the fact that the money multiplier and money demand are very unstable. Since 1999, the interest rate on 28-day National Bank of Poland bills has been the operating target of the central bank and open market operations with these bills are the main monetary policy instrument. Monetary policy has been successful in lowering inflation from almost 250 per cent in 1990 to 3.6 per cent in 2001 (despite unexpected raises in inflation from mid-1999 until mid-2000).

Policy makers resisted completing the liberalization process by the end of the 1990s due to the imbalances in the Polish economy that became evident that year. The decision to first restore equilibrium – and to postpone full liberalization – created a favorable environment for full liberalization two years later. At the time of writing (spring 2002) the draft foreign exchange law liberalizing all capital movements with OECD countries is before the parliament and is expected to come into force by the end of 2002.

By liberalizing capital movements, Poland has become a more open economy and gained the resulting benefits, including FDI flows (Table 12.1). The first visible benefit is the widening of the financial basis for business activities and the extension of freedom for doing business. Resident and nonresident investors are now free to invest in Poland and abroad with very few exceptions. They may lend and borrow long term from Polish and foreign banks, issue and place securities on the Polish and foreign capital markets, grant one another guarantees related to international trade transactions and

Table 12.1   Poland: foreign direct investment inflows (US$ m)

	1995	1996	1997	1998	1999	2000	2001
Equity (cash)	1,807	2,845	2,663	4,323	6,064	8,813	5,733
(non-cash)	298	314	453	281	403	–	–
Reinvested earnings	888	244	25	-264	-453	-400	–
Credits and loans*	666	1,095	1,767	2,025	1,256	929	1,194
Total FDI inflows	3,659	4,498	4,908	6,365	7,270	9,342	6,927
(previous year = 100)	(195)	(122)	(109)	(130)	(114)	(129)	(74)

Note : *Credits and loans directly linked with foreign direct investment.

Source : National Bank of Poland.

transfer personal capital cross-border. In some circumstances, residents may also open bank accounts abroad and nonresidents can open zloty accounts with resident banks (with some exceptions regarding short-term transactions).

The inflow of FDI has also been beneficial for the national economy. New sources of business financing are available and the economy has access to new technology, managerial skills and jobs. The stock of FDI reached US$40 billion at the end of 2001 (Table 12.2). Inflows were US$9.4 billion (including the privatization of Polish Telecom for some US$2.9 billion) in 2000 and US$6.9 billion in 2001. Inflows have been sustainable and relatively high since 1997, the year following accession to the OECD. FDI inflows helped to restructure the Polish economy, to strengthen the equity position of companies and to improve international competitiveness. Some 14 per cent of total investment in Poland in recent years (excluding privatization) is accounted for by FDI inflows. It has also allowed the remarkable growth in exports on the demanding OECD markets (Table 12.3).

The value of invested capital per company increased from US$0.556 million in 1992 to US$2.290 million in the year 2000 (Table 12.4). The manufacturing sector benefitted most from FDI inflows; food processing and car production sectors attracted 14.5 per cent of the total value of invested capital (Table 12.5). FDI in the financial sector amounted to over 20 per cent of the total FDI stock by the end of 2000 and as a result a strong banking sector has emerged. The trade and services sector attracted more than US$5.7 billion of investment and telecommunications some US$2.9 billion. The labor market also benefitted through the creation and maintenance of jobs in

Table 12.2 Poland: foreign direct investment stock level (US$ m)

	Equity investment in Polish companies	Share of FDI stock	Credits and loans granted	Share of FDI stock	FDI stock level	Previous year = 100
1992	1,135	82.8	235	17.2	1,370	100
1993	1,661	72.0	646	28.0	2,307	168
1994	2,840	75.0	949	25.0	3,789	164
1995	6,130	78.1	1,713	21.8	7,843	206
1996	8,697	75.8	2,766	24.1	11,463	146
1997	10,125	69.4	4,462	30.5	14,587	127
1998	16,063	71.4	6,416	28.5	22,479	154
1999	18,986	72.8	7,089	27.1	26,075	116
2000	25,353	75.4	8,355	24.8	33,603	128
2001	31,086	76.5	9,549	23.4	40,635	121

Source : National Bank of Poland.

privatized companies. Companies with foreign capital ownership employ almost 20 per cent of the total labor force in Poland and provide training for both employees and managers.

Investment other than direct, such as portfolio investment, short-term credits and loans, commercial credits and nonresident deposits with resident banks, amounted to 20 per cent of the total foreign capital inflows to Poland and were more volatile than direct investment flows. Nevertheless, the ratio of short-term inflows to foreign exchange reserves amounted to about 35 per cent by mid-2001 and was close to the full-safety ratio of 29 per cent.[12]

The Polish experience with capital movement liberalization is positive. It shows that if liberalization is adequately sequenced and linked to developments in the real sector of the economy and is backed by regulations and adequate institutions, it is a beneficial process for supporting economic growth and smoothing the transition process.

Table 12.3 Poland: trade by FDI-companies (US$ m)*

	1995	1996	1997	1998	1999
FDI inflows	3,659	4,498	4,908	6,365	7,270
Exports of FDI companies	7,936	9,315	11,077	13,527	14,134
(share in total exports)	*38.1*	*38.1*	*43.0*	*47.9*	*51.5*
Imports of FDI companies	12,305	17,720	21,120	25,122	25,612
(share in total imports)	*42.4*	*47.7*	*49.9*	*53.3*	*55.7*
Trade balance of FDI companies	-4,369	-8,405	-10,043	-11,594	-11,479
Overall trade balance	-6,155	-12,697	-16,556	-18,825	-18,504
(share of FDI companies)	*70.9*	*66.2*	*60.6*	*61.5*	*62.0*
Current account balance	5,310	-1,371	-4,312	-6,858	-11,569
(share of FDI inflows)	*69.0*	*328.0*	*114.0*	*92.8*	*63.0*

Note :* FDI companies refers to companies with foreign capital participation.
Sources : National Bank of Poland, Foreign Trade Research Institute and own calculations.

Table 12.4 Poland: foreign direct investment per company (US$ m)

	Number of companies	Total invested capital	Average capital per company
1992	2,462	1,370	0.556
1993	2,743	2,307	0.841
1994	8,775	3,789	0.432
1995	10,235	7,843	0.766
1996	11,307	11,463	1.014
1997	12,377	14,587	1.179
1998	12,649	22,479	1.777
1999	13,400	26,075	1.946
2000	14,668	33,603	2.291

Sources : Own calculations based on the National Bank of Poland and Central Statistical Office.

Table 12.5 Poland: structure of foreign direct investment

| | Foreign direct investment inflows | | | | FDI stock value | |
| | 1996 | | 2000 | | 2000 | |
	(US$ m)	*(%)*	(US$ m)	*(%)*	(US$ m)	*(%)*
TOTAL	8,697	*100.0*	9,342	*100.0*	33,602	*100.0*
MANUFACTURING	5,160	*59.3*	2,085	*22.3*	13,190	*39.2*
Food processing	1,258	*14.5*	407	*4.3*	2,869	*8.5*
Car production	801	*9.2*	280	*3.0*	2,070	*6.2*
Chemicals etc.	503	*5.8*	176	*1.9*	1,398	*4.2*
Wood products etc.	528	*6.1*	283	*3.0*	1,496	*4.4*
Rubber and plastics	390	*4.5*	127	*1.3*	793	*2.4*
Metal production	276	*3.2*	93	*1.0*	677	*2.0*
Machinery	192	*2.2*	64	*0.6*	448	*1.3*
Audio, TV, etc.	102	*1.2*	85	*0.9*	378	*1.1*
Textiles production	152	*1.7*	4	*0.4*	246	*0.7*
Other manufacturing	958	*10.9*	–	–	–	–
Energy, gas, water	–	–	350	*3.7*	408	*1.2*
FINANCIAL	1,270	*14.6*	1,970	*21.1*	6,818	*20.3*
TRADE AND SERVICES	1,335	*15.4*	–	–	5,679	*16.9*
REAL ESTATE	331	*3.8*	444	*4.7*	2,125	*6.3*
CONSTRUCTION	178	*2.0*	157	*1.7*	1,429	*4.2*
TRANSPORT, STORAGE , TELECOMMUNICATIONS	276	*3.2*	3,421	*36.6*	3,333	*9.9*
OTHERS	147	*1.7*	44	*0.5*	165	*0.5*

Source : National Bank of Poland.

NOTES

1. I would like to thank Prof. Zbigniew Polanski (NBP) for valuable comments.
2. Box 12.1 summarizes the key steps taken during the reform process.
3. OECD, Economic Surveys – Poland, 1997.
4. OECD, Economic Surveys – Poland, 1997.
5. OECD, Economic Surveys – Poland, 1994.
6. OECD, Economic Surveys – Poland, 1997.
7. National Bank of Poland data.
8. Of these 46 banks, 15 are fully foreign owned, 20 have a majority foreign partner and the remaining banks are indirectly foreign controlled.

9. See Bednarski and Osiński (2001) for additional information on the banking sector.
10. This subsection is based on Bednarski and Osiński (2001).
11. National Bank of Poland data.
12. The ratio for the emerging markets amounted to 66 per cent in mid-2001.

References

Alexander, W.E. et al. (1995), 'The Adoption of Indirect Instruments of Monetary Policy', IMF Occasional Paper No. 126, Washington, DC: International Monetary Fund.

Argy, V. (1987), 'International Financial Liberalization – the Australian and Japanese Experiences Compared', *Bank of Japan Monetary and Economic Studies*, **5** (May), 105–67.

Ariyoshi, A. et al. (2000), 'Country Experiences with the Use and Liberalization of Capital Controls', IMF Occasional Paper No. 190 Washington, DC: International Monetary Fund.

Arteta, C., B. Eichengreen and C. Wyplosz (2001), 'When Does Capital Account Liberalization Help More Than It Hurts?', NBER Working Paper No. 8414, Cambridge, MA: National Bureau of Economic Research.

Bacchetta, P. (1996), 'Capital Controls and the Political Discount: The Spanish Experience in the Late 1980s', *Open Economies Review*, **7** (October), 349–69.

Bakker, Age F.P. (1996), *The Liberalisation of Capital Movements in Europe*, Dordrecht: Kluwer Academic Publishers.

Bakker, A.F.P. and B.R. Chapple (2002), 'Advanced Country Experiences with Capital Account Liberalization', IMF Occasional Paper No. 214, Washington, DC: International Monetary Fund.

Baliño, T.J.T., J. Dhawan and V. Sundararajan (1994), 'Payments System Reforms and Monetary Policy in Emerging Market Economies in Central and Eastern Europe', *IMF Staff Papers*, **41** (3), 383–410.

Bednarski, P. and J. Osiński (2001), 'Financial Sector Issues in Poland', paper prepared for the workshop on Financial Sector Issues in Accession Countries, European Central Bank, Frankfurt am Main, 24–25 October.

Berger, H., J.E. Sturm and J. de Haan (2001), 'Capital Controls and Exchange Rate Regimes: An Empirical Investigation', CESifo Working Paper No. 433, Munich: CESifo.

Berglof, E. and P. Bolton (2002), 'The Great Divide and Beyond: Financial Architecture in Transition', *Journal of Economic Perspectives*, **16** (1), 77–100.

Bhagwati, T. (1998), 'Why Free Capital Mobility May Be Hazardous to Your Health: Lessons from the Latest Financial Crisis', paper presented to NBER Conference on Capital Controls, Cambridge, MA, 7 November.

Boote, A.R. and J. Somogyi (1991), 'Economic Reform in Hungary Since 1968', IMF Occasional Paper No. 83, Washington, DC: International Monetary Fund.

Calvo, G.A. and E. Mendoza (2000), 'Contagion, Globalization, and the Volatility of Capital Flows', in S. Edwards (ed.), *Capital Flows and the Emerging Economies*, National Bureau of Economic Research, Chicago: University of Chicago Press, pp. 15–41.

Chang, R. and A. Velasco (1997), 'Banking Fragility and Exchange Rate Regime', Working Paper 97-16, Atlanta: Federal Reserve Bank of Atlanta.

Claessens, S., S. Djankov and D. Klingebiel (2001), 'Stock Markets in Transition Economies', in L. Bokros, A. Fleming and C. Votava (eds), *Financial Transition in Europe and Central Asia: Challenges of the New Decade*, Washington DC: World Bank, pp. 109–138.

Cooper, R. (1999), 'Should Capital Controls Be Banished?', *Brookings Papers on Economic Activity*, **1**, 89–141.

Coricelli, F. (2001), 'Financial Liberalization in Economies in Transition: Tales of Success and Failure', in G. Caprio, P. Honohan and J.E. Stiglitz (eds), *Financial Liberalization: How Far? How Fast?*, Cambridge: Cambridge University Press, pp. 208–32.

Cottarelli, C., T. Krueger, R. Moghadam, P. Perone, E. Ruggiero and R. van Elkan (1998), 'Hungary: Economic Policies for Sustainable Growth', IMF Occasional Paper No. 159, Washington, DC: International Monetary Fund.

Darvas, Z. and G. Szapáry (2000), 'Financial Contagion in Five Small Open Economies: Does the Exchange Rate Regime Really Matter?', *International Finance*, **3** (1), 25–51.

Dooley, M.P. (1996), 'A Survey of Literature on Controls over International Capital Transactions', *IMF Staff Papers*, **43** (4), 639–87.

Dooley, M.P., Y.C. Park and R. Dornbusch (2001), 'A Framework For Exchange Rate Policy in Korea', paper presented at the IMF-KIEP Conference on Financial Crisis and Recovery in Korea, Seoul, 19 May.

Dornbusch, R. (2001), 'Malaysia: Was It Different?' mimeo, Cambridge, MA: Massachusetts Institute of Technology.

Drees, B. and C. Pazarbasioglu (1998), 'The Nordic Banking Crises: Pitfalls in Financial Liberalization?', IMF Occasional Paper No. 161, Washington, DC: International Monetary Fund.

EBRD (1998), *Transition Report 1998: Financial Sector in Transition*, London: European Bank for Reconstruction and Development.

EBRD (2001a), *Transition Report 2001*, London: European Bank for Reconstruction and Development.

EBRD (2001b), *Transition Report Update 2001: Cross-border Capital Flows*, London: European Bank for Reconstruction and Development.

EBRD (2002), *Transition Report Update 2002: Cross-border Capital Flows*, London: European Bank for Reconstruction and Development.

Edey, M. and K. Hviding (1995), 'An Assessment of Financial Reform in OECD Countries', OECD Economics Department Working Paper No. 154, Paris: Organisation for Economic Co-operation and Development.

Edwards, S. (2000), 'Capital flows, real exchange rates, and capital controls', in S. Edwards (ed.), *Capital Flows and the Emerging Economies*, National Bureau of Economic Research, Chicago: University of Chicago Press, pp. 197–254.

Edwards, S. (2001), 'Capital Mobility and Economic Performance: Are Emerging Economies Different?' NBER Working Paper, No. 8076, Cambridge, MA: National Bureau of Economic Research.

Eichengreen, B.J. and P. Masson (eds) (1998), 'Exit Strategies: Policy Options for Countries Seeking Greater Exchange Rate Flexibility', IMF Occasional Paper No. 168, Washington, DC: International Monetary Fund.

Eichengreen, B.J. and M. Mussa (1998), 'Capital Account Liberalization: Theoretical and Practical Aspects', IMF Occasional Paper No. 172, Washington, DC: International Monetary Fund.

Feldman, R.A. and H. Temprano-Arroyo (1998), 'Trade and Financial Effects of EMU on Selected Transition and Mediterranean Countries', in R.A. Feldman (ed.), 'Impact of EMU on Selected Non-European Union Countries', IMF Occasional Paper No. 174, Washington, DC: International Monetary Fund, pp. 20–69.

Fischer, S. (2001), 'Exchange Rate Regimes: Is the Bipolar View Correct?', *Journal of Economic Perspectives*, **15** (2), 3–21.

Fries, S. and A. Taci (2002), 'Banking Reform and Development in Transition Economies', EBRD Working Paper No. 71, London: European Bank for Reconstruction and Development.

Fukao, M. (1990), 'Liberalization of Japan's Foreign Exchange Controls and Structural Changes in the Balance of Payments', *Bank of Japan Monetary and Economic Studies*, **8** (September), 101–65.

Furman, J. and J. Stiglitz (1998), 'Economic Crises: Evidence and Insights from East Asia', *Brookings Papers on Economic Activity*, **2**, 1–136.

Ghosh, A., T. Lane, M. Schultze-Ghattas, A. Bulir, J. Hamann and A. Mourmouras (2002), 'IMF-supported Programs in Capital Account Crises', IMF Occasional Paper No. 210, Washington, DC: International Monetary Fund.

Haggard, S. and L. Low (2001), 'The Political Economy of Malaysian Capital Controls', mimeo, San Diego: University of California.

Hood, R. (2001), 'Malaysian Capital Controls', World Bank Working Paper, No. 2536, Washington, DC: World Bank.

Hoshi, T. (2000), 'What Happened to Japanese Banks?', IMES Discussion Paper No. 2000-E-7, Tokyo: Institute for Monetary and Economic Studies, Bank of Japan.

IMF (various issues), 'Annual Report on Exchange Arrangements and Exchange Restrictions', Washington, DC: International Monetary Fund.

IMF (1995) 'Controls on Capital Flows: Experience with Quantitative Measures and Capital Flow Taxation', in *International Capital Markets*, Washington, DC: International Monatery Fund, pp. 95–108.

IMF (2001), 'International Financial Integration and Economic Performance: Impact on Developing Countries', *World Economic Outlook: The Information Technology Revolution*, Washington, DC: International Monetary Fund, pp. 145–73.

Ishii, S. et al. (2002), 'Capital Account Liberalization and Financial Sector Stability', IMF Occasional Paper No. 211, Washington, DC: International Monetary Fund.

Ito, T. (1992), *The Japanese Economy*, Cambridge, MA: Massachusetts Institute of Technology Press.

Johnston, R.B., S. Darbar and C. Exheverria (1997), 'Sequencing Capital Account Liberalization: Lessons from the Experiences in Chile, Indonesia, Korea and Thailand', IMF Working Paper, WP/97/157, Washington, DC: International Monetary Fund.

Johnston R.B. and I. Otker-Robe (1999), 'A Modernised Approach to Managing Risks in Cross-border Capital Movements', IMF Policy Discussion Paper No. 6, Washington, DC: International Monetary Fund.

Johnston, R.B., M. Swinburne, A. Kyei, B. Laurens, D. Mitchem, I. Otker, S. Sosa and N. Tamirisa (1999), *Exchange Rate Arrangements and Currency Convertibility: Developments and Issues*, Washington, DC: International Monetary Fund.

Jomo, K. (2001), 'Capital Controls', in K. Jomo (ed.), *Malaysian Eclipse: Economic Crisis and Recovery*, Singapore: Select Books Pte. Ltd, pp. 199–215.

Kaplan, E. and D. Rodrik (2001), 'Did the Malaysian Capital Controls Work?', NBER Working Paper, No. 8142, Cambridge, MA: National Bureau of Economic Research.

Klein, M. and G. Olivei (1999), 'Capital Account Liberalization, Financial Depth, and Economic Growth', NBER Working Paper, No. 7384, Cambridge, MA: National Bureau of Economic Research.

Kim, S., S. Kim and Y. Wang (2002), 'Macroeconomic Effects of Capital

Account Liberalization: The Case of Korea',Working Paper No. 02-01, Seoul: Korea Institute for International Economic Policy.

Kraay, A. (1998), 'In Search of the Macroeconomic Effects of Capital Account Liberalization', mimeo, Washington, DC: World Bank.

Krugman, P. (1999), 'Recovery? Don't Bet on It', *Time (Asia)*, June 21.

Lane, T., A. Ghosh, J. Hamann. S. Phillips, M. Schulze-Ghattas and T. Tsikata (1999), 'IMF-supported Programs in Indonesia, Korea, and Thailand: A Preliminary Assessment', IMF Occasional Paper No. 178, Washington, DC: International Monetary Fund.

Laurens, B. and J. Cardoso (1998), 'Managing Capital Flows: Lessons from the Experiences of Chile', IMF Working Paper No. WP/98/168, Washington, DC: International Monetary Fund.

Mauro, P., N. Sussman and Y. Yafeh (2000), 'Emerging Market Spreads: Then Versus Now', IMF Working Paper No. WP/00/190, Washington, DC: International Monetary Fund.

McCallum, B.T. (1997), 'Inflation Targeting in Canada, New Zealand, Sweden, the United Kingdom, and in General', in I. Kuroda (ed.), *Towards More Effective Monetary Policy*, London: Macmillan, pp. 211–41.

McKinnon, R. (1973), *Money and Capital in Economic Development*, Washington, DC: Brookings Institution.

McKinnon, R. (1993), *The Order of Economic Liberalization: Financial Control in the Transition to a Market Economy*, Baltimore: Johns Hopkins University Press.

Mishra, D., A. Mody and A.P. Murshid (2001), 'Private Capital Flows and Growth', *Finance and Development*, **38** (2).

NBH (2000), 'Annual Report', Budapest: National Bank of Hungary.

Oblath, G. (1998), 'Capital Inflows to Hungary in 1995–96 and the Accompanying Policy Responses', *Empirica*, **25**, 183–216.

OECD (various issues), 'Economic Outlook', Paris: Organisation for Economic Co-operation and Development.

OECD 1994–2000, Economic Surveys of the Czech Republic, Hungary, Korea, Mexico, Poland and the Slovak Republic, Paris: Organisation for Economic Co-operation and Development.

OECD (2002), *Forty Years' Experience with the OECD Code of Liberalisation of Capital Movements*, Paris: Organisation for Economic Co-operation and Development.

Park, Y.C. (2001), 'The East Asian Dilemma: Restructuring out of Growing Out?', Essays in International Economics, No. 223, Princeton: Princeton University Press.

Park, Y.C., and J. Lee (2001), 'Recovery and Sustainability in East Asia', NBER Working Paper No. 8373, Cambridge, MA: National Bureau of

Economic Research.

Perotti, E. (1998), 'Inertial Credit and Opportunistic Arrears in Transition', *European Economic Review*, **42** (9), 1703–25.

Pistor, K. (2000), 'The Standardization of Law and Its Effects on Developing Economies', G-24 Discussion Paper Series No. 4, New York and Geneva: United Nations Conference on Trade and Development, and Center for International Development, Harvard University.

Quirk, P. and O. Evans (1995), 'Capital Account Convertibility: Review of Experience and Implications for IMF Policies', IMF Occasional Paper No. 131, Washington, DC: International Monetary Fund.

Rodrik, D. (1998), 'Who Needs Capital-account Convertibility?' in P.B. Kenen (ed.), *Should the IMF Pursue Capital Account Convertibility?*, Essays in International Finance, No. 207, Princeton: Princeton University Press, pp. 55–65.

Rogoff, K. (2002), 'Managing the World Economy', *The Economist*, August 3, 62–4.

Simone, F. and P. Sorsa (1999), 'A Review of Capital Account Restrictions in Chile in the 1990s', IMF Working Paper No. WP/99/52, Washington, DC: International Monetary Fund.

Sundararajan, V. et al. (1997), *Coordinating Public Debt and Monetary Management*, Washington, DC: International Monetary Fund.

Sundararajan, V. et al. (2002), 'International Capital Mobility and Domestic Financial System Stability: A Survey of Issues', forthcoming, Washington DC: International Monetary Fund.

Svensson, L.E.O. (1992), 'An Interpretation of Recent Research on Exchange Rate Target Zones', *Journal of Economic Perspectives*, **6**, 119–44.

Svensson, L.E.O. (1997), 'Inflation Forecast Targeting: Implementing and Monitoring Inflation Targets', *European Economic Review*, **41** (6), 1111–46.

Svensson, L.E.O. (2000), 'Open-economy Inflation Targeting', *Journal of International Economics*, **50**, 155–83.

Takeda, M. and P. Turner (1992), 'The Liberalization of Japan's Financial Markets: Some Major Themes', BIS Economic Papers No. 34, Basle: Bank for International Settlements.

Tamarisa, N. T. (1999), 'Exchange and Capital Controls as Barriers to Trade', *IMF Staff Papers*, **46** (1), 69–88.

Temprano-Arroyo, H. and R.A. Feldman (1998), 'Selected Transition and Mediterranean Countries: An Institutional Primer on EMU and EU Relations', IMF Working Paper No. WP/98/82, Washington, DC: International Monetary Fund.

Tivakul, A. and P. Sventarundra (1993), 'Financial Innovation and Modernization of the Thai Financial Market', paper presented at the

OECD Workshop on Financial Innovation and Modernization of Financial Markets, Paris, 2-3 December.

Valdes-Prieto, S. and M. Soto (1998), 'The Effectiveness of Capital Controls: Theory and Evidence from Chile', *Empirica*, **25** (2), 133–64.

Vichyanond, P. (1994), 'Thailand's Financial System: Structure and Liberalization', Research Monograph No. 11, Bangkok: Thailand Development Research Institute.

Vujčić, B. and M. Lang (2001), 'Determinants of Growth in Croatia', paper prepared for the Global Development Network 3rd Annual Global Development Conference, Rio de Janeiro.

Williamson, J. (2000), 'Exchange-rate Regimes for East Asia: Reviving the Intermediate Option', Policy Analysis in International Economics No. 60, Washington, DC: Institute for International Economics.

Wyplosz, C. (2001), 'How Risky is Financial Liberalization in the Developing Countries?', *Comparative Economic Studies*, **2**, 1–26.

Index